The Political Economy of European Integration

This is the first book to present a balanced and accessible introduction to diverse political economy perspectives on different aspects of European integration, demonstrating both the importance and the potential of research in this area.

The Political Economy of European Integration includes three types of chapters: broad literature reviews, narrower applications of existing arguments, and new syntheses of competing claims. The authors also present a critical appraisal of how scholars in the EU and US use theory to understand European integration and examine issues such as citizens' attitudes; perceptions and preferences of actors; the role of non-state actors; principal–agent questions; and the role and the autonomy of European institutions.

This empirically informed and methodologically rigorous volume, written by highly regarded contributors, provides an important overview of the state of play in the EU political economy in North America and the EU. It will be of great interest to students and researchers in the fields of comparative political economy, EU studies, international political economy and international organisations.

Erik Jones is the Resident Associate Professor of European Studies at Johns Hopkins University, Bologna Center, Bologna, Italy. He is the author of *The Politics of Economic and Monetary Union* and co-director (together with Amy Verdun) of the EU Political Economy Interest Section of the European Union Studies Association in the US.

Amy Verdun is Jean Monnet Chair in European Integration Studies and Associate Professor in the Department of Political Science, University of Victoria, Canada. She is the author of *European Responses to Globalization and Financial Market Integration: Perceptions of EMU in Britain, France and Germany*; and editor of *The Euro: European Integration Theory and Economic and Monetary Union.*

The Political Economy of European Integration

Theory and analysis

Edited by
Erik Jones and Amy Verdun

Routledge
Taylor & Francis Group

LONDON AND NEW YORK

First published 2005
by Routledge
2 Park Square, Milton Park, Abingdon, Oxon OX14 4RN

Simultaneously published in the USA and Canada
by Routledge
270 Madison Ave, New York, NY 10016

Routledge is an imprint of the Taylor & Francis Group

© 2005 Erik Jones and Amy Verdun for selection and
editorial matter; individual contributors their chapters

Typeset in Times New Roman by
Newgen Imaging Systems (P) Ltd, Chennai, India
Printed and bound in Great Britain by
The Cromwell Press, Trowbridge, Wiltshire

British Library Cataloguing in Publication Data
A catalogue record for this book is available
from the British Library

Library of Congress Cataloging in Publication Data
A catalog record for this book has been requested

ISBN 0–415–34063–2 (hbk)
ISBN 0–415–34064–0 (pbk)

Contents

Illustrations

Contributors

Maria Green Cowles is Assistant Professor at the School of International Service, American University, Washington, DC, USA.

Mary Farrell is Senior Researcher at the United Nations University, centre for Comparative Regional Integration Studies (UNU/CRIS) in Bruges, Belgium.

Erik Jones is Associate Professor of European Studies at Johns Hopkins University, Bologna Center, Bologna, Italy.

Hussein Kassim is Senior Lecturer in Politics at Birkbeck College, University of London, UK.

Anand Menon is Professor of European Politics and Director of the European Research Institute, University of Birmingham, UK.

Jonathon W. Moses is Professor at the Norwegian University of Science and Technology (NTNU), Department of Sociology and Political Science, Trondheim, Norway.

Robert Pahre is Professor in the Department of Political Science and Associate Director in the European Union Center at the University of Illinois-Urbana Champagne, USA.

Marcus Pistor is a Research Officer in the Research Branch of the Library of Parliament in Ottawa, Canada.

Waltraud Schelkle is Lecturer in Political Economy in the European Institute at the London School of Economics, UK.

A. Maurits van der Veen is Assistant Professor in the Department of International Affairs, School of Public and International Affairs, University of Georgia, USA.

Amy Verdun is Jean Monnet Chair in European Integration Studies and Associate Professor at the Department of Political Science, University of Victoria, Canada.

Abbreviations

[C]ESDP	[Common] European Security and Defence Policy
ACP	African, Caribbean and Pacific States
ADR	Alternative Dispute Resolution
APEC	Asia Pacific Economic Cooperation
ASEAN	Association of South East Asian Nations
ASEM	Asia–Europe Meeting
BAs	business associations
BEPGs	Broad Economic Policy Guidelines
CAP	Common Agricultural Policy
CEECs	Central and Eastern European Countries
CFSP	Common Foreign and Security Policy
COG	Chief of Government
CPE	Comparative Political Economy
CPE	Critical Political Economy
DPG	Deutsche Postgewerkschaft
EADS	European Aerospace, Defence and Space Company
EB	Eurobarometer
EBA	'Everything But Arms'
EC	European Community
EMU	Economic and Monetary Union
EPAs	Economic Partnership Agreements
EPT	Endogenous Policy Theory
ERM	Exchange Rate Mechanism
ERT	European Roundtable of Industrialists
EU	European Union
FPÖ	Freiheitliche Partei Österreichs (Austrian Freedom Party)
FTAA	Free Trade Area of the Americas
GATT	General Agreement on Tariffs and Trade
GBDe	Global Business Dialogue on e-commerce
HIS	Historical Institutionalist Supranationalism
HZDS	Hnutie za demokratické Slovensko (Movement for a Democratic Slovakia)
IGC	Intergovernmental Conference

II	Institutional Intergovernmentalism
IPE	International Political Economy
IR	International Relations
LI	Liberal Intergovernmentalism
NAFTA	North American Free Trade Agreement
NAP	National Action Plan
NATO	North Atlantic Treaty Organization
NGO	Non-governmental Organization
OECD	Organization for Economic Co-operation and Development
OMC	'Open Method' Coordination
ÖVP	Österreichische Volkspartei (Austrian People's Party)
QMV	Qualified Majority Voting
RCS	Rational Choice Supranationalism
SDL	Strana demokratickej l'avice (Democratic Left Party Slovakia)
SGP	Stability and Growth Pact
SNS	Slovenská narodná strana (Slovak Nationalist Party)
SPÖ	Sozialdemokratische Partei Österreichs (Austrian Social Democratic Party)
TABD	Transatlantic Business Dialogue
TRIPs	Trade-Related Intellectual Property Rights
UK	United Kingdom
UN	United Nations
US	United States
WIPO	World Intellectual Property Organization
WTO	World Trade Organization

Introduction

Erik Jones and Amy Verdun

As the title suggests, this book is about the political economy of European integration. We chose that subject for two reasons. The first is empirical. The European Union (EU) has changed a lot over the past decade. It will change even more over the decade to come. The enlargement of membership, the reform of institutions, and the expansion ('deepening') of policy competency all promise to make the Europe of the future very different from the Europe of the past. Anything that changes so much, so quickly, is interesting – certainly to us and hopefully to our readers as well.

The second reason for choosing to write this book has more to do with political economy than with European integration. There are many good books already in print about this new Europe. Our goal is not to add to the burgeoning mountain of contemporary and forward-looking analysis. Rather we hope to provide illustrations that will make that new literature a bit easier to grasp. We believe that much of what is happening in Europe cannot be understood from a single point of view. More than ever before, students of European integration must look at their subject from a range of perspectives, they must use different toolkits, and they must be willing to challenge their own assumptions.

The problem with embracing such a variety of analyses is that it is so easy to make mistakes and so difficult to figure out what others are actually doing. The more disciplines you add into the mix, the greater this problem becomes. Thus while we believe it is important to adopt a range of different viewpoints, we accept that there are practical constraints on how much diversity we should expect any single analyst to apprehend. That is why we focus on political economy.

The term 'political economy' has two different connotations. Sometimes it refers to the interface between economics and politics in the real world – as in the politics of economic policymaking or the economic motivations behind electoral choice. When classical writers like Carr (1981 [1939]: 106–10), Schumpeter (1962 [1950]), or Polanyi (1957 [1944]: 135–50) decry the separation of politics and economics, they usually focus on this real-world dimension. For them, politics and economics are inextricably intertwined.

Such empirical issues are largely uncontested with respect to European integration. Few would object to the assertion that European integration is both political and economic. From the European Coal and Steel Community to the single currency, politics and economics have always intertwined. Moreover, analysis of European integration has reflected this real-world overlap between economic and political concerns. In this regard, the early work by Albonetti (1963), Haas (1958), Hoffmann (1966), and Willis (1968) is little different from the later work by Milward (1992), Moravcsik (1998), and Scharpf (1999). Such writers may make competing claims about what drives European integration and where it is going, but they all accept that the process has both political and economic dimensions.

This empirical consensus extends into the major journals on European integration as well. Virtually all of these journals accept submissions from a range of disciplines. The *Journal of Common Market Studies* has two editors, one from economics and the other from political science. The *Journal of European Public Policy* and the *Journal of European Integration* each have only one editor but still attracts a variety of submissions. *European Union Politics* has run special issues on 'economic and monetary union and fiscal policy' and 'the winners and losers of EU decision-making'. The journal *Current Politics and Economics of Europe*, that has been publishing articles on those two broad topics, is changing its name to *Journal of European Political Economy* as of 2005. One would expect it to generate a larger interest in the area of 'political economy' rather than merely emphasizing the two separate fields of study.

The second meaning of the term 'political economy' is more narrowly methodological. It implies the adoption of assumptions and tools from one discipline in order to answer questions or address phenomena usually restricted to the other. Examples here include the textbook by Drazen (2000) or the reader by Frieden and Lake (1995). Such works invariably draw attention to areas in the real world where politics and economics intersect. However, their goal is to encourage a change in perspective from the disciplinary norm. This collection of essays falls in that more methodological camp. We realize that economics and politics are intertwined in the real world. However, we are more interested in illustrating different possible perspectives than in describing specific instances of overlap.

This emphasis on political economy perspectives is particularly important in the context of European integration. The literature is replete with excellent descriptions of the economics and politics of Europe – not to mention the institutions, ideas, policies, political system, member states, history, and so on. Except for the slim volume by Michelmann and Soldatos (1994), however, the literature on European integration does not provide many surveys of the different perspectives that can be taken on contemporary problems of politics and economics. The new journal *European Political Economy Review* encourages interdisciplinary synthesis, but its contents are determined by submissions and not by editorial commission. Hence, it can offer specific contributions from particular points of view, but it does not provide an omnibus survey.

Our objective with this collection is to fill that gap in the literature, at least in part. In the chapters that follow, we have assembled a range of perspectives on European integration from within the broader ambit of political economy. The essays build on different assumptions, incorporate different analytical tools, and reflect different styles of writing. As editors, we have insisted that all chapters be accessible to interested readers from a variety of backgrounds. However, we have been more concerned to preserve the authenticity of difference than to reshape the contributions as so many pieces in a puzzle.

The resulting picture is incomplete in some areas and overlapping in others. Such shortcomings are inevitable, but perhaps not really relevant. Our aim is to encourage students of European integration to experiment with different points of view, but be firm on adopting a clear theoretical and methodological approach. If that message comes across we will have achieved our goal. Students or academics hoping to find a more systematic coverage of the various institutions and policies of the EU should look to any of the major textbooks on the market.

The remainder of this introduction makes the general case for interdisciplinary research on European integration. Although we are keen to encourage experimentation across disciplinary divides, we are equally concerned to avoid accusations of relativism or eclecticism. The point we want to make is not that any perspective is just as good as another. Rather it is that no one point of view is adequate in all areas. To torture a phrase, 'no matter how good the hammer, not every problem is a nail'.

The introduction has four parts. The first sets out the challenge of combining tools from different disciplines. The second describes the anatomy of a 'perspective'. The third focuses on how to measure relative success or failure (and considers the possibility that not all measures of success are the same). The fourth part concludes with some words of advice and acknowledgment.

The perils of interdisciplinary research

Interdisciplinary research is all the rage at the moment. Most of the funding councils list it as either an advantage or a priority when allocating funding for research projects. The EU made it a precondition for participation in its Sixth Framework programme to create a European research area. Policymakers are constantly talking about the need for 'greater interdisciplinarity'. Even an increasing number of students seem to be more eager to follow interdisciplinary degree courses instead of conventional ones.

Yet for all this hype, most academics remain stubbornly within the confines of their disciplines. Economists study economics, political scientists study politics, and so on. Different groups may borrow a few ideas or tools from one another. But they rarely try to cross disciplinary boundaries, nor do they easily adopt each other's methodology or theories, and they almost never try to create a grand synthesis of different traditions.

Such academic conservatism is born of caution. Interdisciplinary work is easier to get wrong than to get right. It is important to understand the advantages of working within the boundaries of a discipline. To begin with, there is so much to be taken for granted. Virtually every economist will have some familiarity with Keynesian demand management and virtually every political scientist will know something about the redistributive politics underlying the welfare state. While the debates within each discipline tend to be straightforward, the debates between them do not. The problem is that few economists or political scientists have a clear understanding of the links between Keynesianism and the welfare state. Moreover, these links are not intuitive. Most welfare state outlays are not very useful for demand management, and demand management in itself offers little that is of interest to the distributive coalition underlying the welfare state. Hence many historic welfare states (such as Germany) have little experience with Keynesianism and a few of the more Keynesian countries (such as the United States) have underdeveloped welfare states.

Shared familiarity is not the only advantage of working within a discipline, or even the most important. A common appreciation for the rules of the analytic game is even more beneficial. Consider the economic modelling of welfare. Most economists are ready to accept that welfare functions can be modelled in two-dimensional space as a stable, continuous, linear-homothetic trade-off between alternative combinations of goods or services for consumption. Most political scientists would have a hard time unpacking what that long string of modifiers actually means. If they did, they would be quick to point out objections. Welfare functions are unstable (sometimes I want more jam on my toast, and sometime less). They are discontinuous (I can spread the same pot of jam on one piece of toast or two, but I am unlikely to break up one of the pieces to achieve an optimal covering given the amount of jam available). They are non-linear (if I have enough jam, I will have two pieces of toast, but if not I will only have one and I do not really care either way). They are non-homothetic (if I have two pieces of toast I am happier with more jam, but if I have only one piece of toast, I am happier with less). Economists would be quick to point out that it is very difficult to model welfare functions that do not have convenient mathematical characteristics. Political scientists would counter that such modelling is unrealistic. Both would be right.

Such differences can play an important role in analysis. Popular attitudes toward economic policy are a case in point. Economists prefer to assume popular preferences that are easy to model – usually centring on a trade-off between inflation and unemployment (or stable prices and employment to parallel the bread and jam above). Political scientists may be willing to accept more complex preferences even if the results are less clear cut. For the moment, let us leave aside the question whether one form of analysis is somehow 'better' than another. The only point we want to make here is that economists will find the choices made by economists easier to accept and to argue over than those made by political scientists, and the reverse. Moreover, it would be hard to find a compromise position that either group will find as acceptable as their own analytic conventions (in this case, 'easy to model' versus 'more realistic'). Welfare functions either have certain characteristics or they do not. If we assume that they do, we cannot easily extend the argument to cover real-world cases where preferences behave differently. If we assume that they do not, then we have little reason for accepting conclusions drawn from the simplified mathematical argument.

Of course we could just choose to ignore the significance of common understandings and shared analytic conventions. However, the danger is that we will introduce contradictions into the analysis or, more prosaically, that we will start saying things that do not make sense. For example, most arguments for central bank independence centre on popular perceptions of the trade-off between inflation and unemployment (suggested above). By implication, there are few reasons to advocate an independent central bank (or a central banker more conservative toward inflation than the population at large) if we do not believe that the population will accept a trade-off between inflation and unemployment or if we reject the view that the population, on average, is more afraid of unemployment than inflation. An independent central bank may even be redundant in a society where the population is always and openly inflation-averse. Curiously, though, it is precisely those societies – like Germany – in which independent central banks tend to occur. This leaves us with two problems. First we have to explain why Germans are more inflation-averse than our assumptions. The usual argument is that the Germans experienced hyperinflation in the period 1920–1923 and a currency reform in 1948 (when the Reichsmark was abandoned and the D-mark was introduced, which also had a major negative effect on savings), but this effect seems to be uniquely German and is not manifest in any of the many other countries that have suffered from hyperinflation. Then we have to explain why negative correlations between inflation and central bank independence suggest the importance of central banks and not the anomalous influence of cultural preferences. Here the usual rejoinder is to refer to large sample correlations, but without controlling for other anomalous inflation-averse societies. The danger of contradiction looms on both sides of this conundrum.

Contradiction is the real peril of interdisciplinary research. It is not an insurmountable obstacle. For each of the examples above, we could point to excellent works by economists and political scientists that have brought together insights from both disciplines. However, avoiding contradiction is difficult. The more original the synthesis, the more concepts that are combined across disciplines, and the more analytic conventions that are challenged, the more difficult avoiding contradiction becomes.

Fortunately, originality is usually unnecessary. Although interdisciplinary research is in vogue, as said, academics have for many years been combining disciplines (albeit often at the fringes of the profession or after receiving tenure). Even better, the more ambitious the synthesis, the more likely it is to have been tried in the past. These combinations are not as well established as the disciplines from which they borrow. They tend to be more eclectic in that they reflect both the requirements of particular problems and the predilections of the authors themselves. Many similar syntheses exist without reference to one another (which is to say there is a lot of reinventing the wheel). Nevertheless interdisciplinary syntheses do exist and they can provide a storehouse of examples of how to avoid contradiction in new research and analysis.

The anatomy of an interdisciplinary perspective

The first step in interdisciplinary research is to find out what others have done before. This is not as easy as it seems. Because interdisciplinary work takes place outside disciplines, it does not often appear in textbooks. When it does appear, the textbook writers are usually more interested in making the links back to the discipline than in explaining the origins and evolution of the particular synthetic tradition. That explains why there is so much reinventing the wheel.

Yet it is possible to navigate the world of interdisciplinary research. The trick is simply to know what landmarks to focus on. These landmarks constitute what we refer to as the anatomy of a perspective. They are anatomical in the sense that all syntheses have them. They are perspectives because they tend to be more individual than collective and because they lack the coherence of the disciplines from which they emerge. This anatomy can be described in terms of six elements:

1   the structure of borrowing across disciplines;
2   the predominant assumptions about the nature of the real world;
3   the preferences for analytic forms;
4   the ambitions of the analysis;
5   the intellectual centre of gravity; and
6   the underlying research agenda.

The essays in this volume all borrow more heavily from political science than from economics. By implication, they tend to introduce economic concepts more carefully while taking for granted some familiarity with the building blocks of political science. If the structure of borrowing were otherwise, the balance of attention would be reversed. This asymmetry of treatment can have perverse effects on the uninitiated. Often what is taken for granted in the predominant discipline is more important to the analysis than what is explained as being borrowed. Therefore identifying the structure of the synthesis is useful not so much for what it reveals, but for what it suggests might be hidden from view.

Assumptions about the real world are usually among the most important of these hidden factors. In the essays here, we have asked our contributors to be as explicit as possible in setting out what they believe to be fundamental. For example, Kassim and Menon focus on patterns of delegation or institutionalized power relations. Cowles is interested in the influence of different types of agency. Van der Veen is concerned with ideas, Pistor with ideologies, and Pahre with self-interest.

Such assumptions are often tightly bound up with analytic preferences. Therefore it is also important to note how arguments are structured within a given perspective. Verdun tackles this issue directly by looking at the presumed tension between modelling and description. Jones is more inclined to admit to complexities and Moses is predominantly interested in identifying recurrent patterns. The point to note is that analytic preferences are not just about the presence or absence of equations. They also concern the balance between general theory and specific description. Hence Farrell tends to situate events within a general theoretical context while Schelkle is more concerned with identifying developments as they have occurred.

Having said that, description does not exist for its own sake. All the political economy perspectives that we illustrate (and all interdisciplinary perspectives) have underlying analytic ambitions. Recognizing these ambitions is important not just for understanding the arguments, but also for interpreting why some things have been described while others have not. For Schelkle, the ambition is to distinguish between what is new and what is not. Farrell's ambition is to see what fits within particular heuristic frameworks. This distinction is subtle and yet still has important implications for what each author chooses to describe. Of course the same point could be made with respect to each of the chapters. The implication is not that our contributors have selected only that data which proves their point. Rather it is that they have not selected data irrelevant to the point that they are trying to make. They have not described what (outgoing) European Commission President Romano Prodi had for breakfast this morning either.

Each of the chapters in this volume also draws upon a slightly different strand in the literature. Moreover, identifying the differences in the strands is an important part of identifying the perspective as a whole. Some of the traditions are very easy to locate because they have such a clear centre of gravity. The critical school discussed in Pistor's chapter centres on the Canadian University of York and the Dutch University of Amsterdam. Jones focuses on that group of comparative political economists that draws inspiration from the writing of Karl Polanyi. Moses points to the influence of Albert O. Hirschman and Verdun examines the analytic divide between Europe and the United States.

In turn each of these communities has an underlying research programme. Such programmes are different from the specific analytic ambitions of particular authors. However, they are related insofar as they provide the context within which such ambitions are formed. Van der Veen's work on the influence of ideas is part of a larger effort to reintroduce real-world complexity into political and economic analysis while Pahre's emphasis on preference mapping is part of a programme to extend the application of insights from simplified models. Hussain and Kassim fall somewhere in between. The principal–agent models they favour are often too complex for formal treatment and yet too simple to satisfy those who believe that bureaucratic relations extend far beyond the act of delegation. Yet, as Verdun and Cowles suggest, there is no necessary contradiction between different research programmes. Simple models can yield important insights on a complex reality, and real-world complexity can help to extend simple regularities to encompass unexpected anomalies. The point is that whether or not they contradict, these research programmes remain distinct tendencies within the literature. The challenge is to figure out what such tendencies imply about the structure and meaning of the research itself.

Measuring success and failure

The most important implication of the different tendencies in the literature is found in the measurement of success and failure. As we mentioned at the start of this introduction, we do not believe that all explanations are equally valid. However, we do believe that the validity of an explanation should be understood within an appropriate context. Of course all arguments should be internally consistent.

By the same token, any description of the real world should be accurate insofar as it is detailed. However, beyond these universal standards for validity, an argument can be assessed only with reference to its own perspective: its consistency with similar arguments and with its own foundational assumptions; the relative sophistication of its analysis; the ambitions of its author; its engagement with the literature from which it emerges; and its contribution to the larger research programme.

The strong claim that we wish to make in this context is that no single standard for validity predominates over all others. Verdun makes this case in more detail in her chapter. For the moment, it suffices simply to contrast the two predominant decision-rules that have polarized political science over the past decade and more – one emphasizing parsimony and the other emphasizing completeness. The advocates of parsimony draw support from Occam's razor, which is the principle that, all things being equal, the simpler explanation is the better. The advocates of completeness draw support from the observation that all things are rarely equal and nothing in the real world is ever simple. Obviously, both sides are right and both are wrong. Simple explanations can be useful even when incomplete. Sewage may not cause cholera in any strict sense, but you can greatly reduce the incidence of cholera by treating sewage. By the same token, the motives behind European integration may not be purely economic, but you can understand a lot about what has happened in Europe over the past five decades by focusing on who got what, where, when, and how.

More complete explanations get closer to the real world. Economics have been important in European integration, but ideas have also played a crucial role as have the individuals who promoted those ideas. The disadvantage of introducing this notion of ideational and individual influence is that it complicates the learning process by increasing what we need to know about EU and by reducing what we can learn from European experience about the way the world works in general. From the parsimonious perspective, such increased complexity constitutes a bad trade-off. From the perspective of completeness, the increased complexity is the objective. Moreover, the suggestion of a compromise does little to change the different measures of validity. We could argue that scholars should strive to maximize the 'leverage' of their analysis by including only those variables where the return in terms of explanation exceeds the complexity of adding to the argument as a whole. However, by doing so, we are more likely to create a third tradition than to reconcile the advocates of parsimony or completeness.

The conclusion to draw from this multiplicity of standards for argument is that we need to be familiar with many different perspectives on European integration if we are to evaluate their respective contributions to the literature. Along the way, we should not lose sight of the fact that our goal is to understand what is happening in Europe and perhaps also to discover whether what is happening in Europe can increase our understanding of the larger world. The good news is that Europe is changing rapidly at the moment, and anything that changes so quickly and so completely is bound to be interesting. The bad news is that the problems we have to address are complicated, even if the arguments we wish to make are relatively simple. The implications of enlargement and institutional reform, the challenge of decision-making at the European level or across multiple levels of governance, the stability of the single currency, the threat of right-wing extremism, the crisis of the welfare state, and the impact of slow growth and high unemployment – these are all problems that require the insights of many disciplines. At a minimum they require an understanding of politics and economics. This understanding of political economy should be free of internal contradiction, it should accurately reflect developments in the real world, and it should be appropriate to the problems addressed and the wider analytic tradition. This is no mean task. We hope that the essays to follow will help as an introduction to a solution.

Advice and acknowledgment

In drafting this introduction, we chose not to provide a brief summary of each of the chapters. Rather than encourage readers to flip back and forth through the book, we thought it would be easier to provide an abstract at each chapter start. This may break up the flow of the volume. However, given our ambition to introduce a variety of perspectives, we doubt that there is much flow to disrupt in any event. That said, the chapter organization in this volume is not arbitrary. The first four chapters originally formed a part special issue of the *Journal of European Public Policy* (vol. 10, no. 1 (2003), pp. 84–158; http://www.tandf.co.UK/journals/routledge/13501763.html) and are intended to be more encompassing. The following six chapters are slightly more specific. This distinction does not hold entirely. The chapter by Jones focuses primarily on two writers and one causal argument. By contrast, the chapter by Pistor has a much wider ambit. Nevertheless, we retain the view that the first four papers provide a good background for any reading of the chapters to follow. We chose not to organize the volume around an arbitrary division between formal modelling and thick description. Indeed, the first two chapters argue explicitly against this distinction. Readers may nonetheless be interested to know that the more formalized chapters are those by Moses and Pahre. Van der Veen and Pistor have a more linguistic, ideational focus. Farrell and Schelkle are more grounded in current events.

In addition, we have chosen these ten chapters as an introduction to the variety of perspectives available for understanding the political economy of European integration. This collection is not comprehensive, but it should be comprehensible and it should also be relatively complete. Suggestions for additional areas of coverage are always welcome and would make useful fodder for future editions.

We would like to thank all our contributors for their hard work and for their willingness to respond to numerous requests for revisions. Jeremy Richardson provided terrific support and encouragement both of the original special issue and of the later edited volume. The membership of the EU Political Economy interest section of the European Union Studies Association (EUSA) of the United States has supported this project all along and provided both the editors and the contributors. Melissa Padfield and Stefanie Fishel, both graduate students at the University of Victoria, made it possible for us to complete the manuscript by providing excellent editorial assistance. Financial support for this assistance was provided by a SSHRC grant (410-2002-0522) held by Amy Verdun. Our partners and children made it possible by providing the space and support that we needed to pull things together.

Finally, we should point out that this volume has an introduction but not a conclusion. We debated long and hard over this point. In the end, however, we decided that like many a textbook the last chapter rarely is the one that sums up. However, it is hard to do well without some introduction into the different perspectives of analysis. We hope that this volume will help stimulate further interdisciplinary research and encourage the use of political economy approaches in such research design. Whether we succeed in that ambition, however, cannot be written in these pages. If we succeed, it will be written elsewhere.

1 An American–European divide in European integration studies

Bridging the gap with international political economy (IPE)

Amy Verdun[1]

Abstract: There appears to be a divide in the literature between American and European approaches to European integration studies. This chapter discusses the differences between the two types of approaches, and what problems occur from having this divide. It is argued that IPE offers a venue for dialogue between those who focus exclusively on the EU (labelled here as 'European approaches') and those who see the EU case to be part of more general phenomena and who seek to produce general theories ('American approaches'). The chapter suggests that IPE offers a useful body of literature to narrow the gap between 'American' and 'European' studies of European integration.

Introduction

The field of European integration studies has gone through a turbulent fifteen years in terms of its scholarly analysis and its implications for European integration theory. Whereas the origins of European integration theory can be traced back to American International Relations literature, present day theories are inspired by a wide range of approaches and case studies produced on both sides of the Atlantic. Though we see many fascinating theoretical approaches in the literature, the relationship between the empirical case studies and theory is not always clear. Some scholars are mainly interested in describing the phenomenon in which they are interested. They want to reflect on the theoretical approaches available in order to place matters in perspective, but are not necessarily interested in developing or improving existing theories. Others use the case of European integration and policy-making in the European Union (EU) as a way to develop new theoretical approaches or to amend existing theories. As a result there appears to be a gap between these case study-oriented and theory-oriented approaches. Furthermore, it seems to be that the former often comes out of European schools whereas the latter proliferates in the United States. Thus, one could provocatively claim that there is a split between European and American scholarship, which is characterized by how theory and empirics are treated.

This chapter examines why there is a gap between the more theory-oriented American and case study-oriented European scholarship in the field of European integration/EU studies and how the gap can be narrowed. It suggests that the IPE literature can serve as a vehicle to bridge the gap. To develop this argument the chapter is structured as follows. The first section offers an analysis of the split between American and European scholarship in the field of European integration/ EU studies. The second introduces the field of IPE and reviews four of its schools of thought: neorealism, institutionalism, social constructivism and a collection of approaches critical of the status quo referred to here as the critical school. The third section discusses how IPE can contribute to bridging the gap between the two approaches in the field of European integration. The last section draws some conclusions.

The EU as *sui generis* case? Views from both sides of the Atlantic

The developments in European integration theory mirror the rapid changes that have occurred in contemporary Europe, in particular those that have taken place since the late 1980s. In Europe this sea change has led scholars to being interested in understanding this process, which to many observers seems excessively complex and not easily comparable with other political processes at the national level, or indeed elsewhere in the world. Frustrated with the inability of the traditional integration theories to explain, predict or clarify the outcome of the European integration process, numerous scholars have moved to focusing more narrowly on the EU as a unique case and develop specific theories about the European integration process (for a review of European integration theories, see Verdun 2002).

It has long been questioned whether the European integration process should be considered to be a *sui generis* case or a case that resembles others (cf. Wallace 1983). A number of scholars – usually Europeans – tend to treat it as the former (see *inter alia* Shaw 1999). These scholars argue that the integration process is sufficiently distinct that it merits being conceptualized differently and requires specific theories. In doing so, they offer explanations that are often exclusively applicable to the EU. Others do not argue the case quite as forcefully, but argue instead that the European integration process is in-between a *sui generis* case and a case like many others (see *inter alia* Kohler-Koch 1997). Scholars on the other side of the Atlantic, however, tend to focus on the European integration process as an example of a process of institution building and policy-making not dissimilar to those in other parts of the world (see e.g. the debate in a 1997 issue of *ECSA Review*, i.e. Caporaso *et al.* 1997). They see the European integration process as a reaction to pressures that many countries, also those outside Europe, are facing (see also Cohen 1998; Mattli 1999). Countries in some parts of the world may make different choices than those in other parts, and hence do not proceed towards regional integration in the way that Europe has done. These scholars would argue that the EU is not fundamentally different from other forms of governance. It is just in a different stage of institutionalization (see also Jupille and Caporaso 1999).

In terms of their contribution to the literature, the studies that adopt a *sui generis* approach to the study of the EU tend to move away from contributing to the wider Political Science literature.[2] Instead, they develop theoretical approaches that are derived from European integration studies, and typically assume that their approaches are not necessarily applicable to studies beyond those related to the EU. Even though there are notable exceptions, this development has had the effect, in particular in American circles, of making European integration studies less important because the connection between it and the broader Political Science literature has become less obvious. As Simon Bulmer has put it: 'The *sui generis* assumptions of some political integration theory and the lack of interdisciplinary dialogue have risked confining European integration to an intellectual "ghetto" within the social sciences' (Bulmer 1997: 8).

As a result of their view of the European integration process as being comparable to processes going on elsewhere, 'American scholars' tend to place their study of the EU within a broader framework of theoretical approaches that are of a more general nature. Their aim typically is to show that the European integration process is yet another case with which they can show that a particular theoretical approach can be proven to be right or wrong. In other words, their aim is to contribute to the general theoretical literature using the case of the EU.

By contrast, many 'European scholars' seem more inclined to invent a new *ad hoc* approach, or label, to signal their specific approach, which they have derived from their exclusive study of the European integration process. These European scholars often aim at making a new contribution to the more narrow literature on European integration. In doing so they do not concern themselves too much with questions regarding what European integration studies can contribute to the overall Political Science literature.

The categories 'American' and 'European', mentioned above, are introduced here for purely analytical reasons and also to be provocative. The terms 'American approach' and 'European approach' (or 'American scholar' versus 'European scholar') should be seen as terms that are used to capture a group of scholars that fit broadly into these categories. In this chapter we understand a 'European approach' to be aiming at examining the European integration process as separate from processes in other parts of the world. In the extreme case this approach considers Europe to be a *sui generis* case. The theoretical contribution to the literature that this approach makes applies only to the case of Europe. It does not aim at taking the integration process to be an example of a phenomenon that exists outside Europe. In turn, the 'American approach', as we use it here, aims at fitting into the broader approaches of Political Science literature. According to this approach, the European integration process is only one case, and hence one should examine other cases as well. These studies aim at contributing to the wider Political Science literature.

Though the dichotomy is clearly artificial and provocative, the names of these categories are selected to reflect the apparent cultural differences in academia on both sides of the Atlantic. There are of course Americans who contribute to the European approach (Peterson 2001), and Europeans who apply an American approach (Hix 2002).[3] Furthermore, let us be clear that there are indeed European integration scholars who adopt approaches that speak to the general Political Science approaches and/or who make broader comparisons in their studies (*inter alia* Börzel and Risse 2002; Hix 1994; Knill and Lenschow 2001; Majone 1997, 2001a,b; Scharpf 1997). Likewise, there are numerous American-trained scholars who have a keen interest in European integration as such and who have incorporated European scholarship in their research (*inter alia* Ingebritsen 1998; McNamara 1998; Mattli 1999; Moravcsik 1998; Pierson 1996; Pollack 2001).

The above-mentioned two trends – to examine European integration merely from either a European perspective or an American perspective, that is, too much specificity or too much examining Europe as just another case study – are each unrewarding. A criticism of the American approach is that these scholars are so busy trying to prove to their fellow (American) political scientists that they are eager to make a contribution to the general literature that they are unable to appreciate the complexity, diversity and uniqueness of the European integration process. Also, they often choose their case studies in such a way that they can contribute most easily to that literature, rather than that they are necessarily genuinely interested in the European integration process as such. They shy away from the fact-finding, descriptive, explorative research or research with inductive methodologies designed to gather information about the integration process. By contrast, one can criticize the European approach for being overly inward-looking or for reinventing the wheel. One sometimes wonders to what extent the new approach is really all that new or significantly different from what more general approaches offer. Furthermore, it is often unclear how these theoretical approaches can be falsified or tested, as it is not clear that they could apply to other cases. In fact, the authors of these approaches often state that it is not their intention or ambition that their theories be generalizable beyond the scope of the EU.

So why would authors stick to one or the other trend? Sometimes it appears that scholars are merely signalling to one another to what body of literature they belong rather than fully engaging with one another in a scholarly debate. The process that seems to be going on is one in which debates are happening in distinct academic territories. This behaviour can be found in the way the research problem is identified, the literature to which one wants to make a contribution, the academic references cited, and the theoretical and methodological approaches chosen. It may be that this territorial divide is logical if one takes into consideration the academic criteria in both Europe and North America. In Europe it is broadly felt that one needs to contribute to the overall literature, and preferably find a label/approach that will be associated with one's name, thus contributing to one's fame in the field. In North America one's reputation depends on how well-known one is in the general field study, such as Political Science. In North America the field journals are typically rated lower than general journals (thus *American Political Science Review* is considered to be a 'higher ranked' journal than *International Organization*). More importantly, contributing to regional studies is considered of even less scholarly value than contributing to a general field journal (thus a publication in *International Organization* is considered to be of higher scholarly value than a publication in a regional journal, such as *Journal of Common Market Studies*).

The divide in European integration studies seems to have also been taking place in the area of International Political Economy (IPE). Scholars in this field study the processes that lie in the broad intersection of international politics and economics. IPE deals with questions such as why actors (states, sub-state actors and international institutions) collaborate. Research questions include regional integration, financial market integration, regulation (deregulation and re-regulation), transfer of sovereignty, multilateralism and so on. We shall argue below that IPE offers a venue for dialogue between those who focus exclusively on the EU and those who see the EU case to be part of more general phenomena. It is, of course, not the intention to profess that IPE is the only body of literature that can be of use to studies of European integration, nor that others would be less valuable. Rather the aim is to address how we can make sure the various approaches continue to have a dialogue together. IPE is seen as 'one' route to get there. Let us now turn to a brief introduction of that literature.[4]

The field of IPE

The IPE literature has typically been composed of work by authors at the crossroads of international politics and international economics, and as such the field contributed importantly to the understanding of the integration process (Lawton, Rosenau and Verdun 2000). Throughout the early post-war period IPE was not yet developed as a field of study of Political Science, but rather was occupied by scholars in the Economics discipline. With the increasing quantification of the Economics discipline and the increasing use of mathematics and formal models in that discipline, the study of the intersection of international politics and economics slowly became abandoned by Economists and increasingly occupied by Political Scientists. They included in particular scholars who studied the realm of international trade, finance and regional economic cooperation. Among the early scholarly work we find Baldwin (1971), Cooper (1968), Keohane and Nye (1972), Kindleberger (1970) and Strange (1970, 1971, 1972).[5] IPE continued to grow, particularly as the world experienced global recession and hyperinflation in the 1970s, the debt crisis, and increasing international interdependence. Before the word 'globalization' had gained popularity, IPE scholars were already studying the effects of increasing interconnectedness of international economics and politics (Gilpin 1987). Topics that remained of interest to IPE scholars were in particular international finance, monetary policy, exchange rate policy, trade, economic cooperation, regional economic integration and so on.

In the 1980s IPE became more attractive as a field due to the eagerness of scholars to understand prominent processes in the international domain: the debt crises, increasing interdependence, policy learning, and slowly but surely regional integration, together with changes in policy-making signalled, for example, by the prominence of neoliberal politics and its accompanying processes of liberalization, deregulation and financial market integration. The growth of financial markets was another important characteristic that had taken off in the 1970s and continued to influence world politics throughout the 1980s and beyond. In the 1990s, after the end of the cold war and with the rise of 'globalization', IPE obtained yet more popularity amongst Political Scientists. The concept of globalization emerged even though it is often argued that the world may not be quite as globalized as it was in the late nineteenth and early twentieth century. Though the concept is often not carefully defined, it is generally accepted that it includes three things: (1) internationalization, (2) the information and technological revolution, and (3) liberalization. States, markets and non-state actors reacted to these phenomena in a number of ways. Increasingly national governments have been moving towards further opening up of their economies to selected other countries and markets, whilst at the same time not wanting to open up completely. The easiest way to open up whilst protecting is by creating an institutional framework which includes some states and/or markets, but excludes others. Non-state actors, such as large corporations, have also gained importance in recent years. They too have been keen to have an institutional framework of this nature (see Maria Green Cowles, Chapter 2 below). IPE deals with these topics, and the European integration process is a typical example of a response to these challenges posed by globalization and financial market integration. But before IPE started to take off in European integration studies it was the field of IR that made the first major contribution to the theorizing about the European integration process.

As is well known, IR theories developed by scholars in the United States lay at the heart of the two most widely cited traditional integration theories: neofunctionalism (Haas 1958, 1964, 1968) and intergovernmentalism (Hoffmann 1966). Neofunctionalism tried to offer an alternative to the Realist school of thought. It saw the European integration process as a direct response to functional needs of states. It also foresaw that domestic, transnational and supranational actors would engage in regional integration to improve their efficiency in governance, given their relative close proximity and the various possibilities for collaboration. In studying the European integration process, it had in mind comparisons with other parts of the world. Ernst Haas's neofunctionalist approach was soon challenged by Stanley Hoffmann's intergovernmentalism. This approach, in contrast to neofunctionalism, belonged to the Realist school. It argued that the European integration process could only be understood if one examined the interests and power positions of various national state leaders and their interests. The obstructive behaviour of the French President Charles de Gaulle in particular lay at the basis of Hoffmann's work. Another theoretical approach promoted in this period was an approach developed by Karl Deutsch. He examined groups of elites, and the communication amongst them (Deutsch *et al.* 1957, 1967). Deutsch's approach did not attract the attention that neofunctionalism and intergovernmentalism did. However, it has been argued that constructivism, which gained popularity from the 1980s onwards, in fact follows in the footsteps of Deutsch. The two dominant integration theories lost their appeal in the 1970s (Haas 1975, 1976; Webb 1983).

In their overview of IPE literature since the 1950s Katzenstein, Keohane and Krasner (1998) argue that European integration theory was strongly influenced by

American scholars until the early 1980s Since then American scholars have been less inclined to create their own general theories of European integration based on their own research, but rather have relied on the empirical work conducted by the Europeans (Katzenstein *et al.* 1998: 655). Though fewer in number, contributions to the European integration literature by American scholars have been quite prominent, such as Moravcsik (1998), Pierson (1996), Tsebelis (1994). Numerous publications in fact have come out in the IPE flagship journal *International Organization* (*inter alia* Moravcsik 1991; Pollack 1997; Sandholtz 1993). Since the early 1990s, both European and American scholars have published scholarly pieces on European integration that have adopted theoretical approaches that borrowed concepts and insights from Comparative Politics, Public Policy, but also from International Political Economy.

Four schools of thought in IPE

Although IPE scholars have traditionally been subdivided into three schools, Liberalism, Mercantilism and Marxism (Woods 2001), this chapter will focus on the schools of thought (and divisions amongst them) that have become more dominant in the past decade. Based on the ongoing debates in the IPE journals, such as *International Organization*, one could say that it is fairly common to subdivide the IPE approaches into four categories: neorealism, neoliberal institutionalism, social constructivism and the critical approaches.

Neorealism

The neorealist approaches are among the IPE approaches that take the state as the dominant actor in determining the outcome of international politics. The seminal work by Waltz (1979) argues that the international system can be understood only by looking at the actions of states. They act in their own self-interest, and try to maximize their interests based on fixed *ex ante* preferences. The outside world is perceived as being in a state of chaos in which anarchy prevails. At times a major player can impose order on this chaos. But that state will do that only when it is in the interest of that major player. The original work by Waltz did not allow for any role for domestic politics or international organisations. However, in reply to its critics (Keohane 1986) neorealism opened up to the possibility of domestic forces possibly affecting state preferences and perceived interests. Yet, for the outcome of international bargaining and cooperation, the locus of attention remained the state. Realist approaches have found their way into the study of the EU, especially to explain the behaviour of inter-state bargaining (Garrett 1993; Grieco 1995).

Neoliberal institutionalism

The neoliberal institutionalist approaches accept that states are the primary actors in the world and thus that neorealism 'provides a good starting point for the analysis of cooperation and discord [in the international system]' (Keohane 1984: 245). However, in addition one should recognize that institutions can have an effect of their own. Institutions are defined by Keohane as 'sets of practices and expectations'. They can facilitate interstate agreements and enable states to pursue their own interests through cooperation (Keohane 1984: 246). More recent institutionalist approaches have emphasized a larger role for institutions. They have emphasized the importance of path dependence, socialization and policy learning (Hall and Taylor 1996). Institutions, in this more recent view, set the path for the development of policies, rules and procedures. By having this historic precedent and standard operating procedures, the policy-making process is influenced. Sometimes emphasis is placed on the fact that international institutions can be more effective in imposing rules and regulations. Thus nation-states will be inclined to follow those rules and regulations more frequently, consistently and without clear direct links to self-interest, than realist accounts would lead us to believe. In recent years institutionalism has been frequently adopted in studies of European integration (*inter alia* Bulmer 1994a,b; Pierson 1996).

Social constructivism

Since the second half of the 1990s the social constructivist school has gained a lot of terrain and has appeared to be a 'new' school of thought. However, as always with so-called 'novelties', the approach had been around for quite some time. Already in the 1960s Berger and Luckmann (1966) outlined their social constructivist approach. They identified three core assumptions. The first concerns the nature of the individual. He/she is taken to be a social creature that creates and institutionalizes new knowledge about 'reality' and finds his/her personal identity based on social processes. The second assumption is that our observation of 'reality' may be an artefact, as it is coloured by whoever observes or interprets it. The third concerns how social scientists study social action. They are involved in the process, and hence their action and previous socialization colours their findings. Social constructivism was made more prominent in IPE literature through the work of Ruggie (1975, 1998) and others (*inter alia* Checkel 1998, 1999a; Finnemore 1996a; Risse 2000). More recently European integration scholars have adopted the social constructivist approach in their studies (Christiansen *et al.* 1999; Diez 1997; Marcussen 2000).

Critical approaches

There is not one uniform school of thought that encompasses the so-called 'critical approaches'. Often reference is made to a number of them, such as various forms of Marxism, the British critical school (Palan 1992), the Amsterdam School (Van der Pijl 1998), the neo-Gramscians (Cox 1981, 1983a, 1995), but also various forms of post-materialists, such as reflectivists (Jørgensen 1997) and post-structuralists (Walker 1989). These approaches all have in common that they criticize the traditional approaches of IPE and IR. They argue that the traditional schools focus too much on the state and fail to understand how the underlying structure divides power and wealth. They are critical in that they see the status quo to benefit the rich and the already well-off. Moreover, they argue that the international structure widens the gap between the 'haves' and the 'have-nots'. These approaches not only criticize the traditional approaches for their normative values and their objects of study, but also criticize the academic method of rationalism and causal models with hypotheses testing. They share with the social constructivists the assumption that there is no clear 'reality out there' but that this world is to be interpreted, and that the researcher plays an important role in that process. In recent years some European integration studies have been inspired by some of these more critical approaches in their studies. In particular the work of European scholars has been more open to these approaches (*inter alia* Van Apeldoorn 2002).

These four approaches have in common that they focus on the questions regarding the role of the state and the interaction between the state and the system. The neorealists place the most emphasis on the state. Neoliberal institutionalists add to that the importance of institutions, as either rules and regimes or more formal organizations. The social constructivists add to these factors the fact that the actors (states, policy-makers, social scientists) are all influenced and formed by their culture, education, socialization and identity, and thus these factors will influence the role they play in this interplay between states, institutions and the system. The critical schools underline that those interactions are not value free, and that the outcome ought to be taken into consideration when politics are made, and are studied.

IPE and European integration studies

IPE approaches were a welcome addition to IR approaches. The latter typically focused on foreign policies and on the policies of states vis-à-vis other states. IPE offered to look at economic interactions between states which opened up the 'states' and included many more actors and factors, in particular the transnational and domestic actors (state and non-state actors). European integration theories have built on the original two integration theories in a number of ways, and in so doing have taken on important IPE characteristics.

As mentioned above, intergovernmentalists were originally pure realists. However, the most recent intergovernmental approach to European integration, by Andrew Moravcsik, gradually took on a more liberal perspective on the integration process. It incorporates the role of domestic interest groups in helping to define national state preferences. Economic factors are taken very seriously. However, even though the incorporation of domestic politics in this approach is a real innovation compared to the traditional approach, the approach still stresses that the states have the ultimate influence over the process. The effects on the process of the actions of institutions, supranational actors and the like are dismissed (Moravcsik 1998). This approach is very useful in studying treaty negotiations and intergovernmental bargaining as well as examining the state preferences of EU Member States. It offers scholars conceptual tools to analyse the state-specific characteristics and interests as well as the power-play that goes on among them.

The observation that EU Member States have no longer felt the need to protect sovereignty at all costs has puzzled many neorealists, and in turn has given more ammunition to studies of institutionalism. Institutionalisms in all kinds of dimensions have been used to explain why states give up their sovereignty or 'pool their sovereignty' (Keohane and Hoffmann 1991). Regimes, sets of rules and formal organizations are able to offer services to states that they in turn would be unable to safeguard by merely focusing on national state preferences. Neofunctionalism, has some similarities with neoliberal institutionalism, focuses on the degree of 'order' in society. It hypothesizes under what conditions societal actors, the state and the supranational actors would transfer their loyalties to the supranational level. It theorizes about interstate cooperation from a functional perspective. Thus it hypothesizes the transfer of sovereignty on the basis of policy-making efficiency and effectiveness. In recent years the study of the EU by those who are broadly favourable to the claims of neofunctionalism increased dramatically (Burley and Mattli 1993; Stone Sweet and Sandholtz 1997, 1998a; Tranholm-Mikkelsen 1991). Various authors, in a number of different ways, have each made persuasive accounts of the European integration process by adopting a historical institutionalist approach (*inter alia* Bulmer 1994a,b; Pierson 1996; Wincott 1995). These approaches are able to examine the European integration process that continues to go on outside the grand bargaining and the intergovernmental conferences (see in this context also the multilevel governance approaches[6]). It offers conceptual tools to examine the role of institutions, be they actual organizations, a regime or set of rules. The concept of path dependence offers us insights in how some processes are influenced by decisions made in the past. It offers us an approach that is suitable for examining the ongoing policy-making process, and the role of supranational institutions in this process.

Social constructivists have further refined their object of study. They argue that the integration process falls prey to the visions and images that the politicians, policy-makers, but also social scientists have in mind. They also argue that the role of socialization, knowledge, and perceived reality is helping to create the Europe of tomorrow. More recently scholars with this inclination have been arguing forcefully against some of the assumptions of rationalist approaches, in particular those of intergovernmentalism, arguing that a lot of socialization and preference formation occurs in between the moments of intergovernmental bargaining. In this view the bureaucratic politics and interdepartmental politics (e.g. competition between various Directorate Generals within the Commission) are as important as the grand bargains that take place at Intergovernmental Conferences or at European Summits (Christiansen *et al.* 2002). These approaches offer conceptual tools to examine the process behind the process. That is, the subtleties within institutions, Member States, and the policy-making process. It questions the capacity of the state-centric and institutionalist approaches to identify unambiguous preferences, interests, policies and so on. These approaches are inclined to consider more factors that aim at describing the process. In so doing, they want to keep open the option that ideas, culture, language, personalities, sub-entities may be of crucial importance, thus leading to different variables (often many variables) as being important.

The critical school argues that the integration process has become too much focused on economic integration within the context of a neoliberal regime. It also argues that the kind of integration created in Europe benefits the already well-off. Critical approaches aim at correcting the imbalance. They also work at conceptualizing how a fair and just Europe can be created. Critical approaches are concerned that the European integration process will weaken state–society relations. Numerous neo-Gramscian perspectives question the underlying hegemonic nature of the European integration project (Bieler and Morton 2001; Van Apeldoorn *et al.* 2003). Finally they call for strengthening of democratic processes in the EU and increasing accountability, transparency and legitimacy of EU governance. These approaches are in many ways in opposition to the 'mainstream' approaches. They question the rationality of market forces and the 'choice' that it assumes. Instead they develop concepts that can assist the analysis of how the integration process may be influenced by power relations that have been built up in the course of the integration process.

Most of these IPE approaches, especially those applied to the EU, have also managed to incorporate domestic factors, something for which the field of IR has been strongly criticized (Hix 1994; Jupille and Caporaso 1999; Kassim 1994). IPE has for that matter been able to overcome the problems that critiques have identified with 'pure' IR approaches. Each of these approaches offers analytical tools and plausible suggestions (indeed sometimes hypotheses) that social scientists interested in the integration process can reflect on. The strength and weaknesses of these approaches are quite different from one another. But each of these approaches offers tools and concepts that are generalizable within the context of the broader IPE approaches, and as such offer a possible entry point for general discussion.

So what would be the benefit of adopting IPE approaches in European integration? First, it offers a range of diverse theoretical frameworks, which in turn facilitate an implicit or explicit comparison of the European integration process with other processes. Hence it offers tools for broader theorization. Second, IPE is sensitive to insights from various fields, such as Comparative Politics, IR, Public Policy literature and so on. As such it caters to the European approach, in that it is sufficiently open to the specificity of the European integration process; the specificity or uniqueness of the European integration process can be analysed and discussed with IPE approaches. To advocate IPE as a venue for debate is to aim at finding a middle ground where the debate can take place. In recent years there have been claims that IR would no longer be useful for explaining European integration (Jachtenfuchs 2001: 259). What we argue here, however, is that IPE would offer a suitable body of literature to explain European integration. In another contribution to the literature there has been a move away from the diversity set out above. It is not very useful that the debate in the literature has moved to one on the dichotomy between the so-called 'rationalists' and the 'constructivists'

(Pollack 2001) or the 'rationalists' versus the 'reflectivists' (Smith 2001). Pollack argues that rationalists broadly speaking hold the same rationalist assumptions about research design:

> I would argue that liberal intergovernmentalism, rational-choice institution-alist analyses and even Grieco's purportedly neorealist voice opportunities hypothesis are all part of an emerging rationalist research programme which is rapidly establishing itself as the dominant paradigm in European integra-tion theory, at least in the United States.
>
> (Pollack 2001: 233)

This debate obscures the fact that there are cultural differences, and fundamentally territorial divides about the theoretical culture and body of literature one wants to belong to. The rules of the game in academia on both sides of the Atlantic seem to differ, and this split does not benefit the genuine exchange of ideas. But what that dichotomy also does not emphasize is the degree to which some approaches do not reflect on the case of the EU/European integration process to be informing the lit-erature broader than that of the EU/European integration process alone. As we have seen in the review of the IPE literature above, the constructivists offer as legitimate an IPE approach as the rationalist approaches. What we want to argue here is that the case of the European Union is just one amongst many cases. We would argue here that IPE offers a good body of literature for examining the integration process exactly because of its openness to rationalist and constructivist approaches, its general interest in the very thing that the integration process is often deals with, namely international economic cooperation.

Conclusions: bridging the gap

This chapter has argued that the 'American' and 'European' scholarship on the European Union and the European integration process is divided. It has been argued that there is a split between the cultures of scholarship on both sides of the Atlantic. In fact, a comparison could be drawn between the behaviour of scholars and that of dogs peeing to demarcate their territory. The European approach has been increasingly moving away from general theories and has been more inward focusing, thereby only seeing the case of Europe as the one that is interesting to study because of its inherent characteristics. In order to appear on the radar of the more general Political Scientists as well as American scholars with an interest in EU studies, these approaches need to be more outward looking and consider how their theories can be applicable to cases other than that of Europe. The American approach by contrast has been moving toward less case specificity in favour of contributing to the more general literature in Political Science. The chapter is also critical of the American approach that is overly preoccupied with theory and with making a contribution to the general Political Science literature and in doing so fails to appreciate the specificities of the case of Europe. The chapter suggests that an IPE approach will enable American scholars to do justice to the uniqueness of the

European integration process whilst at the same time allow them to focus on more general theorization. Overall the chapter argues that IPE as a field offers useful analytical and theoretical tools for EU/European integration studies to become more visible in the eyes of the generalists, whilst still respecting the diversity of theoretical approaches that exist on both sides of the Atlantic.

The benefits of using IPE approaches in European integration studies are three-fold. First, IPE approaches focus the research design on seeing the EU/European integration process as one case in the broader study of regional integration. They thereby transcend the *sui generis* or N = 1 debate. Second, IPE approaches as applied to the EU have responded to the critics from Comparative Politics and public policy in that their focus is on many more actors than on states alone. IPE approaches allow for the study of both state and non-state actors (domestic, transnational, supranational and international actors). Third, the kinds of debate going on in the European integration literature are also present in the IPE literature. These are the ones referred to above, that is, rationalists versus constructivists/reflectivists, but also the issue of generalizability and falsifiability of theoretical approaches. The advantage of using the IPE approach is that it continues to strive to place these debates within a broader framework, and not only focus on the case of the EU/European integration. It also means that similar theoretical discussions regarding other areas of study can have their influence on the debates that are taking place about the study of the EU/European integration.

In conclusion, though it may be natural to be signalling to what body of literature and what academic community one belongs, it would be beneficial if the transatlantic debate remains lively. Let us hope that in the years to come the two approaches will come closer together. This chapter has suggested that IPE could offer a useful bridge across the emerging divide.

Notes

1 The author wishes to thank James A. Caporaso, Rachel Cichowski, Christine Ingebritsen, Maria Green Cowles, Markus Jachtenfuchs, Erik Jones, John Keeler, Mark Pollack, Mark Thatcher, Michael Webb and two anonymous referees for comments, criticisms and suggestions on earlier versions of this article. The usual disclaimer applies.
2 This article reflects on how European integration studies contribute to the Political Science literature, even though academic scholarship in the area of European studies can and does contribute to interdisciplinary knowledge and thus will also contribute to other disciplines such as Law, Economics, Public Administration, Environmental Studies and so on.
3 An example of this inverse advocacy could be seen in action at a conference co-sponsored by UACES and the Central European University held in Budapest in April 2000. John Peterson (an American national) and Simon Hix (a British citizen) were each advocating the virtues of respectively 'European' and 'American' approaches. At some point it was so amusing to see them profess the benefits of the 'other' approach that the Chair of that panel, Helen Wallace, jokingly suggested that they should switch passports.
4 New journals have also been set up to try to bridge the gap. For example, the journal *European Union Politics* was founded with an almost exclusive aim to become a regional journal that will be taken seriously by mainstream American Political Science.

Thus it seeks to include pieces that discuss research on European politics that adopt methodologies and theoretical approaches from mainstream American Political Science.

5 It is generally argued that International Political Economy is a subfield of International Relations – scholars such as Strange argued that this statement should be reversed (see e.g. Strange 1988).

6 Note that multilevel governance approaches have a lot in common with these institutionalist approaches. It is the view of this author that they can also be considered IPE approaches in so far as they are aiming at more generalizable knowledge claims.

2 Non-state actors and false dichotomies

Reviewing IR/IPE approaches to European integration

Maria Green Cowles[1]

Abstract: Many IR and IPE theories marginalize non-state actors in a manner inconsistent with their role in EU integration, governance, and policymaking. Yet multinational firms, NGOs, and advocacy networks are increasingly important players in today's global economy. This review chapter examines four theories/approaches that tend to ignore this development: neorealism, institutionalism, constructivism, and the critical school. To shed light on the literature's marginalization of non-state actors, I identify three false dichotomies: (1) the international versus domestic, (2) the public versus private, and (3) the 'good' versus 'bad'. The chapter provides empirical evidence to demonstrate why these dichotomies must be transcended and discusses theoretical developments that better account for non-state actors. Finally, I recognize a fourth false dichotomy between the American IR/IPE theories and the European comparative, political economy, and governance approaches. Rather than adopting one approach over another, this chapter suggests that both schools of thought can benefit from one another.

Introduction

There is a temptation to argue that the heyday of firms and other non-state actors in European Union (EU) integration theories and policymaking occurred during the Single Market years.[2] The political role of multinational firms behind the 1992 programme (Cowles 1995; Sandholtz and Zysman 1989; Van Tulder and Junne 1998) and the subsequent mobilization of other interest organizations produced a flurry of writing, often in the pluralist vein, on these non-state actors (Anderson and Eliasson 1993; Coen 1997; Cowles 1996; Greenwood 1997; Greenwood *et al.* 1992; Mazey and Richardson 1993). Scholarly accounts of 'history-making events' (Peterson 1995) since the Single Market programme, however, have not involved these non-state actors to the same extent. Today, the sole focus of many International Relations (IR) and/or International Political Economy (IPE) scholars analysing the EU is on the nation-state. Indeed, if one only looks at the 'historic decisions' – the Maastricht, Amsterdam, and Nice treaties and the current convention on the future of Europe – as the summation of European integration since 1992, one might question the importance of non-state actors in our theoretical and methodological approaches to the EU today.

As Verdun notes in this volume, IR and IPE theories are crucial to our under-standing of international economic cooperation and the EU integration process itself. Yet the scope of non-state actors in these IR/IPE theories and approaches remains somewhat marginalized or, more precisely, 'ghetto-ized'. There is a ten-dency to narrow non-state actors' functions by limiting their activity to a single level of governance, by confining certain roles to the realm of traditional state and insti-tutional actors, by pre-assigning normative labels to them, and/or by restricting our analysis to certain kinds of policy analysis.

This ghetto-ization of non-state actors is nothing new. The role of the firm, for example, has been largely undertheorized in IR and IPE theories in general (Eden 1991; Sally 1995; Strange 1988, 1996). Yet the increasingly global economy, the transnationalization of markets (Newman and Bach 2002a), and the role of the EU as both a promoter of and bulwark against this transnational and global economy suggests the need to incorporate firms and other non-state actors more explicitly in our political economy approaches to the EU. Indeed, while the literature on global-ization is vast, one of its common strands is the recognition that global economic change creates new and different kinds of alignments of non-state actors around core issues and across borders (Weber 2001: 289).

This chapter reviews a specific set of IR/IPE literature in terms of its incorpo-ration of non-state actors given their relatively new and varied roles in the EU today. There are, of course, many IPE theories and approaches that focus on state and non-state actors. Examples would include the hegemonic stability theories surrounding international monetary policy (Krasner 1976), the classic work beginning with Dunning (1958) on the impact of foreign direct investment by multinational firms, and the more recent work on transnationalism (see Risse 2002). My focus is on those IR/IPE theories and approaches discussed by Verdun (Chapter 1 above): neorealism, institutionalism, social constructivism, and the critical school. Scholars have applied all four theories and/or approaches – individually or in various pairings – to European integration and EU studies in recent years.

The purpose of the chapter is not to suggest that one or more of these theories/ approaches are better than another, or to suggest an alternative theoretical frame-work (e.g. transnationalism). Rather, the purpose is to explain how this literature marginalizes non-state actors in a manner inconsistent with their roles in EU inte-gration, governance, and policymaking today. I focus on three false or artificial dichotomies, inherent in one or more of the theories/approaches, as a mechanism to explore this 'ghetto-ization'.[3] The first is the international/domestic dichotomy which appears in neorealist accounts. The second dichotomy is the public versus private debate, upheld in the rational choice strand of institutionalism and its offshoot, principal–agency theory. The third dichotomy is that of 'good versus bad' found in the constructivist and critical school approaches.

The chapter concludes with a fourth false or artificial dichotomy – the debate between IR/IPE approaches versus comparative and public political economy approaches to the EU. Many of these European governance approaches (Jachtenfuchs 2001) have made important advances in moving the study of non-state actors beyond the pluralist discussions of the 1990s. While one might be tempted to simply set aside the IR/IPE approaches in favour of the EU governance theories, I argue that such action would be premature. Indeed, this essay suggests that both schools of thought can benefit from one another.

Neorealism and the international/domestic dichotomy

Realists and neorealists focus their attention on states and their power to explain international cooperation. Liberal intergovernmentalism, the EU variant, argues that domestic actors, including non-state actors, inform the preferences of member states.[4] The Putnam model of two-level games, for example, focuses on the chiefs of government (COGs) or negotiators who bargain with their foreign counterparts to reach international agreements (Moravcsik 1993b). The COGs' 'win-sets' – their bargaining margin of manoeuvre – are determined by domestic interests alone.

Liberal intergovernmentalism makes a careful distinction between the functions of domestic and transnational interests/social groups. First, transnational interests can strengthen or undermine domestic support of a chief of government, but, unlike domestic actors, cannot impact the COGs' bargaining positions *per se* (Moravcsik 1993b: 32, 1993c). Second, when domestic interests are not able to organize themselves effectively, transnational actors may provide support to 'supranational entrepreneurs' who, under certain other conditions, influence EU history-making events (Moravcsik 1999a).

There are, however, two basic problems with this line of reasoning. The first problem centres on the capacity of non-state actors at the transnational level. To argue that transnationally organized interests matter only when domestic interests are disorganized is misleading. To maintain that the only role these transnational actors can then play is one of supporting supranational entrepreneurs is simply wrong. Transnationally organized interests, in fact, may have greater incentive – and thus work to organize and represent themselves more effectively – than domestic interests to encourage government cooperation. The supranational governance approach, for example, emphasizes how the firms' transnational market activity brings about pressures for governments to cooperate – with or without the participation of supranational entrepreneurs. Firms have an interest in seeking decisions being made at the supranational (EU) as opposed to national level (Stone Sweet and Sandholtz 1998a). Walter Mattli (1999) makes similar arguments and his political economy approach clearly suggests that the role of firms in EU cooperation and decision-making need not be limited to domestic or meso-level activity. Firms themselves may be part of the history-making phases of EU integration.

Indeed, transnationally organized actors will likely figure in the future development of European Security and Defence Policy (ESDP). Put another way, one cannot ignore the restructuring of the European defence industry and the subsequent creation of new transnational actors when assessing the future of defence cooperation. German DaimlerChrysler Aerospace, French Aérospatiale Matra, and Spanish CASA created the European Aerospace, Defence and Space Company (EADS) – the second largest private aerospace company in the world. While domestic constituencies like European taxpayers and lawmakers might influence COGs' decisions to 'buy European', decisions made by transnational corporate actors 'may well be the cement which will make permanent, or irreversible, the watershed decisions on defence integration' (Collester 2001: 386).

The false domestic versus international dichotomy

A second related problem with this line of reasoning is the false dichotomy between national and transnational/international interests. What liberal intergovernmentalism does not address is that consumer groups, environmental organizations, multinational firms, and transnational advocacy groups can participate simultaneously in international and domestic politics (Cowles 1995; Keck and Sikkink 1998). To claim that domestic social groups matter but transnational interests do not misses the point that increasingly these two groups are one and the same. For example, as domestic regulatory issues such as beef hormones and genetically modified organisms are placed on the EU and international negotiating table, domestic consumer groups mobilize at the European level or even at the transatlantic level, as in the Transatlantic Consumers Dialogue (Pollack and Shaffer 2001). EU and US businesses with extensive transatlantic investment meet in the Transatlantic Business Dialogue (TABD) to develop a 'transatlantic consensus' on key regulatory issues. This transnational consensus is, in effect, the firms' domestic consensus as well (Cowles 2001a).

To recognize this false dichotomy means to acknowledge the changing dynamics of state–society relations. In the first place, interest groups mobilize at different levels at various times in history. European multinational firms, for example, did not organize themselves in Brussels until the late 1970s to early 1980s. Thus the creation of a group like the European Round Table of Industrialists (ERT) and its support of the Single Market programme was a watershed event (Cowles 1994). It is not surprising, therefore, that one finds no evidence of large corporations influencing 'history-making events' prior to the Single Market programme. Since then, however, companies and other non-state actors have increasingly promoted their interests simultaneously in national, European, and international arenas.

While liberal intergovernmentalists rightly call on scholars to specify better the conditions under which non-state actors' representation matters, liberal intergovernmentalism in turn would be strengthened if it developed a more robust understanding of the multiple arenas in which non-state actors participate. This theory must also recognize that non-state actors do more than articulate their preferences or support supranational entrepreneurs. Increasingly, these actors set agendas, participate in negotiations, implement and/or have the authority to make policy in the first place. In other words, one must recognize the second false dichotomy between public versus private actors.

Institutional and the public/private dichotomy

Institutionalism explains why and how formal organizations, regimes and rules can facilitate interstate cooperation and, at times, encourage countries to pool their sovereignty. The three strands of institutionalism – rational choice, sociological and historical (Steinmo *et al.* 1992; Hall and Taylor 1996) – have all been applied to the EU. As discussed later, sociological and historical institutionalism are often coupled with the constructivist approach in various EU studies, and have been incorporated into many European governance and public policy approaches. Rational choice institutionalism remains more firmly anchored in the IR theoretical approach, and it is the institutionalist strand that is examined here.

Rational choice institutionalism and its offshoot, principal–agency theory, focus on why member states delegate powers to these supranational agents or institutions. It has been applied, for example, to explain why EU member states might confer certain powers and programs on the European Commission.[5] Principal–agent models generally identify four key functions for which member states might delegate authority to supranational institutions: (1) to monitor member state compliance, (2) to solve problems of 'incomplete contracting', (3) to serve as a genuinely independent regulator, and (4) to initiate policy proposals and set the agenda for the principals (Pollack 1997). Yet nowhere in this discussion of institutionalism and the delegation of authority is there a stated role for non-state actors.

However, non-state actors – organized below and/or above the state in transnational groups or coalitions – also participate in important ways in the principal–agent model. First, non-state actors, together with institutions, can influence the calculus of principals to delegate authority, to carry out 'incomplete contracting' and to serve as independent regulators. At noted above, the ERT publicly supported the Commission's Single Market programme. While the companies did not influence the Single European Act negotiations *per se*, they threatened to move their operations out of Europe if member states did not support effective institutional changes to carry out the 1992 project (Cowles 1995).

Second, non-state actors also participate in the shaping of policy proposals and agendas prior to, during, or even after the delegation of authority. Transnational coalitions and actors have been critical in shaping proposals and changing policy outcomes in East Asian economic dynamism, then-Soviet security policy, and African ivory conservationism (Risse-Kappen 1995). Multinational corporations have mobilized to shape the international agendas of international institutions such as the World Trade Organization (WTO), the World Intellectual Property Organization (WIPO), and the Organization for Economic Co-operation and Development (OECD). Key firms, for example, influenced the creation of the Trade-Related Intellectual Property Rights (TRIPs) agreement during the Uruguay Round (Sell 1995). Indeed, the TRIPs agreement would probably not have been achieved without the 'active agency' of these companies (Higgott, Underhill and Bieler 2000: 8). In the EU, the ERT led efforts to promote the open-method of coordination as part of the Lisbon European Council, and fostered the larger Lisbon goal of making the EU the most competitive and dynamic knowledge-based economy in the world (Hodson and Maher 2001; Sisson and Marginson 2001; Wallace 2001).

Third, non-state actors increasingly assume the traditional state or international institution responsibility of monitoring and enforcing international agreements (Keck and Sikkink 1998). International institutions often lack adequate monitoring and centralized enforcement mechanisms. Non-state actors can appeal to international institutions to promote compliance, serve as 'watchdogs' to report non-compliance, form transnational networks and create global public campaigns against negligent states (Börzel 2002). The work of the International Coalition to Ban Landmines did not end with the awarding of the Nobel Peace Prize. Rather, the NGO now monitors compliance of the treaty (Florini 2000: 213). These same actors can go before the courts to demand enforcement. Women's groups have done this rather effectively in the United Kingdom as a means to ensure that EU law is properly carried out and enforced at the national level (Mazey 1998).

Fourth, although not strictly part of the principal–agent theory, non-state actors can provide legitimacy to the supranational institutions who have received these powers. In recent years, a number of international institutions have brought in non-government organizations and firms to build transnational coalitions around key agenda items. The World Health Organization has forged partnerships with both NGOs and companies to promote key global public policies. In the European Union, where the issue of legitimacy or the democratic deficit is pronounced, the Trade Directorate General has engaged in an ambitious civil society programme to shore up support for its own trade agenda (Meunier 2003).[6] In short, non-state actors are now key players in creating global public policy (Reinicke 1998) and in participating in global governance in general (e.g. Clark 1995; Keck and Sikkink 1998; Price 1998; Ronit and Schneider 1999; Smith *et al.* 1997).

The false public versus private dichotomy

As M.J. Peterson pointed out a decade ago, the state – and for that matter, international institutions – do not monopolize the public sphere (Peterson 1992). Firms and other non-state actors increasingly 'do' what traditional public actors do. An important contribution of European governance and public policy theory in recent years is the recognition of the public and private interaction in EU policymaking (see Héritier 1999; Kohler-Koch 1996; Kohler-Koch and Eising 1999; Kooiman 1993). Yet many IR institutionalist and global governance approaches persist in upholding the false dichotomy between public and private actors who are largely overlooked.[7]

State delegation of authority, however, is not only conferred on public actors (i.e. EU institutions), but on private actors as well. The work of Cutler, Haufler and Porter (1999), for example, challenges traditional IR approaches to explore how governments confer 'private authority' on firms and other non-state actors to set agendas, address incomplete contracting, monitor compliance, and self-regulate or co-regulate. Sometimes this takes place precisely because states and public institutions do not have the proper mechanisms to cope with globalization (Cutler *et al.* 1999: 19). While governments have yet to establish clear rules on the protection of intellectual property rights on the internet, for example, private firms such as IBM are working with other software and hardware companies to create their own rules and interoperable standards to promote digital intellectual property rights worldwide (Spar 1999: 40).

Standards-setting is another area where private actors play an increasingly important role (Abbott and Snidal 2001; Mattli 2003). Indeed, with the shift in regulatory policy following the Single Market programme, firms have become dominant players in the policy-making process (Egan 2001). Private rule-making is also found in the form of new trading codes – the *lex mercatoria moderna* or new law merchant – that provide 'a set of principles and customary rules…[guiding] economic transactions at the national and transnational level' as well as private commercial arbitration to solve disputes (Lehmkuhl 2000; see also Mattli 2001; Stone Sweet 2002). Indeed, private forums for international commercial dispute resolution are becoming increasingly popular (Mattli 2001). For example, the Global Business Dialogue on e-commerce (GBDe), a coalition of e-commerce firms from Europe, the United States, and Asia, is developing on-line alternative dispute resolution (ADR) mechanisms and trustmark guidelines to obviate or at least lessen the need for commercial and private consumers to use national courts for redress (Cowles 2001b).

In addition to the *lex mercatoria moderna*, firms as well as other non-state actors have been a growing force behind the development of soft law in international and global governance (Abbott and Snidal 2000). Soft laws are 'rules of conduct which, in principle, have no legally binding force but which nevertheless may have practical effect' (Snyder 1993: 2). Soft law has been used in EU policy-making in the motor vehicle and state aid policy areas (Cini 2001). More recently, soft law, along with self-regulation, has been featured in the White Paper on European Governance. Depending on the extent to which the White Paper is ultimately incorporated, it could revolutionize EU rule-making by promoting 'policy-making without legislation' (Héritier 2001). The result will be a greater shift from public to private policymaking in key areas such as the 'new' or the 'digital' economy.

Of course, the recognition that non-state actors are important, authoritative, rule-making actors in global governance does not imply that state actors are not. Some scholars have expressed concerns, however, that the delegation of authority to private actors 'implies a decline in state capacity' (Kahler and Lake 2003: 15) or a 'hollowing out of the state' (Rhodes 1996: 661). One could argue that the reality is rather different. The effectiveness of transnational coalitions, for example, often depends on their access to 'key targets' or international institutions. Whether or not a firm or NGO has access to the domestic polity and therefore the means to create 'winning coalitions' may ultimately determine its success (Cram 2001; Risse-Kappen 1995). Similarly, the ability of non-state actors to monitor and enforce international agreements can vary according to the access to state legal systems (Conant 2001). Non-state actors are likely to experience greater success in countries with institutions that facilitate firm and NGO access to the courts. Of course, the success of self-regulation may depend on the 'shadow of the state' – the threat of state intervention should the self-regulation fail (Lehmkuhl 2000;

Newman and Bach 2002b; Scharpf 1997). While firms may develop self-regulatory codes of conduct in the United States, for example, the Federal Trade Commission will intervene, enforce, and punish if unfair trade practices occur. Thus there are limits to the roles and capacities of firms and other non-state actors. Indeed, for some scholars, state sovereignty itself sets those very limits (Clark *et al.* 1998: 33–5).

Yet the recognition of traditional state power and sovereignty in these scenarios does not relegate non-state actors to some form of subservient status. While one can readily agree that 'private governance does not stand independent of public governance' (Kahler and Lake 2003), one could also argue that public governance increasingly does not stand independent of private governance. By focusing only on the former one runs the risk of pushing aside and ghetto-izing the role of non-state actors. In reality, one increasingly finds a complementary relationship between public and private actors – the existence of public *and* private management of international markets, and development of public *and* private mechanisms to coordinate the global political economy. Indeed, there is a 'blurring of public–private spheres' of action (Cowles 2001a: 214). Thus it is not merely an augmentation of public governance, but a qualitatively different kind of governance.

Higgott, Underhill and Bieler suggest this coexistence of public/private actors signifies 'a new way of sustaining capitalist accumulation in an era of global structural change' (2000). The new relationship between states, firms, and non-state actors is part and parcel of the current historical phase of political economy (see Héritier 2002). The challenge remains, therefore, for rational choice institutionalism and other IR theories to address this new reality.

Constructivism, the critical approach, and the 'good' versus 'bad' dichotomy

Constructivism is an ontological approach to social inquiry – not a theory *per se* – that is relatively new to European integration theory. Applied to the EU, constructivism provides a rich understanding of the rules and norms in European governance, political community and identity formation in the Euro-polity, as well as discourses, communication action and the role of ideas in European integration (Christiansen *et al.* 1999).

Touted as a middle ground and not a grand theory, constructivism is based on two assumptions: '(1) the environment in which agents/states take action is social as well as material; and (2) this setting can provide agents/states with understandings of their interests (it can "constitute" them)' (Checkel 1998: 325–6). Constructivism often provides a framework in which one embeds other IR/IPE theories. Thus its range includes radical post-modernism to near-rational choice approaches that take the formation of preferences and the role of discourse seriously. Constructivism has also been closely interwoven with the historical and sociological strands of institutionalism, thus distinguishing between the 'thin' versus 'thick' understanding of norms and institutions in social life (Checkel 2001a). Indeed, new institutionalist and constructivist approaches are sometimes the same.

Constructivist approaches are not without criticism. One is that constructivists sometimes lack a theory of agency. Checkel, for example, argues that early constructivist approaches (Finnemore 1996; Katzenstein 1996a; Klotz 1995) tended to overemphasize 'the role of social structures and norms at the expense of the agents who help create and change them in the first place' (1998: 324).

A second criticism is the tendency of early 'statist' constructivists to focus primarily if not solely on the norms and discourses of public actors, institutions, and elites – thus reinforcing the public versus private dichotomy discussed above. In recent years, liberal constructivists have recognized private actors – or at least certain private actors – in their ontological approach (cf. Keck and Sikkink 1998). In the EU literature, while some scholars tend to look primarily at public actors (cf. Christiansen *et al.* 1999), others constructivists examine non-state actors as well (cf. Marcussen 1998; Schmidt 2001, 2002; Verdun 1996). The growing literature on EU social movements – while not explicitly constructivist – is also in this vein (cf. Imig and Tarrow 2001).

The false dichotomy between 'good' and 'bad'

A third criticism of constructivism is its relative weakness in transcending the false dichotomy between 'good' and 'bad' in the literature. This dichotomy exists in two forms: (1) the subject of inquiry (norms, discourses, ideas) and (2) the demarcation of agents. Referring to the former, Checkel points out that constructivists need to 'give equal attention to the bad things in world [or EU] politics that are socially constructed' (Checkel 1998). There is a pattern – though changing – in the literature to only look at the 'ethically good norms'.

In terms of agents, however, there appears to be an unwritten rule to give recognition only to those who are deemed 'ethically good'. Keck and Sikkink make this clear in their own work. They distinguish between three different categories of transnational actors based on their motivations:

> (1) those with essentially *instrumental goals*, especially transnational corporations and banks; (2) those motivated primarily by *shared causal ideas*, such as scientific groups or epistemic communities; and (3) those motivated primarily by *shared principled ideas or values* (transnational advocacy networks).
>
> (Keck and Sikkink 1998: 30, italics in the original)

This classification is convenient but hardly encompassing. While multinational firms may be guided by instrumental goals, they are not devoid of shared principled ideas or values. Yet traditional constructivist theorists have generally neglected to theorize and document the role of firms in creating norms. Indeed, many constructivist scholars are leery of touching IPE in general (see Kirshner 2000). This neglect nonetheless implies that one group (i.e. NGOs and transnational societal groups) has values and moral authority, whereas another group (namely firms) does not. Hence, the 'good' versus 'bad' dichotomy.

The neo-Gramscian school – also known as the transnational historical materialism approach in the critical school – brings together both the constructivist and critical elements of IR/IPE theory (Bieler and Morton 2001; Cox 1995; Gill 1993c; Jørgensen 1997; Palan 1992; Van Apeldoorn 2002; Van der Pijl 1998).[8] Indeed, neo-Gramscians such as Van Apeldoorn set themselves apart from the liberal constructivists' preoccupation with NGOs and societal groups precisely by focusing on multinational firms and their social construction of norms and discourse. Van Apeldoorn's ERT study, for example, reveals how the group's discourse production shaped EU socio-economic governance and policymaking in the 1990s (Van Apeldoorn 2002). The critical element of this approach, relating back to its Marxist roots, is the explicit assertion that the structure of society, especially in today's global capitalism, is inherently biased in favour of capitalist groups such as firms and banks. In Gramsci's terms, it is the hegemony of the firms' discourse production, the firms' ability to appeal to others, which further enables capital to dominate to the detriment of other societal actors (Bieler and Morton 2001).

Whereas neo-Gramscians implicitly refer to firms' negative impact on society, other critical school approaches are more explicit. The English critical school, the normative school (also known as the 'humane governance school'), and many post-modernists often emphasize these 'bad' non-state actors.

In the end, the inability or unwillingness of constructivists and critical school approaches to adequately address firms and other state actors respectively results in this false dichotomy between 'good' and 'bad'. This false dichotomy becomes untenable, however, in the face of empirical observations and theoretical developments. For example, not all NGOs and transnational advocacy networks have moral authority all the time. Norms and practices may be mutually constitutive (Keck and Sikkink 1998: 35), and sometimes, bad practices harm the norms one claims to uphold. Greenpeace International, for example, suffered a normative setback in 1995 when the multi-million-dollar group lost sight of its principled ideas, worrying more about the confiscation of its high-priced boats than its anti-nuclear agenda (Johnson 2000). Similarly, anti-globalization protesters who smash windows and throw stones at police in the streets of Seattle, Göteborg, and Genoa might do more harm than good to their cause.

The false dichotomy also becomes more difficult to uphold when one recognizes that NGOs, transnational advocacy groups, and multinational firms increasingly work *together* to develop new discourse, ideas, and norms within international and EU institutions. Within the EU, for example, BP-Amoco has been an active participant in the climate change discourse with NGOs and Commission officials.

The literature on multinational firms and norms outside the critical school approach is slowly emerging in IR theory (cf. Haufler 2000, 2001; Prakash 2000). Haufler, for example, focuses on firms' self-regulation, arguing that these business norms structure 'the environment within which political action takes place, thus affecting both the direct participant in a business regime, and also structuring activity outside of it' (Haufler 2000: 199–200). Recognizing that it is method-ologically and theoretically possible to examine firms' social construction of norms from a liberal perspective – as opposed to solely a critical one – is impor-tant. In the past, theorists could easily pigeon-hole multinational corporations into the critical school as 'the bad guys' of IR theory. The recent work by Haufler, Prakash and others allows one to avoid this ghetto-ization of non-state actors in the IR/IPE literature.

A fourth dichotomy? IR/IPE versus comparative/political economy approaches

For some scholars, the relevance in reviewing the literature on the role or non-role of non-state actors in IR/IPE theories/approaches may not be immediately apparent. A number of scholars, after all, have collapsed many of these false dichotomies in their treatment of the EU as a polity and in their application of comparative and political economy approaches (Hix 1994). The growing work on policy network analysis has added to our understanding of regulatory policymaking and the meso-level or day-to-day decision-making in the EU (Börzel 1998; Jordan and Schubert 1992; Kohler-Koch and Eising 1999). The EU 'governance' literature (cf. Jachtenfuchs 2001) has embraced the sociological and historical strands of institutionalism and developed accounts of EU policymaking that emphasize the interaction between public and private actors (Héritier 1999; Kohler-Koch 1996). Armstrong and Bulmer, for example, convincingly argue that the Single Market programme – and the non-state actors engaged in it – matter more today than fifteen years ago (1998). Public policy theorists point out how societal, techno-logical and scientific developments pose significant new challenges for EU - governance that, in turn, necessitate new public/private dynamics (Kooiman 1993). As Beate Kohler-Koch notes, given the new actors, new strategies, and multi-levels of governance in the EU today, different theoretical approaches were needed to take into account the 'real world' (Kohler-Koch 1996).

What then is the value of IR/IPE theory and approaches when the governance, comparative politics, and political economy approaches have emerged as power-ful alternatives, arguably more attuned to the realities of EU integration and policymaking?

In examining the state of both literatures today, three arguments emerge for revisiting the role of non-state actors in IR/IPE theory and approaches. The first is that the governance literature tends to limit itself to 'everyday' policymaking (Héritier 1999: 13–14; see also Peterson 1995). The explanatory power for 'high politics' or 'history-making decisions' such as intergovernmental conferences is largely deferred to neorealist or liberal intergovernmentalist theoretical accounts where ' "national preference formation and intergovernmental decisionmaking" is strictly observed' (Héritier 1999: 14). Thus, by automatically turning to this literature, the false dichotomies of international versus domestic, public versus private continue to be promulgated in the liberal intergovernmentalism approach.

A second argument for continuing to examine the IR/IPE literature is that the national experience – and the dominant comparative politics and public policy approaches that theorize about it – do not always correspond adequately to the European experience. EU scholars might correctly point out, for example, that the governments' willingness to confer private authority on firms and NGOs to set agendas, monitor compliance, and self-regulate was well established by neocorporatism in the 1970s (Lehmbruch and Schmitter 1982; Schmitter 1974), and the related Organisation of Business Interests project in the early 1980s (Streeck and Schmitter 1985). Yet, the make-up of many European interest groups and their relationship with EU institutions is rather different from that found in most European capitals. Indeed, the business–government relationship in Brussels is modelled on a more pluralist Anglo-Saxon model – not the neocorporatist relationship found in many continental countries (Coen 1997; Cowles 1996). It is not surprising to find, therefore, that when discussing self-governance and business associations in EU policymaking today, Knill refers to the 'private governance' work of Cutler and colleagues as most relevant in explaining these 'everyday' developments in Brussels (Knill 2001). Importantly, Knill also notes the contribution of Lehmbruch's work on administrative interest intermediation to explain the Commission's active support of certain business associations.

That scholars such as Knill refer to both the IR/IPE and governance literatures leads to the third argument. Just as IR/IPE approaches can benefit from a better understanding of the dynamics behind the comparative politics, political economy, and public policy approaches to EU studies, so too can this European literature learn from the evolving IR/IPE literature After all, one can discuss the EU as a polity *and* an international actor, a process of integration *and* a policymaking body. Moreover, those who look at the two sets of literature recognize that there is a growing convergence between the two. Indeed, the two literatures often use different terminologies for similar phenomena, while still not taking sufficiently into account the contributions of other literatures.[9]

Clearly, one must move beyond this schism in the literature. Rather then setting up a false dichotomy between the IR/IPE and governance approaches, one can consult both to guide and understand one's empirical work and findings. For example, one could examine how the operation of non-state actors at various levels impacts the formation of preferences that shape government leaders' bargaining margin of manoeuvre. To what extent do the strategies of non-state actors differ from one level to another to define the parameters of negotiation? What are the resulting implications for those groups who do not operate at multiple levels? One could also identify the conditions under which states confer private authority at the national, European, and international levels. Are these conditions vastly different? Why or why not? One could also examine the manner in which norms are constituted at the national, European, and international levels. How do these various settings inform agents with an understanding of their interests? What does this tell us about norm creation in the EU as compared to the national level?

Conclusion: reflecting on reality

This review essay identifies some of the weaknesses in the IR/IPE theory and approaches to the EU today. It does so through the identification of three false or artificial dichotomies in the IPE literature that delimit and indeed ghetto-ize non-state actors in European integration and policymaking: (1) the international versus domestic, (2) the public versus private, and (3) the 'good' versus the 'bad' false dichotomies. The purpose in reviewing this literature is not to claim that firms and other non-state actors are all-powerful, all-pervasive, or all-important actors. Rather, it is to suggest that our scholarship would probably be enhanced and enriched if we became more cognizant of how these actors fit in the reality of the EU as polity and global actor today.

Of course, the governance literature that embraces comparative politics, public policy, and political economy approaches also challenge these false dichotomies. The EU governance approach incorporating historical institutionalism in particular has developed important insights into public/private interaction in the EU. While it might be tempting to forsake the IR/IPE scholarship and, in turn, embrace the governance literature, I have argued that it is not necessary to set up yet another artificial dichotomy between the two. Indeed, by consulting both sets of literature, one can better guide and understand one's empirical work and findings and contribute to a more comprehensive understanding of how all actors influence, are constrained by, and are constituted in the national, European, and international settings in which they operate.

Notes

1 I am grateful to Tanja Börzel, Jeffrey Checkel, David Bach, Barbara Haskel, Christoph Knill, Sophie Meunier, Vivien Schmidt, Mitchell Smith, Paul Taggart, Bastiaan van Apeldoorn, the editors, and two anonymous reviewers who provided comments on subsequent versions of this chapter. Of course, any errors or omissions are mine.
2 By non-state actors, I am referring to profit-oriented actors such as firms and banks, to public interest-oriented non-governmental actors such as consumer organizations and environmental groups, and, more broadly, to social movements. I do not include intergovernmental organizations in this definition (cf. Arts *et al.* 2001).
3 I am not arguing that each dichotomy is found in each of the four theories/approaches under review. Indeed, neorealist theories largely sidestep the 'good' versus 'bad' dichotomy; the historical and sociological strands of institutionalism generally avoid the public versus private dichotomy. The neo-Gramscian approach, by focusing on transnational agency, moves beyond both the international versus domestic and the public versus private dichotomies.
4 Scholars disagree with the characterization of liberal intergovernmentalism as part of the neorealist school (cf. Pollack 2001). While liberal intergovernmentalism differs from neorealism on several accounts, it is 'realist' in terms of its focus on state sovereignty, bargaining, and power (see Verdun 1999).
5 See Kassim and Menon in this volume, Ch. 3.
6 Critics point out that international institutions' performance may also suffer from the inclusion of non-state actors if the organizations are 'captured' by NGOs and firms – a criticism levelled at domestic institutions as well. Non-state actors thus can legitimize as well as delegitimize international organizations.

7 As noted above, the neorealist approach also promotes this artificial dichotomy by recognizing only the role of domestic non-state actors in preference formation.
8 As noted above, this approach transcends many of the false dichotomies found in traditional IR/IPE literature, including the public versus private debate. The neo-Gramscian ontological primacy of transnational social forces over states, however, opens it to a different kind of criticism – namely, the failure to address adequately the role of public actors. I thank Bastiaan van Apeldoorn for his valuable comments on the neo-Gramscian approach in this chapter.
9 I thank Christoph Knill for expanding on this point. See also Knill and Lehmkuhl (2002).

3 The principal–agent approach and the study of the European Union

Promise unfulfilled?

Hussein Kassim and Anand Menon[1]

Abstract: The principal–agent model holds great promise for understanding the institutional complexities of the European Union and for moving beyond the sterile debate between intergovernmentalism and neofunctionalism. As yet, however, scholars have failed to exploit the insights that this construct affords. After a brief discussion of the principal–agent model, this chapter offers a critical examination of the way that the principal–agent approach has been deployed by liberal intergovernmentalism, institutional intergovernmentalism, historical institutionalist supranationalism, and rational choice supranationalism. It argues that in all four cases the *a priori* commitments of the theorists, in support either of the view that the member states effectively control their supranational agents and dominate EU governance or of the belief in an inevitable trend towards greater integration, led by supranational institutions, prevent them from making the most effective use of the model. It proposes alternative applications that may prove more fruitful.

Introduction

The principal–agent model and the theory of delegation, which originated in the new economics of organization, have been increasingly applied in the study of the European Union (EU).[2] This chapter critically examines these applications. It argues that the principal–agent model holds significant promise for understanding the complex relationships and interactions that characterize the Union, not least on account of its greater institutional sensitivity over traditional theories of integration. However, its potential has as yet not been fully realized. This is due partly to the prior theoretical commitments of the EU scholars, who have used these models, partly to misunderstandings of the complexity and implications of the approach.

The discussion below is divided into three parts. The first offers a brief overview of, and background to, the principal–agent model.[3] The second discusses the promise that the model offers for understanding European integration and governance, then examines in detail its deployment by authors writing from four theoretical perspectives – liberal intergovernmentalism (LI), institutional intergovernmentalism (II), historical institutionalist supranationalism (HIS), and rational choice supranationalism (RCS).[4] The final section discusses general weaknesses in how the principal–agent model has been applied to the EU and suggests future research possibilities.

The principal–agent model in economics and political science

From its origins in the new economics of organization as a theoretical construct devised to examine relations within the firm (Moe 1984), the principal–agent model became the dominant framework for examining the difficulties that arise from contracting in any setting. Agency relationships are created when one party, the *principal*, enters into a contractual agreement with a second party, the *agent*, and delegates to the latter responsibility for carrying out a function or set of tasks on the principal's behalf. In the classic representation, the principal is the shareholder of a company that contracts an executive to manage the business on a day-to-day basis. However, the principal can be any individual or organization that delegates responsibility to another in order to economize on transactions costs, pursue goals that would otherwise be too costly, or secure expertise.

Difficulties arise on account of the asymmetric distribution of information that favours the agent (Holmstrom 1979; Kiewiet and McCubbins 1991), including adverse selection and moral hazard. The asymmetry of information can allow the agent to engage in opportunistic behaviour – *shirking* – that is costly to the principal, but difficult to detect. The likelihood of shirking is increased by *slippage*, when the very structure of delegation 'provides incentives for the agent to behave in ways inimical to the preferences of the principal' (Pollack 1997: 108). Assuring control and limiting shirking is the 'principal's problem' (Ross 1973). The challenge is to find ways of ensuring perfect compliance, so that agents cannot exploit the costs of measuring their characteristics and performance to act contrary to the preferences of the principal. Economists have focused on incentive structures that discourage opportunistic behaviour on the part of the agent. Contractual restrictions on the agent's operational purview (Doleys 2000) or monitoring the agent are alternative possibilities, but can be costly. Their effectiveness is limited by the extent to which the agent's actions can be observed.

The new economics of organization has been very influential in political science. Rational choice institutionalism, in particular, has drawn from its toolkit in its explanations of how institutions emerge and interact.[5] Scholars of US politics have used the principal–agent model to investigate the relationship between Congress and executive agencies, and the tasks performed by congressional committees.[6] In international relations, delegation has been used to explain why sovereignty-conscious states create international organizations.[7] The basic model has been used to assess the efficacy of mechanisms devised to ensure agent compliance, and extended, elaborated upon, and adapted to take account of cases where there are multiple principals.

Why delegate?

A rich literature has explored the motivations that lead principals to delegate functions and confer authority on agents in the political world. Pollack (1997: 102) suggests that, fundamentally, delegation is a question of institutional design and that 'the question of institutional choice is functionalist': institutions are chosen or created because of their intended effects. The decision is usually motivated by a desire to minimize transaction costs.[8] Delegation also provides a means:

- to overcome problems of collective action, where actors anticipate benefits from long-term co-operation (Axelrod 1984), but want to ensure the transaction costs involved in monitoring compliance do not outweigh the benefits of the agreement and the terms of the contract are respected by other parties (Keohane 1984; Shepsle 1979; Weingast and Marshall 1988);
- to deal with the problem of 'incomplete contracting' (Williamson 1985), which arises in situations where the interaction envisaged by an agreement is long-term, the bargain complex, the negotiating process difficult, and 'the realization of mutual gain... contingent upon the durability of the contract' (Doleys 2000: 535). Rather than writing a fully contingent claims contract, parties will prefer a 'framing agreement' or 'incomplete contract', in which they state general goals, establish criteria for decision-making in unforeseen circumstances (Milgrom and Roberts 1992), and may create an agent that can 'fill in the details of an incomplete contract and adjudicate future disputes' (Pollack 1997: 104);
- to improve the quality of policy in technical areas by delegating responsibilities to an agent with specialist knowledge (Egan 1998);
- to overcome regulatory competition and avoid market failure where interdependent states have incentives to treat their own firms leniently (Egan 1998; Majone 1994);
- to displace responsibility for unpopular decisions (Epstein and O'Halloran 1999; Fiorina 1977);
- to 'lock in' distributional benefits. In contrast to information-based accounts, where the agent is impartial, a second perspective interprets delegation as a mechanism for 'locking in' distributional benefits. Thus the 'industrial organization of Congress' (Weingast and Marshall 1988) is best understood as an efficient way of facilitating 'pork-barrelling' and 'log-rolling'. Members of Congress sit on committees where they are best-placed to secure benefits for their constituents. Similarly, an alternative to Majone's 'search for independence' contests the view that regulators are neutral, arguing instead that the creation of institutions is intrinsically distributive and that the choice of institutions may be motivated by the desire to institutionalize a preferred set of preferences (Stetter 2000);
- to resolve the problem of policy-making instability. The delegation of agenda-setting powers to an agent may prevent the problem of policy 'cycling' that besets systems of majoritarian decision making (McKelvey 1976; Pollack 1997; Riker 1980).

After delegation: coping with the 'Principal's Problem'

Political scientists investigating delegation have focused on how principals have designed institutions that ensure favourable outcomes (Kiewiet and

McCubbins 1991; Moe 1987). Studies commonly begin with the assumption that incentive incompatibility between principals and agents is 'an inherent feature of contracting relationships' (Doleys 2000: 537; Moe 1989), and that asymmetric information allows shirking, leading to agency losses (Weingast and Moran 1983). They examine *ex ante* controls and *ex post* oversight mechanisms that can be used to mitigate this tendency, and assess the cost to the principal of various sanctioning strategies.

Ex ante control typically takes the form of administrative procedures, designed 'to limit the scope of agency activity, the legal instruments available to the agency, and the procedures it must follow' (Pollack 1997: 108). They can be more or less restrictive, and altered in response to agency loss. Such restrictions come, however, at the cost of the agent's flexibility and comprehensiveness of action (McCubbins and Page 1987; McCubbins *et al.* 1987, 1989), and can diminish the effectiveness and overall capacity of the system. *Ex post* oversight falls into two broad categories (Pollack 1997): the imposition of sanctions, where principals attempt to control agency loss through budgetary restrictions, appointments, or revising the agent's mandate through legislative or regulatory means; and monitoring, whereby an attempt is made to rebalance the asymmetry of information by surveillance of agent behaviour. McCubbins and Schwartz (1984) famously distinguish two strategies: 'police patrol' oversight, where the principal engages in continuous and detailed vigilance of agent action; and 'fire alarm' oversight, where the principal relies on third parties to alert it to agency transgressions. The second is less costly, and imposes fewer demands on the principal, than the first, but the comparison highlights a fundamental point: all methods of agency control imply costs to the principal and their cost traded-off against the benefits from limiting non-compliance (McCubbins *et al.* 1987, 1989).

The cost of monitoring is likely to be substantially higher where there are multiple principals. To the cost of co-ordination is added the risk that the imposition of sanctions will involve action that exposes long-standing differences between principals (McCubbins *et al.* 1987). A review of the literature leads Pollack (1997) to identify three factors affecting the likelihood that sanctions will be imposed: the extent to which principals' preferences converge; the decision rules governing the application of sanctions; and the 'default condition' where there is no agreement among the principals. Pollack suggests that a knowing, opportunitistic agent can exploit situations where these barriers are high.

A further issue concerns the type of agency behaviour that the principal is trying to control. Control can be exercised to ensure that agents stay within the remit laid out in the original contract (McCubbins *et al.* 1989). Control can be more intrusive, however, when principals are authorized to interfere in the operation of the agent, even within its contractually defined sphere of competence (Epstein and O'Halloran 1999). The choice of approach involves an important choice. Specifying agency powers 'in excruciating detail...leaving as little as possible to the discretionary judgment of bureaucrats' is obviously 'not a formula for creating effective organisations' since 'cumbersome, complicated, technically inappropriate structures...undermine their capacity to perform their jobs well'

(Moe 1990: 228). At issue, in other words, is the *effectiveness* of delegation: minimize the risk of agency loss or allow the agent the independence to carry out its responsibilities efficiently. The use of budgetary cuts may enable principals to thwart the budget-maximizing ambitions of agents, but is likely to hinder agents in performing the tasks for which they were created (Moe 1987).

A related complication arises when delegation is utilized as a means to establish credible commitments to long-term aims. In such cases, for example, the creation of independent central banks, delegation to an agent is motivated by a concern to secure advantages that depend upon the independence of that agent. Institutional choice has been governed by a concern to protect against coalitional or principal drift (Horn and Shepsle 1989; Shepsle 1992; Shepsle and Bonchek 1997). Where the short- and long-term interests of principals conflict, a decision may be taken to insulate the agent from interference. However, the 'civil servants and political appointees of bureaus insulated from political overseers are...empowered to pursue independent courses of action. Protection from coalitional drift comes at the price of an increased potential for bureaucratic drift' (Shepsle and Bonchek 1997: 375).

Principal–agent approaches to the EU

In recent years, a growing number of scholars have used the principal–agent model in the study of the EU.[9] The principal–agent approach holds considerable promise. First, it is explicitly concerned with complex inter-institutional interactions and need not systematically privilege the role played by one institution or class of actor over others – a trap into which many theoretical approaches have fallen (Menon 2003). It can generate more nuanced hypotheses than the theories that have historically dominated the field. Pollack's use of the model to analyse the power of the European Commission and the European Court of Justice, for example, leads him to the conclusion that the

> autonomy of a given supranational institution depends crucially on the efficacy and credibility of control mechanisms established by member state principals, and that these vary from institution to institution – as well as from issue-area to issue-area and over time – leading to varying patterns of supranational autonomy.
>
> (1997: 101)

This is a more subtle thesis than neofunctionalism or intergovernmentalism can provide. Indeed, Pollack explicitly attempts to 'transcend the intergovernmentalist–neofunctionalist debate' (Pollack 1997: 101) in this way.[10] Second, the principal–agent model offers a way of grasping the institutional complexity of the EU. As Moe has argued, the model 'cuts through the inherent complexity of organizational relationships by identifying distinct aspects of individuals and their environments that are most worthy of investigation, and it integrates these elements into a logically coherent whole' (1984: 757). Third, the employment of theoretical constructs and models that are in more general use may enable EU scholarship to benefit from belonging to the mainstream (see Menon 2003; Moravcsik 1998).

In this section, we review four applications – LI, II, HIS and RCS – of the principal-agent approach to the EU. All four proceed from the assumption that delegation to supranational agents is grounded in the interests of member state principals, but reach different conclusions about the ability of governments to retain their control and the extent to which the Commission and the Court are willing and able to act independently. The first two approaches – LI and II – contend that the member states remain in control of European governance and integration; the third and fourth – HIS and RCS – that the influence of supranational institutions cannot be explained solely in terms of member state preferences.

Liberal intergovernmentalism

Liberal intergovernmentalism explains the creation of the EU's 'strong supranational institutions' (Moravcsik 1993a: 507) in terms of the interests of states, who, under conditions of economic interdependence, recognize the benefits of, and enter into, long-term co-operation, but need to overcome problems of collective action. Drawing on regime theory, Moravcsik argues that international institutions are 'deliberate instruments to improve the efficiency of bargaining between states' (p. 507) and that '[m]uch of the institutional structure of the EC can be readily explained by the functional theory of regimes'. He contends that member states decide on the basis of a cost–benefit analysis of the 'stream of future substantive decisions expected to follow from alternative institutional designs' whether to adopt QMV or to delegate to supranational institutions (p. 509). The calculation involves trading off efficient collective decision making against the risk of being outvoted or overruled. He argues that member states are influenced by the 'potential gains from co-operation', the 'level of uncertainty regarding the details of specific delegated or pooled decision', and the 'level of political risk for individual governments or interest groups with intense preferences' (pp. 510–11). These calculations led to the delegation of agenda setting, enforcement, and external representation. With respect to agenda-setting, Moravcsik (1993a: 511) argues that the interests of the member states are served because the Commission 'assures that [the] technical information necessary for decision is available' and that 'as a neutral arbiter, it provides an authoritative means of reducing the number of proposals to be considered'. In relation to enforcement, Moravcsik (1993a: 511) asserts that '[t]he possibilities for co-operation are enhanced when neutral procedures exist to monitor, interpret and enforce compliance'.

There are, however, several difficulties with the way that LI deploys the principal–agent approach. A fundamental problem concerns the functional theory of delegation. Functional explanation is itself inherently problematic due to its *ex post facto* attribution of motives without empirical investigation, its stress on interests that remain unelaborated, and its lack of precision in identifying the mechanism that links cause to effect.[11] In the case of LI, no empirical evidence is offered in support of the contention that member states engage in a cost–benefit analysis or even that the supranational institutions were created for the reasons that LI alleges. Moreover, the problems that occur with delegation (e.g. conflicting interests or agency loss) are not addressed. The possibility that member state principals and supranational agents may develop divergent preferences, that the Commission may draw on its own resources to pursue its own policy agenda, or that the Court may evolve into a more powerful institution than the original contract envisages is not contemplated.

More importantly, LI assumes that, although the supranational institutions may continue to perform the formal functions that Moravcsik identifies – itself a questionable assumption – there is no reason to suppose that the initial calculations of the original Six about the stream of substantive policy decisions still hold true decades after the signing of the Treaty of Rome. Although he acknowledges that behaviour on the part of the European Court of Justice represents 'an anomaly for the functional explanation of delegation as a deliberate means by national governments of increasing the efficiency of collective decision making' (Moravcsik 1993a: 513),[12] and appears to endorse an explanation put forward by Burley and Mattli (1993), which explains the expansion of the role of the Court in terms of 'a number of factors idiosyncratic to the EC', Moravcsik does not explain how this view might be reconciled with the key tenets of LI. Nor does he account for why supranational institutions continue to serve the interests of the member states or are kept in check by them.

The view that the member states have been able to control the direction of integration is difficult to sustain for reasons identified by Pierson (1996) (see below). There are also empirical grounds for challenging this assumption. The monitoring capacities of the national administrations are frequently overstated. Recent research on the national co-ordination of EU policy (Kassim 2000; Kassim *et al.* 2001) reveals considerable differences in the ambitions and administrative resources of member states, as well as evidence of 'bureaucratic politics' and problems in constructing coherent action. In this light, the image of ever-vigilant principals is difficult to uphold.

Turning to the supranational agents, LI underestimates the Commission's ability to act as a policy entrepreneur. Although the Commission is small and fragmented, it has significant resources at its disposal. As well as its formal monopoly over policy initiation, the Commission has accumulated considerable expertise, technical and legal,[13] occupies a strategic location at the heart of Community decision making as 'process manager' (Eichener 1993), and enjoys access to information that would be difficult for even the best organized and most motivated national administrations to gather (Kassim 2000). A Commission official in a functional Directorate-General might not know more about a sector in a member state than a civil servant, but he or she may well know more about the sector across fifteen member states than any national official.

Finally, it does not follow from the assumption that the member states prefer an independent supranational body to a randomly chosen national government (Moravcsik 1993a: 512) that the Commission will in practice act neutrally.[14] In theory, the Commission embodies the interest of the Community – one could debate whether this represents, in Rousseaunian terms, the general interest, the sum of the particular interests of the member states, or the average interest – but in practice, in seeking to implement the treaties, it acts as a 'purposeful opportunist' (Cram 1993). This often involves partisan behaviour, favouring, for example, free market solutions over protectionist policies, or more Europe rather than less. In several policy areas, including telecommunications and air transport, the Commission has forced the introduction of policy at the European level against some, or even a majority of the, member states by using its competition powers. In other areas, for example, environmental policy, the Commission has actively constructed coalitions with like-minded member states to press a particular agenda. Action of this type is hard to reconcile with the view that it acts as a neutral arbiter.[15] Liberal intergovernmentalism adopts an information-based approach to delegation, ignoring ways in which delegation can produce distributive gains for some member states at the expense of others, thus serving to 'institutionalise partiality' (Menon 2003).

Institutional intergovernmentalism

Institutional intergovernmentalism (Garrett 1992; Garrett and Weingast 1993), by contrast, directly addresses the distributive implications of delegation. Though it also deploys the functional theory of delegation to explain the EU's institutional arrangements (see e.g. Garrett 1992: 533–4), it takes a more critical approach. Garrett (1992: 534–5) argues that functional theory overemphasizes the informational advantages of co-operation and thereby disregards the distributional consequences of the institutions chosen by the member states, when it is precisely these latter considerations that account for why one equilibrium position is selected among the many that are possible.[16] Functional theory takes the view that institutions are constructed as 'informational clearing houses', not as 'governing structures', but the nature of the post-1992 institutions agreed by the member states do more simply than provide the information that allows the states to further their own interests. They challenge nation-state sovereignty and alter the 'political structure of the international system'. The adoption of QMV in the Council abolishes the national veto, while the constitutionalization of the founding treaties by the European Court of Justice has wrought a legal system (Garrett 1992: 535–6).

These changes have not compromised member state control over the EU, according to II, since governments play a decisive role in the legislative process,[17] and the Court does not threaten state autonomy. Indeed, the interests of the Court and the member states coincide. Governments have delegated the task of monitoring compliance and resolved the problem of incomplete contracting by empowering the Court to apply the rules of the Treaty in specific areas (Garrett 1992: 557–8). As an agent, the Court has not struck out independently, aware, like all courts, that its powers are subject to revision by elected politicians and conscious of its particular vulnerability, given that 'its position is not explicitly supported by a written constitution' (1992: 558). Evidence of the Court's quiescence can be found in its jurisprudence. II claims that the Court's decisions are 'consistent with the preferences of France and Germany' (1992: 558, 589). Should a Court ruling go against a particular state, moreover, II contends that that government is likely not to comply (1992: 555–6).

Institutional intergovernmentalism presents a more sophisticated account of institutional arrangements at the European level than LI,[18] but is similarly afflicted by tension between its a priori commitment to member state primacy and the potential problems that arise from principal–agent relationships. Like LI, II discounts the possibility of agency loss, but on different grounds. While recognizing its influence in decision making, II emphasizes that the Commission ultimately depends on the member states among whom it must find a majority, and stresses the Council's decisive influence as last mover.[19] Though II stresses the uniqueness of the Community's legal system, on the one hand, on the other, it posits the subservience of the Court to the member states – a somewhat blatant contradiction. It provides neither an adequate account of the constitutionalization process, nor convincing evidence that Court jurisprudence is congruent with the interests of France and Germany. It does not show how the Court serves the interests of the member states in ensuring compliance with the Treaty, while favouring two of its number in its jurisprudence.[20] Moreover, II has not answered satisfactorily the objection of legal theorists that member states are unlikely to defy the Court on account of the damage that their reputations would suffer (Burley and Mattli 1993).

A historical institutionalist approach

The influence of the principal–agent approach is evident in HIS's critique of intergovernmentalism, even if the terminology is not always used explicitly.[21] In an account that 'stresses the difficulties of subjecting institutional evolution to tight control', HIS argues that the intergovernmentalist approach to integration is flawed, because 'the current functioning of institutions cannot be derived from the aspirations of the original designers' (Pierson 1996: 126–7).

Pierson contends that the member states lose control over the integration process, because gaps emerge that are difficult for them to close. These gaps develop for four reasons:

- the 'autonomous actions of European institutional actors': EC institutions are new actors, with their own interests, which are likely to 'diverge from those of its creators', and have significant resources – 'expertise and delegated authority' (Moe 1990: 121) – of their own;
- the 'restricted time horizons of national decision makers': politicians in the member states are likely to give greater priority to the short-term (Pierson 1996: 136) due to the demands of the electoral cycle and their relatively short periods in office compared to the long-term missions of the supranational institutions;
- the potential for unintended consequences: issue density in the European context generates 'overload' and 'spillover', producing 'interaction effects' that lead to outcomes that are unlikely to have been anticipated at the outset. (Pierson 1996: 136–9);

- shifts in the policy preferences of national governments: the institutional and policy preferences of the member states change over time, while successive enlargements alter policy coalitions.

Once gaps emerge, 'change-resistant decision rules and sunk costs associated with societal adaptations make it difficult for member states to reassert their authority' (Pierson 1996: 123).

Although HIS reveals important weaknesses in the intergovernmentalist approach, it is not without its own problems. First, HIS's account of why member state control cannot be sustained over the long term needs qualification. While governments may have short-term horizons, it does not follow that they neglect developments at the European level. Member states have established specialist mechanisms to co-ordinate their European policies and to manage their inputs into EU decision making (Kassim 2000; Kassim *et al.* 2001). With respect to unintended consequences, though issue densities and overload may make spillover possible, national administrations are present at key stages of the policy process, enabling them to intervene to defend their interests (Dogan 1997; Kassim 2003; Kassim and Wright 1991). In addition, the European policies of the member states do not betray the kind of instability that HIS suggests. On the contrary, the outlook of many member states at the polity and policy level has been remarkably stable.

On other hand, HIS overstates the inability of the member states to reassert their control. The supranational institutions certainly do not control the EU's constitutional agenda, as the European Commission and the European Parliament have discovered at successive IGCs. Even the power of the Court should not be exaggerated. The Barber Protocol, agreed by member governments at Maastricht, was specifically aimed at limiting the impact of a Court decision. In addition, the institutional barriers to member state-directed reform are often not insurmountable. At Maastricht, Amsterdam and Nice, member state principals have reined in the Commission and Court in EMU, in the CFSP, in the development of the ESDP, and in the third pillar. The Lisbon Process and the 'open method of co-ordination' further limit the influence of the Commission. These are powerful counter-examples to the claim that the member states are unable to reassert their control (Kassim and Menon forthcoming; Menon 2003).

Finally, Pierson's sunk-costs argument is not altogether persuasive in that he underestimates the extent to which radical revision of even established policy is impossible. Reform in preparation for the accession of countries from Central and Eastern Europe within the rubric of Agenda 2000, for example, has brought about significant reform in the budget, structural policy and the CAP. Moreover, the way in which 'lock-in' operates is not adequately elaborated. HI needs to explain specifically how the member states are constrained by domestic actors and 'societal adaptations'.

Rational choice supranationalism

Arguably, RCS makes the most sophisticated use of the principal–agent model in the EU literature in its exploration of the conditions under which 'supranational institutions will be delegated authority and will enjoy autonomy from and exert influence on the member governments of the Community' (Pollack 1997: 100–1).[22] Pollack's test of the functional theory of delegation leads him to the conclusion that it can explain the functions attributed to the Commission and the Court – monitoring compliance and enforcing treaty provision, solving problems of incomplete contracting, independent regulation and agenda-setting – if not the Parliament. He challenges the theory's assumptions that 'the institutions adopted are those that most efficiently perform the tasks set out for them' (1997: 107) and argues that institutions can assume roles that were not originally anticipated.

In his analysis of member state control over the Commission, Pollack identifies and assesses the efficacy of four mechanisms:

- comitology (a form of police patrol monitoring), whereby the member states monitor and control the exercise by the Commission of its executive function, but where effectiveness depends on which of the three committee types is in place;
- fire-alarm oversight, involving the EC legal system, the European Parliament's power of dismissal, and the European Court of Auditors, which are designed to enforce Commission accountability;
- *ex post* sanctions, including cutting the budget – costly to member states, since it may have adverse effects for their domestic constituencies; the power of appointment – relatively ineffective, since it can only be exercised every five years (Commission) or six years (judges in the Court); the introduction of new legislation – costly, because it requires mustering a winning majority under QMV or the support of all other member states, where the unanimity rule applies; and unilateral non-compliance – too costly to a member state's reputation;
- revising an agent's mandate though revision of the treaty – 'the "nuclear option" – exceedingly effective, but difficult to use – and ... therefore a relatively ineffective and noncredible means of member state control' (Pollack 1997: 118–19).

On agenda setting, Pollack argues that the Commission has formal power where it has the exclusive right of initiative and where it 'is easier to adopt than to amend a Commission proposal ... differences in member state preferences can be effectively exploited, and ... member states are dissatisfied with the status quo and impatient to adopt a new policy' (Pollack 1997: 124). Its informal agenda-setting influence depends on 'member state uncertainty regarding the problems and policies confronting them and on the Commission's acuity in identifying problems and policies that can rally the necessary consensus among member states in search of solutions to their policy problems' (Pollack 1997: 128).

Pollack's conclusion is that supranational autonomy is determined by four factors: the distribution of preferences among member state principals and supranational agents; the institutional decisions rules for applying sanctions, overruling legislation, and changing agents' mandates; the role of incomplete information and uncertainty in principal–agent relationships with autonomy greater where the

Commission has more information about itself than do others; and the presence or absence of transnational constituencies of subnational institutions, interest groups or individuals within the member states, which can act to bypass the member governments and/or place pressure directly on them (Pollack 1997: 129–30).

Despite its subtlety and sensitivity, in particular, to agent- and sector-specific variation, RCS's deployment of the principal–agent model is problematic. There is, for example, no place for 'learning' on the part of the member states, even though, since Maastricht, governments have found various ways of limiting the influence of Commission and the Court. The frequency of IGCs, moreover, contradicts the view of recontracting as a 'nuclear option'. Most importantly, these developments tend to counter the subtext of Pollack's analysis – that the trend towards further integration is inevitable.

A second point concerns Pollack's reading of comitology, which he sees as a site for a struggle over competence. There is an alternative view, however, which holds that the participants in these committees engage, not in a political battle about the appropriate locus of decision-making, but in problem-solving discussion about technical points.

Finally, Pollack's emphasis on the conditions under which supranational agents can elude member state control leads him to overlook the resources that these institutions command. Studies of EU policy emphasize, for example, the leverage that the Commission can exert by using its competition powers to prise open sectors where national governments prefer the protectionist status quo. Paradoxically, Pollack also overstates the inclination and ability of the member states to control their supranational agents (see above). RCS does not, in other words, accurately represent the respective powers and resources of principals and agents.

Conclusions: the practice and promise of principal–agent approaches to the EU

The four approaches considered above use delegation theory and, in the case of II and two versions of supranationalism, the principal–agent model to present a more sophisticated analysis of European integration than their intellectual forebears, intergovernmentalism and neofunctionalism. These constructs offer greater leverage in understanding the motivation of the member states in creating the European Communities and their preparedness to entrust supranational institutions with key responsibilities, and provide a valuable heuristic for approaching the relationship between governments and those institutions, as well as for assessing the extent to which the Commission and Court have developed independent interests and a capacity for action.

Yet the above discussion draws attention to particular weaknesses in the four accounts. An important difficulty with LI and II, for example, lies in the tension between recognizing the fact of delegation and commitment to a belief in continued member state control. HIS, by contrast, tends to overstate the power of the Commission, while underestimating the ability of the member states to assert influence in European integration and governance. More generally, though, there are weaknesses in the way that these insights have been applied that lead us to conclude that the promise of the principal–agent model in the study of the EU has not yet been fulfilled.

A first problem concerns the degree to which the four approaches simplify the complexity of the EU in their application of these constructs. The assumption that either member states or supranational institutions are unitary actors is extremely questionable. The level of analysis selected by the authors discussed may make this assumption attractive, but even as a convenient fiction it is problematic. Moreover, the focus on member state control of process and institutions – Garrett is the exception – precludes from the outset the possibility of transinstitutional alliances, such as the coalitions constructed with the Commission by member states that are keen to multilateralize their national policy preferences (Héritier *et al.* 1996).

More problematic is the inclination to give a linear reading of integration. Liberal intergovernmentalism and Institutional Intergovernmentalism privilege the role of national governments, while HIS and RCS stress the influence of the Commission and Court and emphasize the inability of the member states to assert their control. The danger is that subtleties of analysis that are promised by the principal–agent model are lost when a prior commitment is made to a view that either national or supranational actors are likely to predominate in the long term. The danger is not only a collapse into the intergovernmentalism– neofunctionalism rivalry, but that intergovernmentalists will continue to disregard evidence that the organizational capacities of national governments are less than perfect, while supranationalists will overlook member state abilities to 'learn', recontract and restrict the Court and Commission, and both will construe the relationship between member states and supranational institutions in conflictual terms – a view that neglects the policy dimension and asserts that the transfer of sovereignty is always the central issue (Menon 2003) and disregards the image of EU decision making, increasingly championed by scholars and practitioners, as co-operative (Lewis 1998, 1999; Wessels 1997) and consensual (Mazey and Richardson 1995).

A second problem is what theorists ignore when they apply the principal–agent approach. The limited focus – on the Commission and the Court of Justice, and to a lesser extent, the Parliament, but not the Court of Auditors or European agencies – is one illustration. The issues that arise from the existence of multiple principals is, similarly, not fully explored – a major failing, given the importance of the question of the extent to which EU membership circumscribes the autonomy of individual states.[23] Only Garrett addresses the question of multiple agents and how they interact. Neither does discussion of principal drift – or what Sokolowski has called (in another context) 'the opportunist principal' (2001)[24] – figure in the approaches discussed above, despite the relevance of principal drift to agency efficiency and independence. The extent to which the efficiency of the Commission is diminished by comitology or its neutrality threatened by infiltration by national officials, typically, at the level of the *cabinets*, also merit closer attention. However, the approaches surveyed above have been more concerned with agency discretion than they have with agency efficiency.[25]

Moreover, the approaches surveyed above – II excepted – are biased towards an interpretation of delegation and principal–agent that focuses on informational aspects. The distributional consequences of institutional design tend be overlooked. The problem here is that distribution is a far more important aspect of European integration and the European Union – indeed of all institutional structures (Knight 1992) – than is generally appreciated. Member states are inclined to support the transfer of competences to the EU or back the Commission, for example, when they are likely to win, but distribution also has implications for continued willingness on the part of principals to delegate significant power. Garrett and Weingast (1993: 186) observe that the influence of an informal agenda setter should be greatest when the distributional consequences of the policy are small. However, the scope, and importance, of Community action has expanded dramatically since 1991 with clear implications, according to such reasoning, for the potential influence of the Commission. Indeed, the sheer longevity of the EC/EU itself poses a serious problem for those interested in utilizing the principal–agent model to explain its development and functioning. Since 1957 various functions have been delegated to Community institutions and the degree of autonomy from member state control varies significantly between different policy fields and functions. Inevitably, there are tensions between these various roles, and hence attempting to utilize one specific form of principal–agent approach – for instance information based – is likely to provide at best only a partial explanation.

Finally, delegation raises the issue of legitimacy. Delegation may improve decision making in valuable ways, but it may complicate or erode well-established lines of democratic accountability. In 1969 Ted Lowi launched a scathing attack on Congress for delegating excessive power to unelected bureaucrats who were entrusted with ever-increasing discretion over their areas of responsibility. In the recent past, however, Majone (1993) has argued that the creation of non-majoritarian institutions is entirely compatible with democratic decision making. Legitimacy is of course related to efficiency, since the effectiveness of an agent and, therefore, of the system as a whole, is usually at least partially a function of the agent's status and the way that it is perceived. Neglect of this question is surprising, not only due to its intrinsic importance, but also in view of widespread concern, especially since Maastricht, to enhance the democratic credentials of the EU (Menon and Weatherill 2002).

The question of effectiveness, the notion of delegation for distributional as opposed to informational purposes, as well as the implications of delegation for legitimacy and democratic accountability are all, therefore, promising avenues for future research on the EU based on the principal–agent model. Such research could complement those approaches outlined above, and help students of the EU ensure that the scholarly achievements of those working with this model match its early promise.

Notes

1 We would like to thank Damian Chalmers, Sara Connolly, Dionyssis Dimitrakopoulos, Morten Hviid, Bill Tompson, Catherine Waddams-Price, the editors, and two anonymous reviewers for many helpful suggestions. Any errors are our own.

2 See for example, Egan (1998), Francino (2001), Garrett (1992, 1995b), Garrett and Weingast (1993), Menon (2003), Moravcsik (1993a, 1998), Pierson (1996), Pollack (1996, 1997), Stetter (2000).

3 Space constraints permit no more than a cursory treatment. Useful discussions are to be found in Moe (1984) and Kassim and Menon (2003).

4 We follow Doleys' distinction between approaches that emphasize the influence of supranational institutions on EU decision making ('supranationalism') and neofunctionalism, which makes additional claims about the process of integration and the inevitability of integration (2000: fn 4).

5 See Hall and Taylor (1996).

6 See Moe (1987) for a critical overview.

7 See Keohane (1984). For application in European politics, see Bergman *et al.* (2000); Thatcher and Stone Sweet (2002).

8 See also Hall and Taylor (1996: 945–6).

9 See n. 2 above.

10 This debate has, in recent years, generated more heat than light and has imposed a straitjacket on theoretical inquiry (Branch and Øhrgaard 1999, Schmidt 1996).

11 See Sandholtz (1996) for a discussion of this problem in relation to LI.

12 Quite unanticipated by the member states, 'the ECJ has constitutionalized the Treaty of Rome, built alliances with domestic courts and interest groups, pre-empted national law in important cases, and opened new avenues for Commission initiative, as in cases like *ERTA* in common commercial policy, and *Cassis de Dijon* in technical harmonization' (Moravcsik 1993a: 513).

13 We owe this point to Damian Chalmers.

14 Exactly the reverse is true in the case of the Council Presidency, where the incumbent member state is expected to play the role of 'honest broker'.

15 See Hooghe (2002) on the orientation of Commission officials.

16 Moravcsik acknowledges this point when he argues that member states take into account the likelihood that future streams of substantive decisions resulting from the pooling or delegation of sovereignty will be to their benefit when deciding on institutional design, but does not discuss the tension between information-based and distributional consequence views.

17 See Garrett (1992, 1995a,b), Garrett and Tsebelis (1996), Tsebelis and Garrett (2001).

18 See n. 17 above.

19 See n. 17 above.

20 We owe these points to Damian Chalmers.

21 In fact, in the first section of his article, Pierson (1996) takes the view that the projection of supranational institutions as agents implies their subservience to the member states. However, he later uses a more familiar construal where asymmetric information enables agents to escape the control of the principal (p. 139).

22 Our reading of Pollack as a supranationalist reflects the position he adopts in his theoretical writings. Although his empirical work (e.g. 2000) highlights the power of the member states, it is not grounded in the perspective elaborated in his theoretical writings.

23 Although Pollack (1997) discusses how divergent interests between the member states enable supranational agents to behave opportunistically, he does not explain how and under what conditions this might occur, and he certainly does not address the question, raised by Marks, Hooghe and Blank (1996), of the impact of European integration on individual, as opposed to collective, sovereignty of the member states.

24 We thank Bill Tompson for drawing this concept to our attention.

25 Though Pollack (1997: 115) does make a passing reference to this issue.

4 Idiosyncrasy and integration

Suggestions from comparative political economy

Erik Jones[1]

Abstract: There is a growing consensus in comparative political economy that 'globalization' is not eliminating the distinctive character of specific nation states. Even in Europe, where formal integration between countries is most profound, nation states remain idiosyncratic. Starting from this consensus, the questions I ask are: (a) how can we explain the coincidence of national idiosyncrasy and international integration; (b) what does our explanation tell us about processes of European integration? The answers, I argue, lie in two theoretical traditions – one stemming from Karl Polanyi's (1957) insistence on the social embeddedness of market institutions and the other from Gunnar Myrdal's (1956) interpretation of the cumulative causality behind integration at the national and international levels. Although well-received in other areas, neither tradition has played much of a role in the study of the European Union. The chapter concludes by suggesting a research programme that could develop from the interface between idiosyncrasy and integration.

Introduction

Students of comparative political economy have reached a consensus that the world's advanced industrial societies are not growing any more alike – at least not necessarily. Globalization, technological development, de-industrialization, demographic change, and a host of other factors all press upon welfare states and social institutions. Nevertheless, the result of this pressure is little or no necessary convergence on some common set of norms, institutions, or practices across countries.[2] Of course parallels do emerge from one case to the next. Yet these are more incidental than indicative in nature. The subtitle of Scharpf and Schmidt (2000b) captures the essence of the argument: 'diverse responses to common challenges'.

The absence of necessary convergence is nowhere more surprising than in Europe, where the remarkable development of the European Union must be added to the list of exogenous and endogenous challenges to national distinctiveness. The countries of Europe nevertheless provide the richest source of empirical support for the persistence of differences. For comparative political economists this juxtaposition of European integration and national distinctiveness under-scores the relative importance of other causal factors affecting the varieties of capitalism in evidence. For students of European integration, the confluence of factors is more fundamentally significant. If integration in Europe does not coincide with some form of necessary convergence between the member states, then what does 'integration' really mean?

The purpose of this chapter is to reflect the consensus in comparative political economy against the backdrop of European integration. My goal is not to survey the application of new institutionalist approaches to the study of the European Union and neither is it to provide some deep methodological critique of the competing frameworks used for analysis. Such arguments have already been pursued comprehensively by authors like Aspinwall and Schneider (2000) and Peterson (2001). In contrast with these authors' efforts to survey the breadth of the literature, my ambitions are more limited to illustrating some of the principal causal mechanisms at work and to suggesting some of the implications of focusing attention on those mechanisms. The questions I ask are two: How can we explain the persistence of national diversity within the common institutional framework of the European Union? What does the explanation tell us about the process of European integration? The answer to the first question conforms closely to the consensus view (albeit in simplified form): using Karl Polanyi's (1957) analysis of the 'double-movement' behind the social embeddedness of market institutions, it is possible to suggest both why countries differ and how European unity might contribute to national diversity.

The answer to the second question represents a departure from the existing consensus in comparative political economy. Rather than bracketing national diversity as something to be explained, it opens up the possibility that the idiosyncratic character of this diversity may be part of the explanation for the pattern of integration witnessed in Europe. The challenge is to develop a framework for analysing the interaction between idiosyncrasy and integration. Gunnar Myrdal's (1956) interpretation of the cumulative causal forces behind integration at the national and international level offers one possible solution. More important, Myrdal's analytic framework provides a basis for research on Europe that is different from the canon of integration theory and yet consistent with the consensus view in comparative political economy.

The chapter is developed in five sections. The first surveys the comparative political economy consensus in order to explain the idiosyncratic nature of national diversity. The second demonstrates the use of Polanyi's 'double movement' in explaining the causality that runs from integration to idiosyncrasy. The third introduces Myrdal's cumulative causality as a means of bringing idiosyncrasy and integration into dynamic interaction. The fourth suggests a research programme that could develop at the interface between idiosyncrasy and integration. The fifth section concludes.

From diversity to idiosyncrasy

The consensus among comparative political economists is at the same time deep and eclectic. It is deep insofar as most comparative political economists agree that countries have remained distinctive despite the many common forces acting upon them. Yet it is eclectic in the sense that different authors tend to highlight different areas of distinctiveness. Hence any broad survey of the literature would turn up a host of resilient 'differences' between countries that are important to economic performance, international competitiveness, institutional adaptiveness, or democratic stability.

The variety is most clearly evident when viewed in terms of horizontal strata. Wage bargaining institutions, monetary authorities (including central banks), distributive policies, tax regimes, political ideologies, and patterns of party-political competition constitute the focus of concern for macro-analysis. Corporate governance, supply networks, infrastructure, labour organization, labor market regulations, and skills development provide a meso-layer for attention. Social capital, interpersonal trust, popular values, and the economics of the family lie at the micro-layer.

The vertical concerns cutting across these strata are less immediately tangible and yet fundamentally no less diverse. For example, prevailing conceptions of distributive justice and patterns of distributive conflict necessarily stretch from the micro- to the macro-level of aggregation. Yet how are we meant to translate 'the spirit of cooperation' or 'the notion of fairness', or even 'social democracy' from one national context to the next without pointing to specific combinations of stratified characteristics – this type of family, this level of interpersonal trust, this pattern of industrialization, this form of corporate governance, these skills, this infrastructure, these policies, these policy institutions, and so forth? The easy answer is to invoke some essential characteristic – Asian values, German inflation aversion, Dutch consensus, and the American work ethic. The more difficult (and yet fortunately more common) answer is to bracket a set of necessary or indicative features for analysing particular problems. Wage bargaining and unemployment, central banks and inflation, social capital and democratic stability, and so forth. Such work has undoubtedly enriched our understanding of why difference matters. Yet it has also had the inadvertent effect of creating a set of functionally specific vertical pillars that are every bit as diverse in content as the horizontal strata they intersect.

The eclecticism at the heart of the comparative political economy consensus derives not from the observation that countries are diverse but from the reality that this diversity is idiosyncratic. It is possible to connect a particular structure of the family with a particular form of corporate governance and a particular pattern of party-political competition – as is often done in studies of French industrialization during the Third Republic. Yet the connections are historically contingent or, more generally, sensitively dependent upon initial conditions. So, for example, if we hoped to recreate French bourgeois capitalism in one of the transition countries in Central Europe, we would have to control for much more than the structure of the family, the form of corporate governance, or the pattern of party-political competition. Indeed, we would have to control for so many factors that inevitably the effort would prove futile. This was the lesson learned by Soviet economists in Central Europe during the 1950s and rediscovered by

Western economists in Central Europe during the 1990s. Countries will develop idiosyncratically or not at all.

The use of the term idiosyncrasy in this context is deliberate. My point is not simply that countries are different in certain respects. Rather it is that even similarities across countries are likely to have arisen for different reasons, along differing trajectories, and with different implications or effects. The scale of these differences need not be tremendous and in metaphorical terms it is easy to imagine that countries will bear family resemblances. However, the significance of the family metaphor should not be overestimated. Even two countries with a long heritage in common – such as Belgium and the Netherlands – should not be expected to resemble one another or even to hold common features – such as consociational democracy – for the same or similar reasons.

The idiosyncratic basis of national distinctiveness is unsurprising insofar as it reflects another deep and yet eclectic consensus in comparative political economy (and elsewhere) known broadly as the 'new institutionalism'.[3] The consensus is that institutions matter. The eclecticism lies in how institutions matter and why. Without digressing too far, suffice it to say that the new institutionalism constitutes a cross-hatch of direct and circular causal mechanisms implicating institutions both in particular outcomes and in their own reproduction. Moreover, this cross-hatch of causal mechanisms is every bit as complicated as the horizontal strata and vertical pillars for national difference suggested above. Institutions matter in ways and for reasons that both reflect and impact upon their broader environment including actors, other institutions, and themselves.

The link between the new institutionalism and the consensus on resilient national distinctiveness is analytic and not accidental. Countries remain different *because* institutions matter. And national differences are idiosyncratic because institutions matter for reasons and in ways that are sensitively dependent on initial conditions, on context, on timing, and on the beliefs or attitudes of the actors that interact through them or within them. At a macro-level this explains why the notion of diverse responses to common challenges has such appeal. The alternative would be inconsistent with the new-institutionalist consensus. In order to anticipate that common challenges should engender common responses, it would be necessary to assume that any response to globalization, demographic change, and so forth could be fashioned as though differences in institutional context (and therefore institutions) do not matter.

The implications here extend beyond the notion of diverse responses to common challenges and encompass the correlation between institutional form and institutional function. In order to insist that only one institutional configuration can guarantee a particular economic outcome it would be necessary to assume that some institutions matter and yet others do not. For example, an equivalent assertion might be that a politically independent central bank can guarantee price stability no matter how politics or markets may be organized. Even the framers of Europe's economic and monetary union could not make that leap of faith and so invested considerable resources in flanking the European Central Bank with a variety of institutional and procedural supports.

The link between the consensus on national diversity and the consensus that institutions matter extends all the way down to the micro-motivational or cultural level as well. In order to regress any type of performance – such as economic growth or political stability – back to some prior or fundamental characteristic – such as interpersonal trust – it would be necessary to assume that institutions matter in some areas but not in others. Continuing with the same example, institutions can reflect or channel interpersonal trust but they cannot shape it, create it, or diminish it.

The reason for highlighting the interconnections between the consensus on resilient distinctiveness and the consensus on the new institutionalism is not to suggest that countries are idiosyncratic and therefore there is no basis for a comparative analysis of institutions, performance, or the link between the two. Neither can my argument be read in any way as some comprehensive survey of new institutionalism and the convergence–divergence debate in comparative political economy. Rather my goal is to suggest only that idiosyncrasy matters as a persistent feature for analysis both in its own right and with reference to the impact it has on institutional arrangements which cross national boundaries. Recognition of idiosyncrasy offers insights both as an effect and as a cause.

Idiosyncrasy and Polanyi's 'double movement'

In order to illustrate the analytic significance of national idiosyncrasy, I need first to resuscitate Polanyi's (1957) 'double movement' as an explanation for the emergence of distinctively national political economies. The reason for going back to Polanyi is that his analysis of *The Great Transformation* that ushered in the welfare state has had seminal influence on the study of comparative political economy generally and on the development of institutionalism in particular. Not every comparative political economist agrees with Polanyi in every detail and few regard him as holding the last word. Nevertheless, Polanyi's argument lies at the foundation of the current consensus. Hence, for example, Hollingsworth and Boyer (1997) dedicate their collection of essays to Polanyi, while Scharpf and Schmidt (2000a) invoke his argument in the first sentence of their introduction. In this sense, Polanyi's 'double movement' is a greatest common denominator among comparative political economists who might otherwise differ on the specifics of how they believe the welfare state has developed subsequently or what they hold to be the most important explanatory mechanisms behind that development.

As an empirical claim, Polanyi's 'double movement' is descriptive and refers to the observation that (1957: 76):

> While on the one hand markets spread all over the globe [during the nineteenth century] and the amount of goods involved grew to unbelievable proportions, on the other hand a network of measures and policies was integrated into powerful institutions designed to check the actions of the market relative to labor, land, and money.

The vast spread of markets was the globalization of the nineteenth century. The emergence of the welfare state was the response. And, in this cause–effect relationship, the paradox for Polanyi (1957: 141) was that: 'while laissez faire economy was the product of deliberate state action, subsequent restrictions on laissez faire started in a spontaneous way'. To paraphrase closely (but anachronistically) the next sentence in Polanyi's argument, the globalization of markets was planned but the structure and functioning of the welfare state was not. From an empirical standpoint, then, it is possible to anticipate the idiosyncratic origins of the welfare states as a prior expression of Scharpf and Schmidt's 'diverse responses to common challenges'. The point to note, however, is that to some extent at least the common challenges were a result of state action.

But Polanyi's 'double movement' is more than just an empirical claim. It is also a theoretical proposition about the politics of economic adjustment. The mechanism at work behind the double movement develops from the logic of distributive politics. Any economic adjustment imposes costs as well as providing benefits. And the distribution of costs and benefits is often inequitable across different groups in society. Hence we should anticipate that groups adversely affected by a change will mobilize in search of redress. As Polanyi explains (1957: 152):

> Sectional interests are thus the natural vehicle of social and political change. Whether the source of change be war or trade, startling inventions or shifts in natural conditions, the various sections in society will stand for different methods of adjustment (including forcible ones) and adjust their interests in a different way from those of other groups to whom they may seek to give a lead; hence only when one can point to the group or groups that effect a change is it explained *how* that change came about.

Moreover, Polanyi is insistent that the motives of these sectional groups cannot be reduced to some objective economic calculation. Rather distributive politics takes place within cultural and institutional environments wherein the values attached to particular strategies or outcomes have a strong subjective component. 'To employ a metaphor, the facts of the economy were originally embedded in situations that were not in themselves of an economic nature, neither the ends nor the means being primarily material' (Dalton 1968: 120).

The implication of Polanyi's argument is that sectional interests necessarily reflect at least some of the idiosyncrasy of their local environment. '[In] any given case, the societal effects of individual behavior depend on the presence of definite individual conditions, these conditions do not for that reason result from the personal behavior in question' (Dalton 1968: 150). In this way, Polanyi's argument does not collapse into a tautology within which societal difference is the necessary product of its own creation. Rather it suggests only that environmental factors influence any calculation of 'rationality'. The more diverse these factors are from one context to the next, the more likely we should expect differences to emerge in separately 'rational' responses to common challenges. Of course there is an element of path dependence leading from difference in one period to difference

in another as the institutionalized responses to one challenge influence the calculation of rationality in responding to another. However, the mechanism behind
this path dependence derives from calculations (and understandings) of rationality
and not from history *per se*.[4]

History matters for our interpretation of Polanyi more in the structure of the
argument than in its content or implications. The force of Polanyi's claim about
the strong subjective component of sectional motivation lies in opposition to the
'class-based interests' that predominated in the Marxist political economy of his
day. His assertion that sectional interests are the natural vehicle of social and
political change underscores that class interests are not. Crucially, the distinction
between a 'section' and a 'class' lies in the sensitive dependence of sectional
interests on local institutional, social, and cultural factors. Where Marxists might
claim that class structures permeate national boundaries, Polanyi would counter
that sectional interests resist strong categorical aggregation or extrapolation from
one context to the next.

The politics of economic adjustment working behind the double movement is
distributive, and yet the rationality at its basis is contextually specific. Moreover,
the context of distributive politics encompasses more than market institutions to
include a range of institutions without explicit economic rationale. In this way,
Polanyi not only explains the institutional reaction to the emergence of world
markets but also the growing diversity of responses to the common challenges
that world markets represent. In Polanyi's empirical account, this diversity ultimately spells the demise of world markets and so ushers in the Great Depression.
And, in turn, the collapse of the world economy facilitated the 'rise of a variety
of new societies' (Polanyi 1957: 252).

However, that great transformation culminating in the 1930s was but a transi-
tory phase in history. In Polanyi's theoretical account, the diversity of national
institutional environments constitutes the defining characteristic of political economics. 'Nothing is more obvious to the student of social anthropology than the
variety of institutions found to be compatible with practically identical instruments of production' (Dalton 1968: 71). Moreover, the ubiquity of such variety
constitutes the link for Polanyi between idiosyncrasy and integration. The problem of integration is not to ensure a strong form of mechanistic determinism in
the form of comprehensive market rules or laws of economic behaviour and neither is it to impose institutional conformism around a single set of structures or
principles. Rather Polanyi invokes the term 'integration' to describe the use of
institutions to structure patterns of behaviour so as to create a sustainable and
self-propagating balance between collective interdependence and individual freedom in a given context (Dalton 1968: 139–74). Moreover, his use of the term is
explicitly normative and contingent: political actors *should* strive to strike a balance between interdependence and freedom; they should do so in full awareness
of the contextual specificity within which they operate; and they should accept
that it is possible to fail.

Polanyi's empirical claim about the origins of the welfare state clearly antedates
the process of European integration. However, Polanyi's theoretical argument has

both positive and normative implications for our understanding of the integration process. In positive terms, European integration lies behind a new double movement for Europe's welfare states. It is a common impetus to which the countries of Europe should be expected to respond differently, contingently, even idiosyncratically. Hence from Polanyi's perspective the consensus among comparative political economists concerning the resilience of national differences is unsurprising. Indeed, the link between integration and idiosyncrasy in Europe is causal.

In normative terms, Polanyi's theoretical argument suggests that European integration *should* result in the achievement of some dynamic and yet sustainable balance between interdependence and freedom for the participating member states. Once Europe's heads of state and government accept the social embeddedness of institutions (including market institutions), they must also accept variation across societies as a necessary constraint on the use of power to 'ensure ... that measure of conformity which is needed for the survival of the group' (Polanyi 1957: 258).

The challenge for theorists of European integration is to reconcile the tension between the positive and normative implications of Polanyi's argument. If the effect of integration is to encourage diversity, and the effect of diversity is to constrain the inducement of that measure of conformity which is necessary for the survival of the group as a group, then how is the dynamic balance at the heart of 'integration' to be achieved? Moreover, what will be the impact of efforts to balance integration at the European level (which is not actually the focus for Polanyi's analysis) on efforts to balance integration at the national or societal level (which is)? These are not questions for which Polanyi has a clear answer. The answers are not manifest in the comparative political economy consensus on resilient diversity or on the new institutionalism. And the answers are almost entirely absent from the theoretical canon concerning European integration. Almost.

Integration and Myrdal's 'cumulative causality'

One theorist who has addressed the dynamic balance implicit in Polanyi's conception of integration both generally and in relation to Europe is Gunnar Myrdal (1956). In his book *An International Economy: Problems and Prospects*, Myrdal sets out a framework for analysing integration as a process that is at the same time cumulative, causal, multilevel and reversible. Moreover, Myrdal's framework builds explicitly upon the normative contrast between conformity and diversity that is analysed by Polanyi. The tension between conformity and diversity exists and the goal of integration is to move toward a particular understanding of balance between these competing forces.[5]

The complementarity between Polanyi and Myrdal is as much analytic and empirical as normative. Both writers are institutionalists who accord a central role in all accounts of social development and political reform to the interaction between individual values and collective institutions. And both predicate much of their analysis on the overwhelming significance of the Great Depression of the 1930s as an episode of international disintegration. The difference between them is that where Polanyi posits the Great Depression at the end of his narrative account, Myrdal places it at the beginning. Both agree that the development of national economic institutions fragmented world markets. Polanyi's focus is on how this came about. Myrdal's is on what should be the appropriate response. Hence where Polanyi reserves his normative arguments until the end of *The Great Transformation*, Myrdal posits his normative emphasis up front. Economic integration, he asserts, is 'the realization of the old Western ideal of equality of opportunity' and ' "international economic integration" is the realization of the same ideal of equality of opportunity in the relations between peoples of different nations' (Myrdal 1956: 11, 13).

The overtly normative emphasis in Myrdal's conception of integration is likely to put off many contemporary analysts of Europe. Nevertheless, it is important not to be distracted by Myrdal's own insistence on the normative or ideological basis of his claim. In the context of more contemporary analysis, the force of Myrdal's normative claim derives from his analytic dependence on the interaction between values and institutions. For Myrdal, institutional reform cannot have effect unless it is somehow accompanied (or even preceded) by a change in values. Hence it makes little sense to analyse processes of institutional development – like integration – without identifying the normative framework within which they are embedded. The resonance here between Myrdal and Polanyi is acute.

Nevertheless, readers familiar with Polanyi and not with Myrdal may anticipate a contradiction in their respective normative frameworks. As a further point of introduction, therefore, it is useful to note that Myrdal's reliance on 'equality of opportunity' and classical Western liberalism does not contradict Polanyi's own rejection of liberal market ideology. Indeed, the similarities between the two authors are striking – particularly given the absence of cross-reference. Myrdal (1956: 25) suggests that 'a purely liberal – i.e., nondiscriminatory and "impartial" – national community is almost a contradiction in terms'; that 'in all advanced countries the secular trend has been away from a free market economy governed by the interplay of market forces'; and that:

> It is a paradox that only a well-integrated community can abide by the rules of economic competition; but that an integrated community will modify the rules if changes in prices impose too drastic a decline in the income of any one sector, or require too sudden shifts of resources or, more generally, if the community favors a course of economic development other than the one that would result from the free play of market forces.

Indeed, Myrdal (1956: 32–3) even has his own version of Polanyi's double movement, within which a principal (though not exclusive) stimulus for the elaboration of many of the institutions of the welfare state can be found in the reaction of social groups within national communities to the risks and adjustments implied by world market forces. For Myrdal as for Polanyi, the result is that 'cultural differences between populations on different sides of state boundaries, which were originally minor, are steadily accentuated as interests are focused on national issues and increasingly institutionalized within the state framework' (1956: 35).

The value that Myrdal adds to Polanyi's argument lies in his elaboration of the 'cumulative causation' behind processes of integration and disintegration. As already indicated, much of the causal force in the argument derives from the relationship between values and institutions. In turn, this linkage is underpinned by Myrdal's assessment of the structure of distributive conflict within conditions of relative scarcity and relative surplus. And it is in the assembly of institutional, attitudinal, and economic forces that the utility of Myrdal's liberal emphasis becomes apparent.[6]

The origins of integration for Myrdal are predominantly attitudinal. Actors choose to equalize opportunities within a group through the elimination of barriers, the redistribution of resources, or (more usually) some combination of the two. The choice may be motivated by collective or complementary self-interest, and yet it must also be underpinned by some more general commitment to the virtues of collective action (in what readers may recognize as an early form of the argument for social capital; 1956: 22). Once the choice for equalization become institutionalized, then the success of the reform measure is contingent upon an identification with the institutions and a willingness to abide by the new rules they imply – two factors which Myrdal describes as comprising 'solidarity' within the given context. Actors must accept to participate in a competitive market and they must agree to contribute to redistribution.

Beyond this point, Myrdal's emphasis shifts from attitudes and institutions to economics and back again. The economic effect of the equalization of opportunity within a group should be welfare enhancing – this is the liberal premise. In turn, the effect of welfare enhancement should be to mitigate the obstacles to a further extension of equality of opportunity while at the same time reinforcing the appeal of engaging in collective institution-building. Distributive conflict is less disruptive and collective action is more attractive in conditions of relative surplus. This is how Myrdal closes the cycle for cumulation. However, given the central significance of attitudes and institutions in the process, the end result is idiosyncratic and not economically (or ideologically) predetermined: 'From this point of view of their cumulative effects upon attitudes and, therefore, possibilities for further advance, even small institutional accomplishments become potentially important' (Myrdal 1956: 55). Processes of integration are path dependent.

A similar cumulation lies behind processes of disintegration. However, the origins of disintegration are predominantly economic rather than attitudinal. Unexpected economic hardship or dislocation undermines the willingness of groups to engage in institutional commitments to equality of opportunity and heightens the significance of distributive conflict. Instead of solidarity, different groups come to struggle over the control of institutions, whether in the form of markets or of redistributed resources. Such conflict in turn impacts upon aggregate welfare and accentuates the unwillingness of groups to commit to equality of opportunity. Here too the process manifests itself institutionally and so exhibits idiosyncratic path dependence.

The cumulative element of these processes is only part of the story. The other part is the fact that processes of integration and disintegration can exist independently in different areas of institutional activity and that they can play out across many different levels of aggregation at the same time. Within a given level of analysis – an individual welfare state, for example – the existence of an institutional arrangement that integrates some members of society while disintegrating others presents no necessary paradox. There may be a normative contradiction between the equalization of opportunities to one group simultaneous to the exclusion of another, but there is no logical or empirical obstacle to such coincidence. The same is true across levels of analysis. A trade union may integrate its own members even if this has adverse implications for other workers outside. And the elaboration of the welfare state can disrupt the functioning of world economy. Indeed, for Myrdal as for Polanyi that is precisely the point. As Myrdal (1956: 33) explains:

> I do not imply the existence of logical elements in conflict between the ideals of national and international integration. I am more convinced than ever that, on the contrary, national economic progress can reach the highest possible levels only in a well-integrated world. But in the severely disintegrated world in which we actually live, there is an obvious lack of institutional balance that works forcefully against international solutions that would satisfy people's cravings for economic progress, equality, and security.

The locus for this tension between integration at the national and international levels lies in the interaction between economic institutions – macroeconomic, regulatory, and market. As different social groups have turned to the state in defence of their welfare, the result has been to elaborate a wide variety of different institutional structures in response to specific problems. And given the territorial boundaries of the state, these institutions have tended to operate only at the national level. Internationally, the effect of these various regimes has been to create obstacles to interaction and to exchange – both institutional and attitudinal – regardless of the explicit intentions behind the original institutional design. Hence the problem is not nationalism or protectionism, *per se*. Rather it is the idiosyncratic manner in which national political communities have addressed shared and complementary values. Hence,

> the ordinary citizen is apt to believe – and very largely with good reason – that the national policies by which [national integration] has been brought about are good, even if they are exactly those which are here pictured as the causes of international disintegration.
>
> (Myrdal 1956: 44)

Resolution of the tension between integration at the national and international levels depends upon the reconciliation of institutional regimes and the preservation of values. In this way, 'international integration becomes … a matter of coordination' wherein '[what] is needed is *an internationalization of these national policy structures themselves, preserving the essential values they represent to the several nations'* (italics in original; Myrdal 1956: 50). In this way, Myrdal anticipates the 'new approach' to voluntary industrial standards that operates at the heart of the internal market programme of the late 1980s as well as the 'open method of coordination' around which the Lisbon European Council built its strategy for welfare state reform in the late 1990s (Hodson and Maher 2001). For Myrdal, such developments should not constitute a departure from the pattern of international integration – they are the pattern, at least insofar as integration is identified with the equalization of opportunity between the member states. Some measure of conformity may be essential, but a wide element of diversity cannot be avoided.

The next phase in Myrdal's analysis in *An International Economy* uses this understanding of integration to explain why efforts to unite Europe during the early to mid-1950s failed to yield the desired result. For Myrdal, the tension between national and international integration was only part of the problem. The other part lay in the excessive ambition of his contemporaries in their efforts to force the pace of integration ahead of the development of popular attitudes and beyond the reconciliation of institutional regimes. Such efforts, he suggests, were doomed to failure. Only a more specific, practical, and incremental project could hope to succeed.

With the benefit of hindsight we might be tempted to agree. The dramatic proposal of a European Defence Community and its concomitant European Political Community could never hope to overcome the attitudinal and institutional obstacles that were present during the first decade of the Cold War. By contrast, a more specific, practical, and incremental pursuit of economic integration might, however, succeed. And it did. But we do not need to appeal to Myrdal to know that. The evidence of the success of European economic integration is all around us. What Myrdal adds to this empirical record is an understanding of the coincidence between the progress of European economic integration and the persistence of national distinctiveness. For Myrdal, the one could not have been possible without the other.

Idiosyncrasy and integration

The insights taken from Polanyi and Myrdal can be drawn together in a research programme that complements the existing work on European integration by emphasizing some of the analytic strengths of comparative political economy – strengths related to the analysis of institutional effects, distributive coalitions, and dynamic systems. The purpose of this section is to suggest how such a research programme could come about and is organized along some of the guiding themes suggested in the work by Polanyi and Myrdal.[7]

From Polanyi, the emphasis in the research programme can be summarized in terms of reactive diversity and distributive politics. When examining any particular facet of European integration, the first step is to look where reactions differ across member states and the second is to attempt to analyse plausible distributive accounts for these differences in reaction. The point is not that integration and idiosyncrasy covary in some direct or linear sense. Rather it is that any aspect of integration may give rise to reactions that differ from one member state to the next for distributive reasons which are strongly influenced by the local structural environment.

Consider, for example, the effects of capital market integration and monetary integration. The predominant expectation in the literature is that these will have a strongly convergent influence on Europe's member states. However, the implications of Polanyi's double movement are that the effect will be divergent and will depend upon domestic distributive politics. In part, this line of reasoning is already well documented in Garrett (1995c, 1998), who analyses the flexibility afforded to left-wing political groups under conditions of high capital mobility. What Garrett (2000) has tended to avoid is the impact of monetary integration, which he concedes will have a convergent influence on fiscal policy.

By contrast, Jones (2003) finds the differential responses to monetary integration anticipated in the logic of Polanyi's 'double movement' in comparative national performance on international current accounts. Simply, the variation in current account performance across countries increases first with capital market integration and again with monetary integration. In turn, this variation in current account performance can be explained with reference to the adoption of differing macroeconomic policy mixes which are possible only under conditions of capital market liberalization and which are reinforced (rather than undermined) by monetary unification. Finally, these differing macroeconomic policy mixes have important distributive consequences which can be traced back to underlying policy coalitions. In the language of Polanyi, we can regress this story about diverse reactions to capital market integration and monetary union through the macroeconomic data and back into those sectional interests that are the natural vehicles for social and political change.

The identification of diverse reactions to common policies or common institutions should not be taken as a challenge to assertions of 'commonality'. With the previous example, my point is not that capital market integration and monetary union have no convergent impact. Rather it is to suggest that they have divergent implications as well. This change in emphasis is important to help round out debates about European integration. For example, where the predominant emphasis in discussions of capital market integration and monetary union is on the convergent features of these policies, then the addition of rules governing fiscal behaviour as in the Stability and Growth Pact can only be viewed as an added constraint. When the emphasis shifts to focus on divergent reactions – and so highlight, for example, the fact that Portugal has run a current account deficit of approximately 8 per cent of gross domestic product for each of the past five years on top of a consistent run of deficits stretching back to the late 1980s – the importance of agreeing standards for fiscal performance increases.

In Polanyi's analysis, distributive politics is mediated not only by institutions but also by ideas. Moreover, the ideational influences on distributive politics are at least partially endogenous insofar as they change over time and as a result of the evolution of political competition. This point is slightly complicated but can be illustrated in the contrast between two prominent accounts of the role of ideas and preferences in the process of European monetary integration. In McNamara's (1998) account, preferences converge across countries under the influence of capital market liberalization. States (or governments) become aware of the implications of high capital mobility for monetary policy autonomy and so come to accept the inevitability (in structural terms) of a neoliberal turn in macroeconomic policymaking. In Moravcsik's (1998) account, the result is much the same and yet the process is more highly contested in the form of distributive negotiations between countries and between competing interest groups within countries. Viewed together these two accounts suggest differing degrees of endogenous influence and therefore differing degrees of convergence across countries: McNamara's account is dominated more fully by the lessons learned from the collapse of Keynesianism; Moravcsik's account incorporates a series of smaller lessons learned by individual countries or groups within countries from myriad events that take place throughout the integration process including the process of negotiating over institutional design.

If we follow the path of contestation to its logical conclusion, multiplying the actors involved and increasing the endogenous influences of past conflicts on current perspectives, then it is possible to restructure much of our understanding of the stability of monetary integration. The predominant assumption in the theory of optimal currency areas is that the choices for entering and leaving a monetary union are symmetrical. Countries (or governments) opt for irrevocably fixed exchange rates when the distributive consequences are favourable – as when trading relations between prospective members are preponderant. But countries (or governments) may also choose to leave the monetary union and opt for flexible exchange rates when the distributive consequences of membership become unfavourable – as under the influence of an asymmetric exogenous demand shock. Assuming that Polanyi is correct in his analysis of the 'double movement', however, this expectation of symmetry in the choices to join and to leave a monetary union should not hold.

Joining a monetary union represents the choice for an exchange rate regime with important consequences for monetary policy. Leaving the monetary union represents a choice for monetary policy with important consequences for the exchange rate regime. The distinction is more than just a semantic one for three reasons implicit in the 'double movement'. First, domestic actors will have changed their institutional environments in order to adapt to the consequences of participation in the monetary union. Second, these actors will have reordered their prioritization of policy instruments by ease of use, with efforts to seek fiscal redress always proving easier than efforts to re-establish a national currency. And third, actors will face a completely different set of distributive calculations – although still difficult, it is far easier to establish the distributive consequences of changing the exchange rate regime than to identify the distributive consequences of changing either the direction or the character of monetary policy. Each of these three reasons is endogenous to the process of monetary integration. And what is important is not only recognizing the precise mechanisms for this endogenous influence of integration on institutions and ideas, but also recognizing the implications of its existence for our understanding of integration as a process.

This discussion of endogenous influences helps to move the research programme from Polanyi to Myrdal, and from the distributive politics of institutionally bounded arenas (like national polities) to the distributive implications of interactions across levels of analysis. What Myrdal emphasizes is the importance of the competition between national and international forms of integration. In practical terms, we should look for this competition to play out in the interaction between systems. As policymaking competencies become institutionalized at the European level, what is the impact on national performance?

One example of research posited in answer to a question like this can be found in Peter Hall's analysis of the implications of monetary integration for German price stability. Hall's (1994) argument is that German price stability during the post-war period is not solely a result of policies of the German central bank, the Bundesbank, but rather results from the complex signalling between the Bundesbank and those actors engaged in wage bargaining. The force of this claim is that price stability derives not from some readily identifiable institutional attribute like political independence, but rather from a more ambiguous distributive equilibrium between powerful forces in German society, namely labour and capital. By implication, Hall speculates as to whether attempts to replace the Bundesbank with a European central bank would somehow eliminate the signalling between monetary authorities and those actors engaged in wage bargaining, and thereby disrupt the distributive equilibrium behind Germany's stable prices (Hall 1994: 17). In turn, such speculation has fed into a well-spring of analyses that have looked at the implications of monetary integration for domestic patterns of distributive conflict, policymaking, and policy adjustment both in Germany and elsewhere.[8] As Hall and Franzese (1998: 526–30) point out, such analysis holds the key to understanding the future of European economic integration.

Myrdal's emphasis on the dynamic interactions between levels of analysis provides a useful window for analysing the relationship between unity and diversity. Not only does it highlight systemic interdependence – such as between the stability of an exchange rate or monetary regime and the interaction between domestic institutions – but it also suggests the importance of identifying operational constraints. As the pattern of European integration adapts to accommodate ever greater diversity among its member states, the importance of such constraints can only be expected to grow. Hence, for example, it is not enough to acknowledge that enlargement will take place on the basis of a 'principle of differentiation', that welfare state reform will be undertaken within an 'open method of coordination', or that the European Union may evolve along lines of 'enhanced cooperation' between subsets of participants. What is also required is more general analysis of where differentiation ceases to facilitate progress, where open coordination ceases to encourage reform, and where enhanced cooperation exacerbates conflict rather than mitigating it (Jones 2001). These are the types of question which Myrdal encourages us to analyse, and in ways that retain our focus on the importance of distributive conflict as influenced by domestic political and economic institutions.

Suggestions from comparative political ecomomy

Students of comparative political economy have arrived at something of a consensus that national economic institutions are embedded in complex and interdependent networks which differ both historically and constitutionally from one country to the next. Moreover, even though countries are integrating within the world economy and within regional groupings such as the European Union, such integration does not entail that the countries themselves are necessarily becoming less distinctive. Existing research on European integration (and globalization more generally) has focused on the conditions within which convergence does take place, on the institutional features that underwrite specific forms of distinctiveness, and on the conditional nature of convergence across national systems. Such research has added much to our understanding of integration in Europe. However, taken as a whole, this body of research also highlights the idiosyncratic character of national political economies.

The persistence of national idiosyncrasy forces us to reconsider processes of integration, particularly within the context of the European Union. Using the insights of authors like Karl Polanyi and Gunnar Myrdal, it is possible to construct an interpretation of events in Europe within which idiosyncrasy and integration are two elements in the same larger process of interaction. The great virtue of such an interpretation is that it focuses attention on the diverse reactions of groups within countries to common features at the European level. The interpretation suggested by Polanyi and Myrdal highlights the significance of distributive politics to understanding the forces behind Europe and it underscores the role of specific environmental factors in shaping this distributive politics. Finally, this interpretation signals the need to analyse the complementarity between levels of integration and it does so in a manner which should allow us to structure case studies that will not only answer discrete questions but that can be relied upon to inform future research. These focal points are all present in the existing research and yet they are not unified within a common understanding of the basic causal mechanisms at work. The suggestions I draw from comparative political economy are about how such insights can be unified and researched on the basis of the standard causal patterns described by Polanyi and Myrdal.

The vice of this interpretation of the political economy of European integration is that any acceptance of idiosyncrasy invites complexity into the analysis. For most comparative political economists this tension between parsimony and complexity is a long-standing feature of research design. And there is no reason it should not be the same for students of integration. Indeed, if we accept the framework posited here, there is a certain poetic justice to the plight of the analyst. For analysis, as for integration, the challenge is to ensure that conformity which is necessary for survival without sacrificing that diversity which is manifest in the world around us.

Notes

1 A preliminary version of this chapter was presented at the European Research Institute of the University of Birmingham. There and elsewhere I was grateful to receive constructive feedback from Robert Elgie, Paul Heywood, Dave Marsh, Anand Menon, Jonathon Moses, Amy Verdun, and two anonymous referees. The usual disclaimer applies.
2 See for example, Berger and Dore (1996), Esping-Andersen (1999), Hall and Soskice (2001), Hollingsworth and Boyer (1997), Kitschelt *et al.* (1999), Scharpf and Schmidt (2000a,b).
3 See for example, Goodin (1996), March and Olsen (1989), Peters (1999), Weaver and Rockman (1993).
4 Note here the contrast between Polanyi and Pierson (2000: 264–5).
5 Note here the contrast with Puchala (1975), who argued that the concept of 'integration' should be understood explicitly in terms of harmonization.
6 See particularly Myrdal (1957: 1–55).
7 See also Jones (2002).
8 See for example, Franzese (2002), Iversen (1998, 1999), McNamara and Jones (1996), Soskice and Iversen (1998).

5 Home alone

Integration and influence in national contexts

Jonathon W. Moses[1]

Abstract: In an effort to reconceptualize the study of European integration this chapter focuses on the effects of European integration on the *nature* of national sovereignty. Currently, there is no clear theory that allows us to generalize about the nature of the influence integration has on sovereignty. In order to fill this gap the chapter develops a framework to test hypotheses regarding this nexus between integration and national sovereignty by modifying Albert O. Hirshman's *Exit, Voice and Loyalty* (1970) argument. Within this new framework the chapter suggests that the concept of exit can be thought of as synonymous with integration, where the level of integration is correlated with the likelihood of exit from the project of integration. As shown in the chapter this approach helps, by means of empirical and theoretical research, to generate micro-level expectations about the effects of integration on political actors and apply this to all political levels affected by integration. As a result it provides a more comprehensive picture of the process of European integration.

Introduction

> A giant step on the road toward an integrated theory of regional integration, however, would be taken if we could clarify the matter of what we propose to explain and/or predict.
>
> (Haas 1971: 26)

The recent history of European studies is intricately linked to the notion of integration. The 1986 Single European Act signalled phenomenal changes that came to inspire a new type of European study: integration itself came back into focus. While empirically-minded students of Europe began to map the new institutional and policy terrain that developed in the late 1980s, our more theoretical colleagues aimed to explain the sundry motivations for this new integration. The result has been a broad church of researchers who have largely traced the evolution of political sovereignty from national to supranational institutions.

This chapter provides a different way of thinking about integration. Rather than trying to explain the nature and motivation of European integration itself, I flip the traditional causal arrow around and ask: how does integration affect the *nature* of national sovereignty? In doing so, my concern is not with how much sovereignty remains at different levels of governance. Rather, I am interested in how integration affects influence on the sovereignty that remains however small or large. While it is possible to find a number of national studies on how European Union (EU) membership and, by implication, integration has affected the nature of domestic policy choices, I am unaware of any theoretical framework that allows us to generalize about the nature of this influence. This chapter aims to fill that void.

I develop a modified version of Albert O. Hirschman's influential *Exit, Voice and Loyalty* (1970) model to generate two stylized scenarios, representing a world with and without integration. The lessons of these two stylized scenarios are contrasted to show how political influence varies with integration.

In this approach, 'exit' becomes a surrogate for integration. For Hirschman, exit represents the ability of consumers, or political actors, to switch their consumption or membership pattern. Thus the possibility of exit is intricately linked to the degree of integration. To understand this linkage, it may help the reader to consider the relationship between exit and integration in more concrete terms. Imagine the possibilities available to an investor. The capitalist's ability to withdraw an investment from a given country (exit) depends on the level of barriers inhibiting this investment elsewhere. If the market for investments is integrated, then the capitalist's cost of exit is small. If the market for investments is not integrated, exit (outward foreign investment) is costly, perhaps unviable. In this way, exit and integration can be understood in Stolper-Samuelson-like terms (but where trade does not need to substitute for factor flows!), such that integration, or liberalization, benefits owners of factors that are potentially more mobile.[2]

This way of thinking about integration is rather different from traditional political economy approaches, as illustrated by most of the contributions to this volume. But the question that motivates this study requires that we shift our analytical perspective. In doing so, integration ceases to be a dependent variable, captured in terms of formal outcomes (institutions, policies, etc.). Instead, integration becomes an independent variable, captured 'informally' – that is, as processes that have effective consequences without formal, authoritative intervention.[3] Thus free movement entails the elimination of barriers to mobility as well as more positive measures for encouraging mobility, for example, institutional harmonization.

My approach generates micro-level expectations about the effect of integration on the nature and effectiveness of citizen influence. These individual influences can be aggregated in any number of ways. As European class cleavages are easier to capture empirically, and because a related (globalization) literature has largely focused on class-based models, I have chosen to close the discussion by speculating about the effects of integration on class influence in member states, across Europe.

Thus in the chapter's final section I sketch the uneven pace of economic integration in Europe measured in class terms. While the public ambition of Europe's political elites has long been to encourage the 'four freedoms', the actual integration of goods, services and capital markets has proceeded much faster than the integration of European labour markets. Compared to other markets, and contrasted against the political and legal rhetoric of European elites, European labour markets remain largely segregated along national lines. These empirical observations provide some basis for speculating about the political effects of integration on influence at home. In particular, I argue that the uneven integration of Europe's markets may be undermining labour's relative influence at home.

This finding is rather counter-intuitive and perhaps politically anathema. For most commentators on the political Left, the maintenance of nationally regulated labour markets is seen as the only effective bulwark for defending policy outcomes that favour workers. In contrast, I argue that the opposite may actually be the case: in the absence of more integrated European labour markets, domestic labour remains home alone with a muted domestic voice.

A theoretical framework

In this section I modify Hirschman's (1970) influential *Exit, Voice and Loyalty* approach. This modification allows us to generate concrete and testable expectations of how integration affects influence on national sovereignty. Hirschman's approach is chosen as a point of departure because it provides us with a useful means for overcoming two conceptual difficulties associated with a project of this type: (1) he offers a novel way of opening up the closed-polity nature of most comparative political economy approaches; and (2) his approach helps us to conceive of and operationalize integration in a way which is novel for political scientists, but perhaps more familiar to economists. In this modified approach, I assume that integration increases the likelihood of exit by reducing the cost of exit. Thus agents with greater access to exit find themselves with new and effective means of influencing political outcomes. Agents that are unable to wield the same threat of exit find themselves home alone, with relatively less influence.

Initial assumptions

I assume that the reader is somewhat familiar with Hirschman's path-breaking book. For that reason, I will avoid a detailed description of his argument and instead present two of his most relevant observations for the argument that follows. These observations allow me to dwell for a moment on the utility of Hirschman's approach for the issue at hand.

Like Pareto, Hirschman begins as a radical pessimist in that he assumes all organizations, regardless of their institutional make-up, are subject to deterioration. Human nature is characterized by entropy, so that:

> Firms and other organizations are conceived to be permanently and randomly subject to decline and decay, that is, to a gradual loss of rationality, efficiency, and surplus-producing energy, no matter how well the institutional framework within which they function is designed.
>
> (Hirschman 1970: 15)

This assumption is critical for Hirschman, who wishes to argue that organizations need an effective feedback mechanism for gauging customer/constituent satisfaction.

I point out this assumption because the motivation for influencing political behaviour in Hirschman's approach is somewhat different from the motivation of actors in traditional political economy approaches. While the latter tend to have an 'offensive' approach to political influence (that political outcomes are a result of agents that actively influence policy outcomes on the basis of their autonomous preferences), Hirschman's approach has a more defensive, rearguard, feel to it. Actors respond to a decline in product quality – a deterioration that is assumed to be endogenous to all organizations, because of the pervasiveness of slack. While these motivational differences reveal themselves in the discussion that follows, they do not affect the outcomes.[4]

The second relevant part of Hirschman's argument concerns the two, competing, 'forces of recovery' by which firms and organizations can learn of this deterioration, and correct it before becoming obsolete: exit and voice. Exit, he suggests, is neat (one either leaves or one does not), impersonal, indirect, and belongs to the field of economics. Voice is messy, personal and direct, and belongs to the study of politics (Hirschman 1970: 15–16).

Exit is the main recourse of consumers responding to a decline in the quality of a firm's product. Voice is the main recourse for citizens responding to a decline in the quality of their state's policies (i.e. citizenship). As member states in Europe become more integrated, we can expect to see states acting more like firms in a competitive market: they will face actors who wield both exit and voice. However, to conceive of state action in this way, we must first acknowledge two very restrictive, common assumptions: (1) citizens/voters act like consumers; and (2) states act like firms.[5]

By recognizing these two modes of influence, Hirschman provides us with an interesting way of addressing the conceptual trade-off concerning sovereignty and integration. In traditional studies of political economy, we tend to think about interests and influence in terms of closed-polity models. Thus, European studies of comparative political economy aim to explain variations in member state policies with reference to a number of domestic attributes, such as the mode of interest mediation (e.g. corporatism/pluralism), the type of electoral system, national history/culture, the strength of specific political parties, sectors (e.g. exposed/sheltered), classes (e.g. Labour/Capital), etc.

If we are to take integration seriously, however, we need to develop a framework for including new, external influences on sovereignty (of the kind we might expect from increased integration). By combining exit and voice as complementary means for influencing outcomes, Hirschman's approach provides us with a device for capturing just this sort of external influence. In this model, influence is not confined to the ballot box, or domestic political institutions; the threat of exit opens up the approach to influences that are more sensitive to the forces of integration.

In the remainder of this section, I follow Hirschman's presentation of the relationship between exit and voice, and extend its implications to states.[6] Hirschman depicts the relationship in two phases: voice as a residual to exit; and voice as an alternative to exit. These two phases correspond to two idealized scenarios of

European integration. The first (voice as a residual to exit) can be used to analyse the effectiveness of voice in a Europe categorized by segregated political and economic markets, that is, one with little integration. The second scenario (voice as an alternative to exit) can be used to analyse the effectiveness of different channels of influence in an integrated Europe.

Segregated influence

We begin by examining the nature of influence in a model where the costs of exit are relatively high. This model corresponds to the way in which we traditionally think about political influence (i.e. where political and economic sovereignty is relatively segregated); it is developed with an eye to elaborating the possibility of exit, but in a context where exit remains relatively costly. It is in this context that traditional models of comparative political economy provide strong analytical purchase: the greater the cost of exit, the larger the role for traditional voice. The lessons of the first scenario are clear: in the absence of a viable exit option, political actors aim to amplify their voice in national venues.

We can adapt Hirschman's model to states by reproducing his quality demand graph with one that is aimed at interpreting citizen demand for variations in citizenship quality.[7] This is done in Figure 5.1. It might be worthwhile to describe the figure, as it is similar to a traditional demand curve, only different. The upper part of the diagram is a traditional demand curve, where the cost of citizenship has been replaced by the quality of citizenship (depicted inversely, in order to maintain the traditional downward slope of the demand curve).

The demand curve, **D**, represents the quality elasticity of demand (or the exit response of citizens to a deterioration in the quality of citizenship). It falls because I assume that a drop in the quality of citizenship will result in a decline in the demand for that citizenship, as residents will seek exit.[8] Like traditional demand curves (which assume that quality remains unchanged when the effect of price changes on demand are considered), we can assume that the 'cost' of citizenship will remain unchanged while we consider the effect of quality changes on citizenship demand.

The quality of citizenship,[9] Q_c, can be understood in terms of a function of the benefits of citizenship (e.g. jobs, wealth, influence, size, role in the world, social and economic ideology, etc.) as well as the opportunity costs associated with choosing another state's citizenship. The cost of citizenship, C_c, is similarly understood as a function of the costs of citizenship – in both economic and less tangible means (e.g. greater responsibilities, military draft, community service, larger tax burden, etc.) – as well as the opportunity costs associated with choosing citizenship elsewhere. Along the horizontal axis we find the quantity equivalent for states: the number of citizens or residents in a country. The demand curve reflects the quality demand elasticity.

To interpret the figure, we can begin by assuming that the quality of a given state's citizenship deteriorates from Q_0 to Q_1. Say, for example, the welfare state is drastically truncated without a (welfare-effect offsetting) tax reduction. The

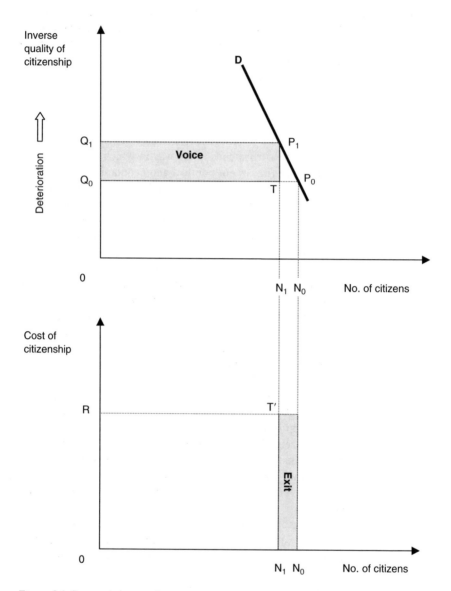

Figure 5.1 Segregated scenario.

figure helps us to map out the effects of this change on citizen and state behaviour. Presumably, the demand for citizenship will drop with the deterioration in quality, and this fall in demand translates into emigration. (Similarly, an improvement in the quality of citizenship will provoke immigration.) Thus in Figure 5.1, outward migration is measured in terms of the decline in the number of citizens (e.g. N_0–N_1). As voice depends on the number of citizens (0–N_1) that remain and the degree of citizenship degradation (Q_0–Q_1), the grey area marked '**Voice**' can be used to capture the amount of voice (of whatever type) that is generated in response to that decline in citizenship quality. Obviously, the larger the size of this area, the more significant the potential voice in correcting for the decline in citizenship quality. Thus, in response to a drastic curtailment of the welfare state, citizens can choose voice or exit, depending on their quality demand elasticities. We can assume that states monitor voice for dissatisfaction to changes in citizenship quality.

The lower part of the diagram reflects the potential costs of exit, in terms of the 'revenues' (broadly defined) that are lost by the state as a result of emigration, sparked by a deterioration in the quality of citizenship.[10] (Similarly, an improvement in the quality of citizenship will induce revenue gains.) When citizenship quality drops from Q_0 to Q_1, and assuming that the unit cost of citizenship does not change, the total revenue loss to the government is depicted by the '**Exit**' rectangle. Of course, these revenues are set arbitrarily in the diagram; their significance lies only in their comparative utility, when we contrast these revenues to those lost under other conditions.

In effect, this first scenario is characteristic of segmented (political, as well as economic) markets. Because of the very high cost of exit, the quality demand curve for citizenship is relatively inelastic. Under these conditions, effective voice becomes essential for the vast majority of citizens who remain: it is their only avenue for addressing grievances. The relative importance of voice compared to exit is clearly illustrated by the size of the corresponding conduit of influence: the amount of voice in this scenario is larger than the potential revenue loss generated by exit (i.e. the '**Voice**' box is larger than the '**Exit**' box). As long as this revenue loss remains relatively small, states rely on voice as the most important conduit for channeling citizen discontent.

Integrated influence

We can now consider how citizen influence might change under conditions characterized by greater integration. In this scenario, exit becomes a more likely (if still costly[11]) option for disgruntled citizens. Therefore exit becomes a real alternative to voice. To show how integration affects influence, this section begins with a general model, like in the previous section, but with a more elastic quality of demand curve. These conditions can be understood as depicting a Europe with greater economic and political integration: here it is easier for citizens to respond with exit to any decline in national citizenship quality. As we shall see, under these conditions citizens enjoy increased opportunities to influence polity outcomes (or respond to quality decline), and states subsequently find it necessary to respond to these influences.

Figure 5.2 depicts the conditions of a more integrated scenario. This integration is reflected in an increase in the elasticity of the quality demand for citizenship (i.e. the shift in demand curves from **D** to **D***, where **D** is the demand curve in Figure 5.1). As in the previous figure, **D*** corresponds to a decline in citizenship quality (from Q_0 to Q_1). The effect of this deterioration in quality (in the new

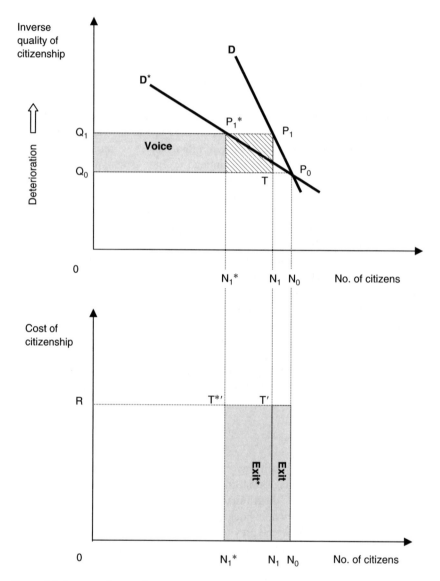

Figure 5.2 Integrated scenario.

context) is a decline in the citizenship population (from N_0 to N_1^*). The more elastic quality demand curve, **D***, shrinks the relative effect of voice and significantly increases the revenue effect of exit (compared to **D**).

In this scenario, exit is no longer subordinate to voice, but can be interpreted as a real alternative to voice.[12] The citizen, in effect, has a new channel through which to respond to deteriorations in citizenship quality (or to generate more 'offensive' policy proposals). It is at this point that we become most aware of the closed-polity handicap in traditional approaches to comparative political economy. Obviously, this new (exit) option complicates the citizen's utility function, as he/she must now decide whether to exit. This decision depends critically on several factors, including the citizen's evaluation of his/her prospects for effective voice.[13] For example, if a citizen believes that his/her voice will be effective in correcting a decline in citizenship quality, he/she may postpone exit. Thus, the quality elasticity of exit (demand) depends both on larger structural considerations (e.g. degree of integration), and on the ability and willingness of citizens to use the voice option.

In this integrated scenario we find that the potential revenue loss to states from exit (**Exit*** + **Exit**) now exceeds the amount of voice that is generated by a deterioration in citizenship quality. It is important to point out that the amount of citizenship deterioration has not changed between the first and second scenarios. What has changed is the ability of a citizen to leave in response to that deterioration. Under these conditions, states find that they can no longer ignore the potential costs associated with exit. Indeed, as integration increases, these costs become so large that states must pay increasing attention to the threat of exit (at the expense of voice).

To the extent that this scenario represents a fully integrated Europe, we can use this framework to generate three explicit expectations about the effects of integration on political influence: (1) citizens will enjoy increased influence on issues of internal sovereignty (while the role of voice has shrunk, they now have access to the threat of exit for articulating dissatisfaction); (2) in response to the increased empowerment of citizens, states themselves need to become more responsive to citizen demands – failure to do so effectively can lead to serious resource and legitimacy losses; and (3) as a consequence of the first two expectations, we should see states begin to compete with one another in attracting mobile citizen resources (like firms in a competitive marketplace).

The discussion thus far has been framed in terms of two theoretical scenarios: a Europe without integration and a Europe characterized by integration. I have used this format to illustrate how the nature of political influence can change under two ideal-typical scenarios. By contrasting these two scenarios, we learn that actors in more integrated markets find their influence strengthened relative to the segmented scenario. In practice, of course, there are varying levels of market integration. These tend to vary across issue areas or markets. The next section will suggest how we might conceive of this (more realistic) scenario.

Complex integration

To capture this mixed scenario, we can consider a second, less speculative, means of interpreting Figure 5.2. Rather than assuming an aggregate shift to **D*** in the context of full integration, we might assume that citizens meet, in effect, different quality demand functions. In the context of European integration, for example, we find that some markets are more integrated than others. Under these conditions, some of the resident population may face rather steep (inelastic) demand curves because their 'markets' are not integrated (e.g. **D**), while other citizens may enjoy access to markets that are more integrated: they face a more elastic quality demand curve (e.g. **D***). For these citizens, voice plays a relatively small role in their response to policy dissatisfaction. Their threat of exit carries with it significant revenue flight. If strategically inclined, these citizens can serve a potent cocktail of political influence: voice mixed with a strong threat of exit. Other citizens, who do not wield a real threat of exit, must confine their dissatisfaction to traditional forms of voice articulation.

State responses to this type of citizen variation will be similar to the aggregate ideal types sketched above. For immobile citizen groups, states are unable to monitor efficiently their dissatisfaction. Even in democratic states, the voice-recovery mechanisms become increasingly ineffective over time (this follows from Hirschman's radical pessimism). In short, states increasingly lack effective responses to those citizens who do not have recourse to exit. For mobile citizen groups, however, the (real) threat of exit amplifies their political influence, ensuring that they are heard in political debates at home.

To conclude, this interpretation of Figure 5.2 suggests that states will respond with varying levels of effectiveness to the dissatisfaction articulated by different citizen groups. This level of response will depend critically on the citizen's ability to exit – which is itself determined by the degree of integration for the asset held by the citizen in question. Most strikingly, citizens who enjoy access to integrated markets have a clear advantage in articulating their dissatisfaction with any deterioration in citizenship quality. (Inversely, citizens without access to integrated markets risk being ignored.) We can expect states to respond most effectively to the concerns of citizens who enjoy both voice and exit options for articulating dissatisfaction, as they must concern themselves with the threatened revenue losses that result from exit.

Owing to space constraints, I will not elaborate on the role of loyalty in this model, though loyalty does have important consequences for evaluating the exit-effect on voice in states that are engaged in varying levels of integration. In short, loyalty can be understood as an important means of raising the costs of exit, thereby securing an important role for voice – even in a context characterized by a cheaper exit option. Loyalty – in the form of nationalism – is, of course, one of the modern state's strong suits. Thus, under conditions with a viable exit alternative, and where loyalty is a strong and real force, we can expect that the citizen's ability to influence policy outcomes will be stronger than under conditions where voice is the only means of responding to a qualitative change in citizenship. In all likelihood, increasing integration will improve the responsiveness of governments to citizen demands that are voiced under the threat of exit.

Thus far the discussion has been very theoretical. I have introduced a modified version of Hirschman's *Exit, Voice and Loyalty* argument to construct two hypothetical scenarios: one that depicts a Europe without integration, the other depicting an integrated Europe. Static comparisons of these two scenarios help us to understand the effect of integration on domestic political influence. The model relies on individual rational actors who exude political as well as economic identities. In doing so, it allows external influences on national outcomes. In particular, the possibility of agent exit allows us a better way of conceiving political influence in the context of international integration.

In the first (segregated) scenario, we find a political context that is not unlike the one depicted by traditional comparative political economy analyses: political influence is secured primarily by domestic voice. The second scenario describes how the channels of influence and their relative importance can change when actors find themselves in integrated markets. By contrasting these two hypothetical scenarios, it is possible to develop explicit expectations of how the level of integration affects political influence at home: increased integration effectively boosts the domestic political influence of actors. More concretely, those agents who wield a real threat of exit into integrated markets have a better chance of influencing the nature of sovereignty at home.

The nature of integration in Europe

The model sketched in the previous section is agnostic with respect to how interests might be aggregated within a given context. This model might be used for mapping the effect of integration on any number of social aggregations (e.g. class, occupation, ethnicity, citizenship, income, sector, etc.). To illustrate the explanatory power of the model, this section will illustrate how a class-based analysis might be employed in this framework. In doing so, I hope to provide an empirical point of departure for evaluating the nature of integration in Europe. With this information in hand, we can begin to speculate about how influence in domestic contexts might be affected by the particular nature of European integration.

While a class-based approach may appear anachronistic to some readers, there are at least two good reasons for using it. First, class-based institutional and political cleavages in Europe are still among the most visible: political parties, interest organizations, media sources, etc. are predominantly organized along class lines (at least more than, for example, sectoral or occupational lines). This makes it a fairly easy task to map the variance in integration across factor lines (e.g. capital market versus labour market integration). The second reason is clearly related to the first: there is an influential literature in contemporary political economy that looks at the effect of (global) economic integration on partisan models of government variation (e.g. Garrett 1995c and 1998; Oatley 1999, etc.). This literature tends to focus on the potential influence of capital in a world characterized by increasing financial integration. Seldom does it explicitly address the other side of the equation: how the absence of international labour mobility decreases the relative political influence of organized labour. For these reasons, the description of European integration that follows will focus on class.

From the very start of the modern European project, economic integration and prosperity have played a central and instrumental role in efforts to create a common European identity: Europe's political elites have always aimed to weave their countries into a fabric of economic interdependence. Since the Treaty of Rome, the explicit motivation of member states has been to integrate European markets across *all* fronts: labour, capital and goods markets.[14] In spite of these legal intentions, there remained significant barriers to market integration in Europe. Consequently, it was not until the mid-1980s that Europe began to think of itself as 'an area without internal frontiers in which the free movement of goods, services, persons and capital is ensured' (Amsterdam Treaty, Article 14). Since the mid-1980s, market integration has proceeded rapidly across several fronts, albeit unequally. Thus, by the turn of the millennium it was increasingly obvious that trade in goods, services and investments had increased dramatically across Europe, while the rate of intra-EU migration had remained largely unchanged.

To illustrate the unequal nature of developments across several areas of economic integration, Table 5.1 reproduces Hansen and Olesen's (2001: 230) integration monitor. From Table 5.1, we can see that the integration of European labour markets is clearly lagging behind the integration of European capital, goods and services markets. I doubt that this depiction is controversial, so I see little need to belabour the point.

Of course, there are a number of fairly obvious reasons for the lack of European labour market integration, and I do not mean to suggest that we can expect labour to float around Europe as effortlessly as capital. Indeed, European social democrats have gone to great lengths to avoid the conditions that characterize US labour markets, where families are often forced to uproot in response to regional economic cycles. My immediate point is not to argue for or against increased labour market integration – it is merely to show how European labour markets are clearly less integrated than European capital, goods and service markets.

It is also important to emphasize that many of the remaining barriers to labour market integration are informal in nature. After all, labour, unlike capital, has commitments after office hours. In addition, cultural and language barriers remain important constraints on mobility. Nevertheless, there remain a significant number of policy-related barriers to mobility (e.g. the lack of integrated European-wide employment, pensions, taxation and educational legislation); and entrenched welfare systems and flexible economic responses by states will provide disincentives to move (as long as they last).

In light of the lessons generated by the model in the previous section, this uneven nature of European market integration bodes significant consequences in national political venues. To the extent that owners of capital are able to exploit the exit option offered by Europe's integrated capital and goods markets, this framework suggests that the relative influence of capital should increase in domestic policy venues across Europe. On the surface, this expectation seems to resonate with the new political realities in Europe, where national politicians find themselves constantly responding to the whims of capitalists, both foreign and domestic, or risk investment flight. In shouting to outbid other member states in attracting mobile investors, governments have been unable to hear the muted and increasingly ineffective voice of European labour.

In this sort of integrated Europe, the influence of labour remains largely limited to the conduit of voice. As labour lacks a real threat of exit, policy-makers in

Table 5.1 Rating the degree of European economic integration

Area	Rating	Comments
Microeconomic convergence		
• Markets for goods and services	+++	Nearly full equalization of prices through intense intra-EU trade
• Markets for factors of production		
– Labour market	0	No mobility across member-state labour markets, and hence no equalization of wages
• Market for real capital	++	Some mobility (ala FDI flows, mergers and acquisitions) which has led to the equalization of real profit rates
Macroeconomic convergence		
• Nominal convergence		
– Price level	++	Price levels continue to vary, for example, labour intensive non-tradables remain cheaper in poor countries
– Inflation rates	+++	Inflation rates have converged because of intense intra-EU trade and stable exchange rates (later, the common currency)
– Nominal interest rates	+++	Massive cross-border financial activities, combined with fixed exchange rates/common currency, have led to a convergence of interest rates
• Real convergence		
– Business cycle synchronization	+	Different economic structures and lack of coordination has led to member-state specific business cycles
– Unemployment	0	No equalization of unemployment because of varying labour market structures and the member-state business cycles referred to above
– Living standards	+	Mixed trends of convergence in standards of living from the ambiguous effects of mobile goods and resource on (national) distribution of economic activity

Source: Hansen and Olesen (2001: 230).

member states can afford to ignore its voice and instead focus on more vocal (and costly) demands. Of course, the very nature of labour suggests that it can never exploit the same threat of exit enjoyed by capital, even in a 'fully' integrated Europe. There are simply too many social and personal costs associated with migration to make its threat of exit viable. Nevertheless, unless capital market integration is rescinded, or labour market integration is deepened, we can expect influence to be unequally distributed between classes, within member states, across Europe.

Thus, to the extent that it is still possible to explain variances in policy outcomes across Europe with reference to the organized strength of labour (or capital), and to the extent that European capital markets are more integrated than those that govern European labour, then the lesson of this chapter are clear: the influence of capital on domestic policy outcomes has been enhanced by the particular character of European integration.

Conclusion

My ambition has been to develop a framework that allows us to generate testable hypotheses about how increased integration affects the nature of sovereign political outcomes in member states. This framework is purposely vague; after all, the effects of integration extend beyond the European Union. Therefore, the model can be easily extended to consider the effects of integration on domestic influence elsewhere. In spite of this level of generality, the framework generates concrete expectations about how domestic policy outcomes should change in the face of integration. These expectations can be easily operationalized and tested empirically in future research.

I have argued that Europe's relatively segmented labour markets handicap labour's ability to influence policy at home. This argument is both controversial and counter-intuitive. While these features provoke, they also generate new research agendas. In this closing section I will comment briefly on both responses.

The main implication of this approach is to suggest that the problem facing European labour is not one of too much integration – but too little. This implication needs to be examined more closely: can the decline in labour's domestic influence in Europe over the past two decades (an assumption that needs to be tested, but that does not appear unreasonable) be explained by the inability of labour to employ the threat of exit as effectively as capital? Alternatively, we might spend more time contemplating the domestic effects of European initiatives. For example, could the creation of Social Europe actually strengthen labour at the *national* level? To the best of my knowledge, these sorts of question are not being addressed in existing research agendas.

This argument also provides us with an impetus for thinking about new ways of comparing polities within Europe. In particular, it is possible to characterize European states in terms of their relative ease of opportunity for emigration. Thus we should expect to find the strongest voice for labour – controlling for various institutional features (e.g. centralization, wage-bargaining institutions, etc.) – in those small states (e.g. Luxembourg, Ireland) where labour enjoys the easiest opportunity for exit (i.e. English-speaking or multilingual states, and/or those with a history of emigration).

Finally, the exit-voice mechanism can help us reconcile conventional wisdom about the increasing strength of capital, on the one hand, and revisionist arguments about the relative absence of large-scale capital relocations in response to significant tax or cost incentives, on the other. From this approach we can expect exit to affect the character of domestic voice and influence. The exercise of voice in a context of integration thus negates the absolute necessity for exit. Rather than being surprised by the fact that investors do not always take flight, we might ask the question, 'what are firms getting by way of voice to compensate for their not exiting?'

At first glance, this argument may appear difficult to bear; a little historical reflection may help lighten the load. It behoves us to recall that some of the greatest political gains by modern labour (e.g. extension of the suffrage, the modern welfare state, shortened work-week, etc.) came at a time when labour was free to migrate internationally and in fact did so! The early twentieth century is full of examples (albeit understudied) of how the threat of exit abroad was used as a powerful lever for securing political gains at home.

The argument is controversial in that it forces us to think in new and different ways about the nature and content of politics in a world where political sovereignty stretches across disparate levels and institutions. Integration radically affects the way that agents can and will influence sovereign outcomes. As political analysts, we need to search for new frameworks that provide us with a better means of capturing the new nature of politics. In this regard, Ulrich Beck's depiction of the changes wrought by globalization is insightful:

> [T]he new power game between national and transnational players is acted out in the familiar rules and colours of the distribution struggle of industrial society. It is as if employees, unions and governments were still playing draughts, while the transnational corporations have moved on to chess. What looks like a draughtsman may thus become a knight in the hand of a corporation, which may then suddenly deliver checkmate to a thunderstruck king.
>
> (Beck 2001: 65)

At this early point, of course, these arguments must remain speculative. Further study can help to establish the empirical legitimacy of this new framework. Until that time, however, it is not far-fetched to depict a right-ward shift in the policies of European member states over the past two decades. Is it unreasonable to explain that shift with reference to the integration of European capital and goods markets, and the increased influence this shift has brought to capital?

Notes

1 I would like to thank Jostein Vik, Thomas Halvorsen, Ole Bjørn Røste, Daniel Jacquerioz, the editors, and the participants of the IPE Forum at NTNU for their useful feedback and comments on an earlier draft. Obviously, any errors that remain are my own responsibility.
2 See Rogowski (1987 and 1989) for a wonderful application of Stolper-Samuelson to the realm of politics.
3 On the distinction between formal and informal forms of integration, see Wallace (1990).
4 To facilitate comparisons with Hirschman's original work, I have chosen to adopt his (pessimistic) perspective in the discussion that follows.

5 Space constraints inhibit me from elaborating on the difficulties associated with both of these assumptions. At a certain point, the analogies to firms and consumers break down, and we must be careful not to push them too far. For example, I realize that it is unreasonable to expect the potential migrant to have the same cold/calculating attitude to social uprooting as he/she does when changing his/her brand of toothpaste. Similarly, firms hire and fire workers, and are not usually required to consider the social consequences (externalities) of their decisions; states do not enjoy this luxury. A number of other conceptual difficulties lay just beneath the surface. For now, however, I will merely note the problem, and add that I employ these assumptions cautiously. After all, I'm simply extending Hirschman's argument to the next natural step. Hirschman assumed that consumers were like organization members, and firms were like organizations; I extend this so that citizens are like organization members, and states are like organizations. In the final analysis, two factors argue for their inclusion: (1) their common employment elsewhere; and (2) the problems associated with them are not crippling enough to inhibit our careful progress. In the end, I believe that the benefits associated with these sorts of assumption (e.g. parsimony and intuitive grasp) outweigh their apparent costs.

6 This theoretical relationship was originally developed in Moses (2004).

7 Like Hirschman, I assume this deterioration to be exogenous and could occur for any number of reasons. For Hirschman's graphical depiction, see Hirschman (1970: 130).

8 Given the likely role of loyalty in this context, the demand curve will probably be broken up and curvilinear. As Hirschman (1970: 90) suggests, there may be one demand schedule for the deterioration in quality (with low demand elasticities at the beginning, and high elasticities as we approach the exit point), and another demand curve for when quality returns.

9 Obviously, this attempt at capturing citizenship quality is a gross simplification. Not only is citizenship quality multidimensional, it is questionable whether we can make inter-personal comparisons about citizenship quality (as we do, e.g. with television sets). Again, the demands of parsimony are my only defence.

10 This model assumes that states calculate revenues equally for all citizens. In practice, of course, states generate more revenues from some citizens than others. In both political and economic terms, the revenue-loss of an exiting unskilled labour might not compare to the anticipated losses of a fleeing CEO. (Neither are these sorts of difference unique to the revenue side of the model: it is possible that states value individual voices differently as well.) As a first approximation, however, we can adopt the assumption of standard revenues.

11 The question of cost is a complicated one. In one way, the cost of exit is smaller than the cost of voice, as the nature of the return to exit is fixed and known. The return on voice, however, depends on the effectiveness of the voice strategy and is therefore more risky. For Hirschman, the costs of exit to the individual consumer are smaller than the costs of voice. See for example, Hirschman (1970: 40). Later, Hirschman (1981: 222) recognizes that he 'took the costlessness of exit too much for granted'. Obviously, when discussing migration as an exit option, we must presume that the perceived costs will be much higher than those facing a consumer deciding between different brands of detergent.

There is a third option that I will leave latent. There is a real possibility that the dissatisfied voter will remain ambivalent and alienated, and might withdraw completely from the political realm. The option of detachment falls between voice and exit. Roger Ko-Chih Tung (1981) replaces loyalty with the notion of *autism*, or self-adjustment, to compensate for this possibility.

12 In *Exit, Voice and Loyalty*, Hirschman assumed that there was an inverse (or see-saw) relationship between exit and voice, especially when the costs of exit were small. See also Hirschman (1992: 91). Later, in his 1993 *World Politics* article, he modifies this position and recognizes cases where exit and voice can work in complementary, or collaborative, ways.

13 Among other things, we might expect the likelihood of exit to increase: (1) given the proliferation of alternative (substitute) states; (2) given the relative ineffectiveness of voice in the home state; (3) the larger the population of the home state; (4) the relative unimportance of citizenship issues to the individual citizen; and (5) the less developed are the cultural and institutional contexts for voicing dissatisfaction in the home state.

14 Although we tend to remember the Treaty of Rome in terms of a customs union, it is important to recall that its Article 48 stipulated the 'abolition of any discrimination based on nationality between workers of member states with respect to employment, remuneration and other conditions of work and employment'; and Article 73b(1) stipulated that: 'all restrictions on the movement of capital between Member States and between Member States and third countries shall be prohibited'.

he purpose of the
uropean Union
Framing European integration

A. Maurits van der Veen

Abstract: Ongoing debates over a constitution for the European Union (EU) underscore the degree to which the future of the European integration project remains up in the air. I argue that differences of opinion in this context are informed by the frames adopted by policy-makers when thinking about the purpose of the EU. The literature in international and comparative political economy increasingly recognizes the importance of ideas held by policy-makers, but has found it difficult to operationalize this insight and to use it to derive testable implications. In this chapter, I propose a model for meeting these challenges. I argue that ideas about the purpose of European integration can be measured by coding legislative debates on the EU, and that these measures, in turn, can be used to explain initiatives and choices by policy-makers that cannot be reduced straightforwardly to material interests. Evidence from recent legislative debates about EU enlargement in Belgium, Ireland, and the Netherlands shows that this approach can improve our understanding of the process of European integration.

Introduction

> Europe is in the first place an idea, and technical translations of this idea come second.
>
> (Flemish representative Van Grembergen, 2002)[1]

There is no shortage of competing policy proposals for the future of European integration. In this chapter, I argue that differences of opinion regarding this future are informed by the frames adopted by policy-makers when thinking about the EU. As I use the concept, frames refer to different ways of thinking about the purpose of a particular policy, institution, or other political initiative. Several potential frames are widely acknowledged to be associated with the European integration project: policy-makers may see the EU as serving to improve the security of their state, to aid its economic growth, to fulfil the historic ideal of European unity, and so on. These frames are not mutually exclusive: the EU can simultaneously improve security and fulfil historic aspirations, for example. However, their mutual compatibility does not imply that they are all equally powerful. Instead, their relative importance is likely to vary systematically, both over time and across countries. That variation is at the core of the model laid out in this chapter.

The concept of a frame formalizes a basic insight shared by most politicians and many observers alike. Charles de Gaulle famously explained his policy choices in terms of his 'certain idea of France'. His statement acknowledges that there is no such thing as an objective national interest for a state; instead, interests are shaped by ideas. In addition, it indicates that there might well be alternative 'ideas of France' which cannot in any objective sense be determined to be more or less accurate. In other words: de Gaulle used a particular frame when thinking about his policy choices; other frames are likely to exist, and they would have resulted in different policies. This claim suggests a way to test systematically a frame-based ideational explanation of EU policy-making against competing explanations not based on ideas.

The model presented here predicts that differences in salience of competing frames across countries will correlate with different patterns of support for specific European integration projects, in ways that cannot be explained by competing models such as those based purely on material interests. For instance, if a security frame is more prevalent among decision-makers in the Netherlands than among their counterparts in Denmark, we would expect greater enthusiasm for joint European defence initiatives in the former, even if their 'objective' geopolitical or material interests are otherwise identical.

This chapter presents a preliminary application of this model. I analyse legislative debates on the enlargement of the EU, focusing on the Treaty of Nice, and show that these debates provide important insights that could not be derived simply by tracing the influence of different material interests. The chapter is divided into four sections. First, I lay out the theoretical justification for focusing on frames. Second, I review the challenges involved in measuring the strength and salience of different frames in particular contexts. The third section presents the basic frames regarding European integration present in the discourse of the member states. Finally, the fourth section discusses the empirical application of the model to the process of EU enlargement.

Framing policy purpose and interests

In so far as it highlights the importance of ideas, the theoretical approach in this chapter is constructivist. Specifically, to borrow the words of a prominent critic of constructivist approaches to European integration, I argue that 'governmental elites choose specific policies...because they (or their justifications) are consistent with more general, deeper, collectively held ideas or discourses' (Moravcsik 1999b: 670). Another way to phrase the same claim (although Moravcsik might well disagree) is: In choosing policies, elites consider *interests specified by* general, deeper, collectively held ideas, or frames. The difference between the two statements highlights a fundamental shortcoming of much of the rationalist literature on European integration (and on policy-making in general). The point is not, *pace* Moravcsik, that constructivists argue about 'ideas or discourses irreducible to material interests' (1999b: 671), but rather that many critics of constructivism assume the existence of an ordering of material interests irreducible to ideas.

Moravcsik's own approach of liberal intergovernmentalism provides a good illustration of the central issue. Liberal intergovernmentalism, as laid out in *The Choice for Europe* (1998), grants that multiple, possibly competing, material interests may be relevant in the area of European policy-making, highlighting in particular geopolitical and commercial frames. Moreover, Moravcsik claims that, empirically, the commercial frame trumps the geopolitical frame any time it is relevant. He makes the point most exhaustively in his discussion of de Gaulle's policies with respect to European integration (Moravcsik 2000). However, as Trachtenberg (2000) and others have pointed out, the empirical evidence suggests that both the geopolitical and commercial frames were prominent in de Gaulle's thinking, and, hence, also in his decision-making. All the more reason, then, to consider the potential impact of other frames not even considered in Moravcsik's account!

Another criticism to be levelled at liberal intergovernmentalism and related models is the assumption that economic interests can somehow objectively be ranked. This assumption draws upon older, realist claims that there is such a thing as an objective national interest, claims that most observers and practitioners have long since rejected (Hoffmann 1978: 133; Waltz 1986: 331). As Dutch Foreign Minister De Hoop Scheffer noted in a debate on the enlargement of the EU, 'The Dutch interest as such does not exist until determined politically.'[2] Most liberal accounts would interpret this statement as implying that the national interest simply represents the material interests of the principals whose agents are in power. However, even a quick perusal of the literature on European integration shows that principals as well as agents are rarely clear about their own putative material interests. Indeed, in a recent book titled *A Certain Idea of Europe*, Parsons (2003) shows that competing ideas about what the EU should look like institutionally could not be ranked in any straightforward, material sense (see also McNamara 1999). More generally, I argue that decision-makers' interests with respect to EU initiatives are shaped by their views of the overall purpose of European integration.

Debates over EU enlargement illustrate the importance of this claim. If the purpose of the EU is to maintain security on the European continent, it is in the Union's interest to accept as new member states those that, left outside the arrangement, could threaten the continent's stability. If, in contrast, the purpose of the EU is to promote the ability of current members to control economic processes that cross national borders, it is in their interest to accept as new member states those which are economically most integrated with us. Those who take the second stance may see security as something to be tackled by NATO, not the EU. Neither of these interests is more 'irreducible' than the other, nor can they be ranked in any objective sense. It follows that the interest(s) considered in a particular decision will be determined by the frame(s) salient in the minds of the decision-makers. As the quotation opening the chapter already indicated, 'Europe is in the first place an idea, and technical translations [i.e. institutional implementations] of this idea come second'.[3]

Frames and discourse in theory

With this general argument in mind, we can now examine the underlying theoretical framework that supports it. Frames are information objects that serve to organize a number of different pieces of information in a coherent fashion (cf. Goffman 1974; Rein and Schön 1993; Surel 2000). In this way they help actors organize information and understand the world around them (Kingdon 1995). Most importantly for our purposes here, frames often specify goals, and thereby determine (or activate) interests. A wealth of empirical evidence suggests that cognitive and normative frames play an important role in human decision-making processes (Nisbett and Ross 1980; Simon 1957, 1982).[4]

Frames have been used most successfully by political scientists studying social movements, both at the domestic and international levels (e.g. Finnemore and Sikkink 1998; McAdam *et al.* 1996; Tarrow 1994). In addition, a number of other scholars have expressed closely related ideas using different terminology. For example, Hall defines a 'policy paradigm' as a 'framework of ideas and standards that specifies not only the goals of policy and the kinds of instruments that can be used to attain them, but also the very nature of the problems they are meant to be addressing' (1993: 279). This emphasis on ideas as specifying goals is echoed in McNamara's work on European monetary cooperation: ideas help policy-makers 'formulate answers to questions of values and strategies: what should the goals of monetary policy be, and what instruments can be used in pursuit of those goals?' (1999: 457). Other related concepts are analogies (Khong 1992), the *référentiel* (Jobert 1992; Muller 1995), and discursive nodal points (Diez 2001).[5]

Another closely related concept is that of a discourse. The most important difference is the emphasis in the study of discourses on public statements by political actors that 'frame the national political discussion' and give an account of the purposes, goals and ideas that inform and justify policy choice (Schmidt 2000a: 279; see also March and Olsen 1995: 46, 62). The emphasis on public statements is valuable, because it makes discourse measurable in ways that frames, as internal mental constructs, may not be. Thus the literature on the nature of discourses helps extend our understanding of the contents and impact of frames.

In a theoretical model proposed by Schmidt, discourse has four important functions:

> ideationally, by presenting a policy programme that is conceptually sound (cognitive function) and that resonates with national values (normative function); and interactively, by serving policy elites as the basis for constructing a policy programme (co-ordinative function) and for persuading the larger public as to its merits (communicative function).
>
> (2000a: 279)

Schmidt is careful to separate her definition of discourse both from the values to which it appeals and from the 'policy programme' it promotes. As a result, her concept maps nicely onto frames as presented above, connecting the core values of the participants to the causal beliefs they may hold about particular policy options. Although Schmidt distinguishes between the cognitive and normative functions of discourse, it is impossible to separate them empirically. Nonetheless, we should keep in mind that frames play both roles, providing convincing arguments in favour of a particular policy programme, as well as legitimating that same programme by appealing to 'long-standing values and... deep-seated structures of national identity' (Schmidt 2000a: 280).

Some of the literature on discourse tends to assume the existence of a single dominant discourse, whose position is similar to that of a paradigm in Kuhn's (1996) theories.[6] For example, Schmidt suggests that the standard context is one of Kuhnian 'normal science', where a new discourse displaces the old one only by demonstrating greater relevance, applicability, or coherence, as well as the ability to solve problems that the previous paradigm could not. 'The change in discourse, then, reflects something of a revolution in world-view for a polity, since it demands a shift not only in the policy paradigm but also in the underlying values of the polity as a whole' (2000a: 281).[7]

This implies that discourses change only when seriously challenged, and Schmidt accordingly emphasizes, as many others have, the importance of crises to changes in the policy discourse (2000a: 283; see also Hall 1989; Hirschman 1989; Kingdon 1995; McNamara 1998).[8] However, wholesale transformations of a discourse are rather rare (Surel 2000),[9] nor are most discourses monolithic. In fact, it is not uncommon for different aspects of a societal discourse to come into conflict with one another (e.g. McNamara 1998: 67). In other words, the overall discourse need be neither fully consistent nor internally coherent.

If multiple frames (or discourses) compete, the challenge for analysis shifts from identifying the relevant frame to assessing the relative strength of alternative frames. Emphasizing frames, rather than a single discourse, underscores the fact that a single policy area can be framed in many different ways, using competing frames present in the general societal discourse. It also reminds us that there will rarely be a single frame within which particular pieces of information can be incorporated. Instead, different frames are continually put forward by different actors, resulting in a competition for prominence both within society and within the minds of decision-makers (Finnemore and Sikkink 1998: 897; Risse-Kappen 1994: 187).[10] This struggle for prominence does not much resemble the Kuhnian image of a battle among paradigms.[11] Instead, the central insight is that different frames generate 'different interpretations of the way things are, and support different courses of action concerning what is to be done, by whom and how to do it' (Rein and Schön 1993: 147). Hence, the way an issue is framed in the minds of the decision-makers can tell us a lot about the shape a policy will take in practice.

Many authors agree that a crucial factor determining the success of a frame is the degree to which a frame meshes with other frames that are already widely accepted and, more importantly, the degree to which it is compatible with an underlying set of core values such as widely shared conceptions of national identity

(Finnemore and Sikkink 1998; Gurowitz 1999; Jobert 2001; Keck and Sikkink 1998: 204; Klotz 1995; Nadelmann 1990; Price 1998). As Schmidt argues, '[c]ulturally and historically specific conceptions ... set the limits to the transferability of new ideas' (Schmidt 2000a: 287; see also Diez 2001; Habermas 1989; Hall 1989; Katzenstein 1996b).[12] Several different competing frames may resonate with different aspects of a state's national experience and identity, however. This suggests that non-ideational factors may be equally, or even more, important in determining the choices of frames by decision-makers (and the appeal of those frames to their audiences). For example, the cost of particular policy choices suggested by different frames is likely to matter, as is the structural position of their proponents within the government (cf. Checkel 2001b).

Learning more about the sources and selection process of frames is an important task, but one beyond the scope of the present chapter, which focuses on their impact once selected. Although frames do not determine policy choice by themselves, the strength of different frames makes particular policy choices more and less likely. Constraints such as the capabilities of the policy-makers as well as their material interests and those of their principals serve to eliminate certain options and may increase the appeal of others. Thus it makes sense to think of capabilities and material considerations as constraints on the policy choices suggested by frames, rather than the other way around. After all, without a relevant frame there is no interest to pursue.

To put it differently, realist and liberal explanatory factors introduce important constraints – and thus also inputs – into the policy-making process, but the relevance (and thus influence) of these constraints will vary greatly along with the salience of different frames. The model thus explains why realist and/or liberal variables can often tell us a lot about policy outcomes. It also shows that to ignore the role of ideas would imply not just excluding a number of potentially important additional variables, but also misunderstanding the process by which these realist and liberal variables affect policy outcomes. Security, power, and wealth matter, but only because policy-makers believe they do. Just how, and how much, they affect policy depends on their salience among the frames of the decision-makers, as well as on the degree to which they are favoured by the various constraints facing those decision-makers.

The independent impact of frames

Challenges to models that emphasize the power of ideas (and thus frames) come in two broad forms. First, there are those who argue that ideas are epiphenomenal – the true causal factors must lie elsewhere. This claim admits of but two alternatives: either social actors are hardwired to have certain interests (and in a certain ordering!), or the constraints they face are such that any differences in their interests cannot find expression. Although there may be a kernel of truth underlying each of these arguments, empirically neither comes even close to explaining the variation in behaviour and policy choice we observe in practice.[13]

This leaves the second, weaker challenge: ideas (preferences) are not epiphenomenal, but the ideas expressed by policy-makers in discussing or explaining their actions are as likely to be rationalizations or convenient 'hooks' (Shepsle 1985) as the actual ideas that inform the actions in question. Moreover, they are likely to under-emphasize the importance of constraints. It is true that one cannot simply reason back from compliance with certain norms to the acceptance or internalization of those same norms (see Payne 2001). Behaviour might well be the result of compellence or coercion, or it might simply be informed by the material self-interest of the actor.[14] Along the same lines, it is problematic to reason straightforwardly from the strength of specific frames to policy outcomes. Decision-makers may appeal to particular normative frames merely to hide their pursuit of their own material self-interest, or situations of compellence.

However, this discussion overlooks the interactive relationship between frames (or ideas more generally) and actors. On the one hand, frames specify the interests of actors and help shape their identities. On the other hand, actors also use frames strategically, to pursue their interests and to shape the interpretations of their actions.[15] From the point of view of identifying the frames that determine the interests of actors, the issue thus becomes one of measurement. Sceptics argue that since reliable measurement of the ideas that *really* matter is impossible, we are better off assuming the strength of particular ideas rather than trying to measure them. However, it is difficult to defend the rejection a priori of attempts at measurement.

One reason to reject measurements of ideas might be that these measurements may point us systematically in the wrong direction. In other words, the common tendency to rationalize or make decisions more palatable to the public would produce measurements that are not just imprecise (noisy), but just plain wrong. This is an empirical question, and one that is difficult to resolve since we are unable to measure the decision-maker's actual ideas informing a particular action. In the end, we can only decide it by comparing the explanatory power of imperfectly measured ideas against assumed ideas. For this reason, it is important always to consider potential alternatives, in particular those appealing to imputed geopolitical or economic self-interest.

A second reason to reject the measurement of ideas might be a desire to maximize causal distance. On this view, a greater distance between causal factor and policy outcome is to be preferred. The appeal of such a stance depends on the question under consideration. Waltz, for example, admits that his neorealist model can explain only 'a small number of big and important things' (1986: 329). Pushing it even further, we can explain an even smaller number of very general patterns by looking to sociobiology. However, neither approach is particularly helpful if we want to explain the political economy of European integration (see Waltz 1986: 331). At the other extreme, causal distance is minimized, and explanatory richness and detail maximized, by observers engaged in 'thick description', but here our ability to generalize across cases is severely limited. In sum, the appropriate causal distance is to some degree determined by the type of question we wish to ask.

In the end, establishing the causal power of ideas in the making of foreign policy depends on our ability to obtain reliable information about those ideas; information, moreover, of greater quality than we would be able to assume or impute, given information about the structural context facing policy-makers. Whether it is possible to obtain such information is, in the end, an empirical question. Fortunately, in many policy contexts empirical evidence suggests we *can* measure ideas reliably enough to provide us with valuable added explanatory leverage. The next section discusses how best to measure the frames that are of interest to students of European integration.

Operationalizing the salience of ideas

Frames are mental constructs, and as such we cannot directly measure them. The question thus becomes: how can we come closest to measuring these mental constructs, given that our only source is statements by policy-makers, that is, discourse? Numerous game theoretic models argue that it is exceedingly difficult to move beyond 'cheap talk' in discourse, since it is nearly impossible for an audience to distinguish reliably between distorted and instrumental argumentation and sincere expressions of opinion (Austen-Smith 1992; Johnson 1993). This implies that we should be sceptical about the possibility of attaining the Habermasian ideal of a deliberative democracy (see Elster 1998), and that we must be careful of placing too much stock in discourse.

However, even if persuasion may be rare (but see Kratochwil 1989; Risse 2000), discourse inevitably plays an important role in the dynamics of the struggle among different frames. Frames may be refined or reinforced, and the repeated appeal to a particular frame may serve to introduce it as a possibly relevant frame into the minds of other decision-makers. Finally, public discourse can serve to 'entrap' decision-makers by forcing them to implement policies consistent with their own rhetoric at least on the surface, unless they wish to bear the political cost of apparently hypocritical behaviour (Schimmelfennig 2001). In other words, non-negligible audience costs may be associated with behaviour that departs from the associated discourse. As a result, even if one were to accept the conclusions of the 'cheap talk' literature, there is no need to reject the notion that discourse can tell us a lot about the ideas informing policy choice. Although we cannot hope to measure the relative strength of different frames in the minds of policy-makers, we *can* obtain a fairly reliable proxy by looking at elite discourse.[16]

The next issue to address is whether we can measure ideas in ways that allow us to quantify their relative strength across cases. Although the constructivist literature has focused more on single case studies, broad cross-national and over-time measurements along these lines do have a strong pedigree in sociological institutionalism (e.g. Ramirez *et al.* 1997; Thomas *et al.* 1987; see also Finnemore 1996b). The more quantitative approach is particularly valuable in assessing the relative validity of competing causal explanations. A particular problem with qualitative analysis is the lack of a systematic procedure for obtaining the appropriate evidence. This problem is particularly acute in some constructivist work, because of its reliance on the statements (oral or written) of actors as measures of their ideas and beliefs. One can almost always find a quotation from a policy-maker to support a particular argument. On the other hand, it is more difficult to establish that such a quotation is representative, and accurately reflects the relevant ideas and beliefs of that policy-maker and her peers. It is not, however, impossible.

For our purposes, we are interested in measuring the ideas of national political elites in the European integration process, since these are the people who will make the official decisions regarding support for different EU initiatives.[17] Unfortunately, it is not easy to determine just who forms part of this elite, nor to get a representative sample of their ideas (cf. Finnemore and Sikkink 1998; Haas 1992; Muller 1995). In general, policy emerges as the outcome of an interactive process involving the government, the opposition, and the bureaucracy. It is crucial, therefore, not to restrict ourselves to the discourse of the executive branch of government, which would provide an incomplete view of the distribution of frames among the full policy-making elite (Milliken 1999). Moreover, public statements by the executive are often targeted at particular groups (including international audiences) and thus, lacking the coordinative function of discourse, may misrepresent the relative importance of different frames in the policy-making process.

Bureaucrats (and 'Eurocrats') are likely to hold a wider range of views than will be present among the governing parties, since many will be career civil servants rather than political appointees. Unfortunately, it is difficult to get a representative sample of the discourse of these groups. I argue that the best alternative is to sample the relative distribution of frames across a representative sample of the policy-making elite. Almost by definition, a directly elected legislature provides such a sample. In other words, the legislative discourse offers itself as perhaps the best single source for measuring the relative strength of different frames across the entire policy-making elite. It provides a cross-section of ideas likely to be an acceptable, albeit imperfect, proxy for those found among the non-legislative members of the elite too.[18]

Taking the legislative discourse as raw material has additional advantages. Since elites are better informed than the general public, the quality of the discourse will often be higher than that of the communicative discourse aimed at the latter. In other words, we are less likely to find unsubstantiable or inconsistent claims about the relative importance of various goals. In addition, since the legislative record is usually public, politicians are mindful of the need to put forward arguments that resonate with the core ideas of the public. In other words, their communication will be both representational and instrumental (De Sola Pool 1959). However, the context of legislative debates – the coordinating function of the discourse, the danger of rhetorical entrapment, the presence of a budget constraint, and a well-informed and representative elite audience – implies that the distortions implied by the instrumental use of communications will be relatively limited (cf. Larson 1988: 248).

It is important to note that the theoretical model presented here in no sense requires that legislative debates be used as the raw material for measuring the relative salience of different frames. At least two other promising alternatives suggest themselves almost at once. First, we can use the Eurobarometer surveys to get a sense of how Europeans think about the purpose of the EU. Respondents can be filtered according to degree of informedness or job category to get a sub-section that closely resembles the elite. The main problem with this approach is that Eurobarometer questions rarely ask for the objectives or motivations that inform responses about support for particular EU initiatives. The second alternative is to use personal or published interviews with important decision-makers. Two obvious issues here are the representativeness of the policy-maker(s) in question, and the truthfulness of their replies. Clearly, each kind of source has its short-comings. In the present chapter, I focus on legislative debates; however, other analyses may benefit more by using a different source.

Finally, it is worth emphasizing that my approach is more one of content analysis than of discourse analysis. These two approaches represent closely related tech-niques based on the general assumption that our beliefs are both (1) reflected in our statements and (2) of causal importance to our actions. However, discourse analysis is more postmodern in nature (see Price and Reus-Smit 1998; also George 1994), often associated with a rejection of conventional methodological and research design criteria. More importantly for the present discussion, discourse analysis tends to focus on different features of a discourse than does content analysis. Inspired by the work of Derrida (1981), Foucault (1980), and Saussure (1974), it focuses most often on the conscious or unconscious use of particular *words* (e.g. through predicate or metaphorical analysis), and on the way that these not only affect action, but also construct perceptions of reality (Milliken 1999; see e.g. Escobar 1995; Weldes 1999). In contrast, content analysis is more inter-ested in particular policy-related *concepts* and goals expressed in a discourse, such as roles (Breuning 1995; Holsti 1970) or specific beliefs about other actors in international relations (Larson 1988). In what follows, I pay little attention to legislators' particular choice of words or phrases in referring to issues of European integration. Instead, I focus on explicit arguments about the objectives of European integration, as described in the next section.

Framing European integration

The discussion until now has been very general. At this point, we need to specify just what frames we expect to be relevant in the context of European integration, and what types of predictions we can derive, given those frames. As a start, I am interested in broad conceptions of the purpose of European integration. Why is European integration a good thing? In the words of one Dutch representative: '[Everyone,] the Netherlands, too, has to arrive at an image of what Europe is sup-posed to be'.[19] Although it is possible that we can gain further by investigating more specific frames associated with particular policy questions, I argue that answers to this broad question already supply us with information of considerable value.

For the purpose of the present chapter, I divide the relevant frames into seven broad categories: security, geopolitics, control, commercial, history, norms, and solidarity. A security frame sees a crucial function of European integration as the promotion of peace and stability on the European continent. It is commonly agreed that this was an important frame in the minds of decision-makers during the early years of the European integration project. Its continued relevance today, however, is often called into question, as the Dutch Minister of Foreign Affairs acknowledged in 2002: 'This is something that becomes ever more distant for representatives of my generation: Never again war'.[20] A geopolitical frame casts the EU as a way to increase an individual country's control over and influence in international outcomes beyond the scope of the Union. This frame is often dominant among those who see the EU as an important international counterweight to the United States in international diplomacy: 'An enlarged Europe is critical in world terms to provide some type of counterbalance to the only remaining world power, the U.S'.[21]

The control frame has similar implications for the intra-European sphere. Here the idea is that European integration allows a country to have greater influence over outcomes that directly affect its ability to shape its own destiny. Arguments about the EU as a forum for macro-economic coordination and a locus of pooled sovereignty flow from this frame. In the words of one Irish Minister of State, 'pooled sovereignty gives us greater influence and control over our destiny'.[22] The commercial frame, on the other hand, privileges an economic cost–benefit accounting of EU membership. To quote a Dutch representative: 'Europe is nothing more than an economic instrument'.[23] Calculations of the net contributions of each member state to the EU budget are quite salient in the European integration literature, and we would not be surprised to find this frame playing a dominant role. This frame also suggests a focus on the economic aspects of European integration more broadly: 'The Nice Treaty is about protecting and securing our economic success'.[24]

This brings us to three frames that emphasize non-material objectives. These are given short shrift in much of the integration literature.[25] Nevertheless, as Schimmelfennig (2001) points out, they have at times featured saliently in the overall European discourse. The history frame points to the integration project as the fulfilment of a centuries-old ideal, dating back, perhaps, to Roman times. More currently, admitting the Central and Eastern European states is often framed in terms of the reunification of Europe: 'Their separation from the rest of Europe was one of the greatest acts of vandalism in history and it is time to remedy that'.[26] The norms frame sees the EU as a project to ensure the spread of norms of fundamental importance (such as democracy and the rule of law) throughout the European continent. The solidarity frame, finally, views European integration as a way to ensure that others in Europe enjoy the same standard of living as the inhabitants of the more fortunate member states: 'It is not right to deny the opportunity for a better life to so many of our fellow Europeans'.[27]

It should be obvious that the different frames generate different expectations about policy choices in different EU contexts. If the EU is seen primarily as an economic instrument, one might expect a distinct coolness towards proposals for cooperation in the defence and security policy issue areas. If control is the main

Table 6.1 Basic predictions for attitudes towards enlargement

Frame	Prediction
Security	Enlarge only if security and stability threatened; if so, admit only those countries whose threat can be contained by membership[a]
Geopolitics	Admit those countries whose membership will add perceptibly to the international weight of the EU
Control	Admit those countries with whom there is non-negligible economic interdependence, as well as those likely to side with you in intra-EU bargaining under qualified majority
Commercial	Admit those who would be net contributors; possibly admit those who would support your position on intra-EU issues with important economic implications; maximize transition period before economic benefits apply to new members
History	Admit all Europeans, but prefer those with whom shared culture or history is strongest
Norms	Admit those who practice the norms and values of the EU, and prefer those who are in greatest danger of regressing away from those norms in the absence of membership; may accept long transition periods that give candidates time to implement and meet norms gradually
Solidarity	Admit all those who wish membership; minimize transition period before economic benefits apply to new members

Note
a Of course, the assessment of which threats can be contained by membership is subjective and hence open to political discussion.

motivation, on the other hand, further integration not directly driven by the need to retain (or regain) a state's influence over what happens within its borders is similarly likely to be resisted. In the next section, we will look at a country's attitudes towards the question of EU enlargement, one of the most salient policy questions on the EU's agenda today. General predictions for a country's stance on the question of enlargement can be derived quite easily, and are shown in Table 6.1.

A preliminary illustration: frames and European enlargment

To provide a preliminary illustration of the application of the model, I coded legislative debates on the EU around the time of the ratification of the Treaty of Nice in three countries: Belgium, Ireland, and the Netherlands. These three were chosen because (1) they share a certain geographic distance from the new candidate member states, (2) they are near the top of the EU in terms of GDP per capita, and (3) public opinion polls show that when their citizens think about enlargement, they have the same countries in mind (primarily Poland, the Czech Republic, and Hungary). This allows us to control for a number of the potential alternative explanations of differences among them in terms of their attitude towards enlargement.

For the present chapter, I coded debates from the period 2000–2002. A larger number of debates were coded in the case of Belgium since Belgian legislative

Table 6.2 Debates on the EU coded, 2000–2002

Country	Debates[a]
Belgium	General budget debate (Foreign Affairs), 19 December 2000
	Treaty of Nice, 12 March 2002 (Committee)
	Treaty of Nice, 27 March 2002
(Vlaanderen)	Flemish Parliament: European Affairs discussion, 6 November 2001 (Committee)
	Flemish parliament: Treaty of Nice, 14 June 2002 (Committee)
	Flemish parliament: Treaty of Nice, 19 June 2002
Ireland	European Union Bill (2001), 26–27 June 2001
	26th Amendment of the Constitution Bill, 2002 (Treaty of Nice), 4, 10, 11 September 2002
Netherlands	State of the European Union, 10 October 2000
	State of the European Union, 17 October 2001
	Approval of the Nice Treaty, 12 November 2001 (Committee)
	Enlargement of the EU, 23 October 2002

Note
a Unless otherwise noted, these are plenary debates in the lower chamber of parliament.

debates tend to be less substantial than those in other countries. In Ireland, the debate preceding the second referendum on the Treaty of Nice was impressive in extensiveness as well as depth. In the Netherlands, thorough annual debates on the state of the EU provide good year-to-year information on the salience of different frames. The full list of debates coded is provided in Table 6.2.

The coding unit was the speaking turn, that is, a speech by a single speaker that was unbroken except for brief, non-substantive interruptions.[28] For each speaking turn, I tallied all references to the objectives associated with (participation in) the European integration project. Moreover, I tallied multiple appeals to the same argument with at least two intervening paragraphs of unrelated discussion. This allowed for a proper relative weighting in cases where different motivations were clearly not of the same importance to a speaker.

Combining expressed arguments for the EU across different speakers raises some difficult issues, as there are several different ways to aggregate the data. The simplest is just to add the total tallies for each argument and for each speaker across all speakers. If one can draw from a larger body of debates (and of statements about the goals of European integration), it may become worthwhile to weigh different speaking turns, for example by their length or by the size of the representation of the speaker's party in the parliament. However, for the purpose of making fairly broad generalizations, and given the relatively limited body of data at our disposal, a simple tally seemed best.

The results of the coding process are presented in Table 6.3. The first data column gives the total number of statements concerning the objective(s) of European integration.[29] The remaining columns give the relative strength of each of the seven frames, as a fraction of the total count. Whereas a large sample of statements for

Table 6.3 Coding results for debates on the EU, 2000–2002

Country	Count	Security	Geopolitics	Control	Commercial	History	Norms	Solidarity
Belgium	37	**0.35**[a]	0.03	0.03	0.11	0.11	**0.24**	0.08
Ireland	216	0.10	0.09	**0.22**	**0.34**	0.04	0.1	0.07
Netherlands	196	**0.25**	0.11	**0.15**	0.10	**0.14**	**0.15**	0.06

Note
a Figures in columns 3–9 are percentages for each frame of the total count. Those highlighted are the most salient.

Ireland and the Netherlands gives us a certain amount of confidence in the relative strength of each frame as suggested in the table, the data for Belgium is sufficiently thin that our predictions cannot be as certain. For each country, the two most salient frames are highlighted. (In the case of the Netherlands, three frames are almost equal in strength in second place, so all three are highlighted.)

The data suggest that the focus of much of the literature on economic calculations alone does the actual decision-making process little justice. It is obvious that a wide range of frames regarding European integration are sufficiently strong to be taken into consideration. Furthermore, the data show that the relative salience of different frames varies quite dramatically across EU member states, even when their imputed economic and geopolitical interests in the EU and its enlargement can be argued to be quite similar, as is the case for our three countries here.

Combining the data in Table 6.3 with the general predictions in Table 6.1 generates several expectations regarding the attitudes of these countries towards enlargement. Overall, we would expect all three states to be, on balance, opposed to the Eastern enlargement. They are likely to be, in Schimmelfennig's (2001) terms, 'brakemen'. For Belgium, where security and norms are the two most salient frames, we would expect to see the implications for the latter dominate, since few of the candidate enlargement states present any noticeable threat to Belgium's security. Hence Belgium is likely to favour enlargement only when applicant states meet the norms associated with membership. This means that Belgium should prefer a limited enlargement rather than the so-called 'big bang' of ten new members at once, as well as long transition periods to make sure that applicants do not become full members until they satisfy the requirements.

The predictions for the Netherlands are similar. However, here the importance of the control frame is likely to make the Netherlands even more reluctant to accept new members, and even more insistent upon a limited enlargement, including only those with which there are non-negligible economic ties. A sense of shared history with some of the central European countries (especially Poland) may make it easier for those countries to satisfy the Dutch. In Ireland, finally, the salience of the commercial frame would, on balance, lead us to expect resistance to any Eastern enlargement at all, since none can be expected to be net contributors to the EU budget. In addition, Ireland would be expected to favour a long transition period *not tied* to meeting specific norms, but simply to minimize the flow of EU funds to the new countries. Finally, in terms of economic organization and size, most of the applicant states are similar, and not too different from Ireland (e.g. in terms of the importance of the agricultural sector), so it is unlikely that Ireland will insist on any particular order of accession.

In fact, these expectations are largely accurate. Throughout the accession process, the Netherlands continued to insist strongly, and virtually until the end, on a case-by-case decision about accession rather than a 'big bang' process. In addition, the Dutch government repeatedly called for re-evaluation of an applicant state's process during a transition period, with the possibility of extending the transition period further if insufficient progress had been made. Belgium's attitude was similar, but the Belgians were relatively less concerned with limiting enlargement. A significant concern that accepting only some of the applicants while leaving out others might threaten European stability (and thus security) made the Belgians relatively more willing to accept the simultaneous accession of all candidates that met a minimal set of norms.

In Ireland, as is well known, the population rejected the Treaty of Nice in a first referendum. However, their reasons for doing so differed in emphasis from those that most exercised their representatives. Polls showed a public concerned more with Ireland's ability to control its own destiny – in geopolitical and control terms (neutrality, for instance) as well as in normative terms (abortion) – than with the commercial frame. Moreover, polls also suggested a public frustrated by the elitism and heavy-handedness of Bertie Ahern's government. Interestingly, however, two EU-wide Eurobarometer polls that addressed enlargement – EB 55.0 of early 2001 and EB 56.3 of early 2002 – reveal two striking features of Irish public opinion compared to that in other EU member states. First, the Irish were far less decided about the particular pros and cons of enlargement than are their fellow Europeans. Second, they were overwhelmingly more likely to expect enlargement to create new jobs for their country than were their counterparts elsewhere in Europe.[30] The former suggests that they were probably more likely to let dissatisfaction with the government affect their referendum vote. The second indicates that highlighting the commercial frame made good strategic sense for the government. Not surprisingly, then, debates over the second referendum continued to be characterized by the salience of the commercial frame. Moreover, numerous opposition representatives repeatedly asked that voters consider the Nice Treaty on its own merits and *not* use the referendum as a vote on the qualities of Ahern's government.

The two Eurobarometer surveys also show that the Dutch were disproportionately in favour of admitting only a limited number of applicant states. Compared to an average across the EU of about 57 per cent in favour of limited enlargement, about 70 per cent of the Dutch had this preference, in both surveys.[31] Interestingly, the Belgians were disproportionately opposed to any enlargement at all, whereas the Dutch tended to favour at least some enlargement more strongly than the EU average, and the Irish came to the same conclusion between 2001 and 2002, almost certainly because of the increasing salience of economic calculations mentioned earlier. Furthermore, as one would predict given the relative unimportance of the commercial frame in the Netherlands, the Dutch were much less concerned with either the level of economic development or the costs likely to be imposed on the EU budget by the prospective member states. Compared to their counterparts in Belgium and Ireland (or, indeed, the rest of the EU), they were about 50 per cent more likely to disagree with the claim that the former was very important, and more than twice as likely to disagree with an emphasis on the importance of the latter.[32]

What about alternative explanations for the observed variation in these three countries? Most of the literature on Eastern enlargement characterizes different states broadly as in favour of or opposed to the process (e.g. Schimmelfennig 2001). Using the load on the EU budget as the sole consideration, all three states considered here would be expected to be opposed to enlargement. However, it is difficult to explain the preference for selective and graduated membership on the part of the Netherlands based on this factor alone. Similarly, the Irish example shows that economic calculations may well be indeterminate – enlargement brings economic opportunities as well as risks, and it is difficult to say *ex ante* which will outweigh the other.

The question of alternative explanations can also be phrased a different way: Is the salience of the different frames in each country determined by some other factor that can be measured without relying on the potentially strategic use of arguments (cheap talk) by legislators? I have already suggested that economic interests alone cannot explain the observed variation. Nor, I would argue, can a combination of security and economic interests. Moreover, any argument along those lines would have to account also for the relative importance of security considerations in the three countries, in a non-*ad hoc* manner. If anything, one might expect Ireland to be more concerned with security issues because it is not a member of NATO. In sum, therefore, the evidence suggests that information about the salience of different frames can provide an important contribution to our understanding of the choices of EU member states.

Conclusions

The objectives associated with European integration are manifold. Integration may promote geopolitical or material interests such as security, power, control over domestic outcomes and prosperity. It may also pursue the fulfilment of a historical ideal, the promotion of an improved standard of living, and the strength of democracy, the rule of law, and other norms throughout Europe. I have argued here that there is no objective way to order these interests. Some would claim that they cannot even be considered interests in the absence of a belief in the value of the specific goal, but that is not essential to my model. Even if we take these interests as exogenously existent, we need to have a theory about the determinants of their relative importance, if we are to understand national policy choices in the context of European integration.

Critics of ideational approaches to European integration miss the point, therefore, when they insist that arguments (or ideas) reflect 'underlying' interests. The empirical evidence presented here suggests that any fixed, assumed ordering will fall short in explaining the observed variation in national decisions. It is up to such critics, therefore, to provide an alternative model explaining the ordering of those interests in a non-*ad hoc* manner. Similarly, one cannot claim that the material used to measure the strength of frames – legislative debates, in this chapter – simply reflects interests of importance to the speaker for other (non-ideational) reasons without providing some alternative measure explaining those interests that is logically prior to the frames in question. Too often, rationalist explanations fall back on revealed preferences, but this, of course, makes the argument circular.

Another way to cast the same criticism is to argue that the causal distance between measure and outcome is too small. In other words, one might argue that the index of the relative salience of frames presented in this chapter is simply a different measure of the dependent variable of interest: national policy. This criticism falls flat for two reasons, however. First, as I argued earlier, the appropriate causal distance depends upon the questions one is interested in. It is clear that increasing causal distance – assuming a fixed ordering of interests, for example – comes at the expense of a loss in explanatory power. If we wish to explain variation in national policy choices, therefore, we have little alternative but to reduce the causal distance and set out to measure the ordering of frames, and thus of the interests they specify.

The second reason the argument about causal distance falls flat is that legislative debates feature the opinions of a representative cross-section of the elite. Policy choices are made by governments, however, and almost by definition governments do not represent the entire national elite. The argument about causal distance would be much stronger if I had sampled only statements by those of governing parties. One might rebut this by suggesting that the two measures are likely to be the same. To do so, however, would be to concede that whatever it is that determines the salience of a particular frame cross-cuts the main political and economic divisions in a polity. Such a concession, in turn, makes it all the more likely that it is in fact the ideas that matter, and not 'underlying' economic or political interests (cf. Parsons 2003).

This chapter presented but one exploratory test of the general approach. However, the same approach can easily be extended to any aspect of the European integration project. Moreover, measuring the salience of more specific frames in particular issue areas is likely to provide us with further explanatory leverage. In other words, the general model is easily generalizable and extendable. More importantly, however, the relative salience of different frames is not subject to frequent changes. The approach championed here carries important cumulative benefits, therefore. Once we obtain measures of the strength of different frames in a particular country or at a particular time, we can use those to shed light on the choices made in a broad set of European integration initiatives.

This brings us, in closing, to the question of the origins and evolution of frames. Why is it that the security frame for European integration is much more salient in Belgium and the Netherlands than it is in Ireland? Why, conversely, is the commercial frame much more salient in Ireland? Answering such questions is beyond the scope of this chapter. I suspect that much of it has to do with how the European integration project was initially conceived of and sold to their publics by national elites. Since we know that ideas in general, and frames in particular, are sticky, we can expect such initial determinants of the salience of frames to cast a long shadow.

When new policy initiatives are introduced, frames can be derived from a variety of sources. Most commonly, policy-makers look to relevant historical experiences for candidate frames. An important alternative possibility, however, is that of international diffusion. As Bleich (2003) shows for the case of race policies, for example, policy-makers may look to states with similar national identities or experiences to see how they have dealt with comparable issues. Thus Dutch and Belgian leaders may have framed the European Coal and Steel Community in security terms given the salience of security questions in the early post-Second World War era. In contrast, Ireland had been neutral during the Second World War . Far more salient in Irish politics at the time it joined the European integration project was the need to catch up with the rest of Europe economically. It is worth noting that the experiences of poorer areas in Belgium and Italy within the EEC would have shown that this was certainly a relevant frame for European integration.

Most of this is speculation, however. Much work remains to be done both in tracking the patterns of salience of different frames for European integration over time and across countries and in explaining the origins and evolution of those patterns. National history and identity almost certainly play a role, as do periods of crisis and reassessment. Whichever factors turn out to matter most, it is unlikely that we will find a simple model that will permit us to bypass frames. How policy-makers think about the purpose of the EU is a crucial factor in determining their stance on any proposal associated with the overall the European integration project; consequently, measuring how they think is essential to our understanding of European outcomes.

Notes

1 Debate on the Treaty of Nice in the Flemish parliament, 19 June 2002.
2 Debate on the Enlargement of the European Union, 23 October 2002. *Handelingen Tweede Kamer*.
3 Representative Van Grembergen, debate on the Treaty of Nice in the Flemish parliament, 19 June 2002.
4 See also Khong (1992) for a review of the relevant cognitive social psychology literature.
5 Surel (2000) provides a useful overview of the use of these and similar concepts.
6 For example, Risse *et al.* (1999). But see Diez for an approach explicitly emphasizing 'contending discourses within states' (2001: 9).
7 Schmidt distinguishes her model from Kuhn's by noting that new information can continue to be evaluated in the context of the old discourse, and that old ideas and values are often retained in the new discourse (2000a: 282; see also Hall 1993).
8 Note that crisis can be generated by the disjunction between the discourse's predictions about what will happen and what actually happens. In other words, discourse may generate its own crisis.
9 Even the classic example of the introduction of Keynesianism into macro-economic policy-making was characterized by a continued struggle between Keynesianism and alternative ideas, many of which retained or gained adherents throughout the period in which Keynesianism can be argued to have been dominant (Hall 1989).

10 The crucial task for norm entrepreneurs, for example, is to convince everyone not that they have the only correct frame, but rather that their way of framing an issue is at least equally defensible and thus as worthy of consideration as more established alternatives.

11 Nor is there a straightforward connection between a particular policy outcome and a single frame. Even those who are interested in the same general policy outcome will at times employ 'greatly disputed, arbitrarily selected, and even contradictory frames' (Payne 2001: 44).

12 The interaction between frames and national identity is not uni-directional. Once frames take hold and become internalized to a considerable extent, they will begin to exert an effect also on the deeper underlying values that constitute a society's national identity (Schmidt 2000a: 281). In this manner, the competition between alternative frames also has a bearing on the competition among different conceptions of national identity.

13 Moreover, translating the argument about hard-wiring to the state level is problematic in itself, notwithstanding neorealist claims about the survival pressures imposed by the international system.

14 See Checkel (1997, 1999b) and Hurd (1999). The three possibilities of compellence, self-interest, and persuasion or internalization cannot be rigorously separated. Compellence may be modeled as a recalculation of the material self-interest by an actor (Coleman 1990: 29). Similarly, non-compliance with particular norms may impose costs as a result of sanctioning by other actors who *have* internalized those norms.

15 For a related argument addressing those who challenge the causal importance of analogies, see Khong (1992). Arguments along these lines are also central to structuration theory (e.g. Giddens 1979).

16 In fact, since we are interested in measuring the political power of frames, elite discourse may tell us more than would the decision-makers' internal frames, since the latter might fail to incorporate the power of rhetorical entrapment (Schimmelfennig 2001). See Snyder (1991) for another model incorporating this effect.

17 This only holds, of course, for government decisions. If we were interested in trying to explain referendum outcomes, we should examine the ideas held by the public at large, instead. Although the two are often closely related, they may well differ in significant ways, as referendum outcomes in Denmark and Ireland have shown. I thank Erik Jones for this point.

18 If there really were a single, coherent elite discourse, as some authors assume, it would be much less crucial to consider the possibility that opposition or bureaucracy have a different set of frames through which they evaluate policy. Along these same lines, the argument that the public is more likely to be convinced by a single, coherent government discourse (Schmidt 2000: 288, citing Zaller 1992: 8–9) is not quite correct. Publics are more likely to be convinced by a coherent discourse on the part of *their own* elites, who form only a subset of the national elites, and rarely a representative subset (especially in societies with relatively deep cleavages; cf. Lijphart 1968).

19 Representative De Graaf, debate on the State of the European Union, 10 October 2000. *Handelingen Tweede Kamer.*

20 Minister De Hoop Scheffer, debate on the enlargement of the European Union, 23 October 2002. *Handelingen Tweede Kamer.*

21 Representative O. Mitchell, Irish debate on the 26th Amendment of the Constitution Bill, 2002 (Treaty of Nice), 10 September 2002.

22 Minister of State in the Dept. of Finance Cullen, debate on the European Union Bill, 27 June 2001.

23 Representative De Jong, in the debate on the enlargement of the European Union, 23 October 2002. *Handelingen Tweede Kamer.*

24 Minister of State in the Dept. of Justice O'Dea, debate on the 26th Amendment of the Constitution Bill, 2002 (Treaty of Nice), 4 September 2002.

25 Mattli (1999: 20) for example, assumes that the objectives of integration are 'improvement of economic growth and the maintenance of political office'. Nor do any of the alternative theories of integration he discusses move beyond peace or prosperity.

26 Representative Burton, Irish debate on the 26th Amendment of the Constitution Bill, 2002 (Treaty of Nice), 4 September 2002.

27 Taoisaach (prime minister) Ahern, Irish debate on the 26th Amendment of the Constitution Bill, 2002 (Treaty of Nice), 10 September 2002.

28 By substantive I mean that the interrupter introduces new information, be it ideational, factual, or otherwise. Non-substantive interruptions may be heckles, quick questions of clarification, etc.

29 This is different from the number of speaking turns, as some speakers made no such statements, whereas others made more than one.

30 Indeed, in the second of the two polls, they were more than twice as likely as Dutch respondents to expect enlargement to create new jobs (39.82 per cent versus 19.8 per cent, respectively). Questions 22.05 in EB 55.0 and 43.06 in EB 56.3.

31 Percentages are calculated as a share of those who had a specific opinion. Adding in 'don't know' answers changes the percentages but not the finding. Question 13 in EB 55.0, 38 in EB 56.3.

32 Questions 42.02 and 42.04 in EB 56.3.

7 Agency, structure and European integration

Critical political economy and the new regionalism in Europe

Marcus Pistor[1]

Abstract: In mainstream debates about which theory is most useful for explaining European integration since the 1970s, critical political economy (CPE) approaches rarely receive much attention. This is particularly unfortunate in the analysis of the role of business associations (BAs) as political agents in integration (such as the European Roundtable of Industrialists or national BAs), or when integration is examined in relation to profound economic changes. Because it is here that CPE approaches, which have contributed much to our understanding of class-based agency and of the relationship between economic and political change, would seem to offer useful alternatives to standard theories of integration, and international political economy more generally.

Introduction

In this chapter I discuss three CPE schools – regulation theory, the York school of global political economy, and the Amsterdam school of international political economy – and examine how they have been used to explain European integration. I argue that all three can be seen as a product of the rejection of both mainstream political economy, and the economic determinism and structuralism of orthodox Marxism. However, many CPE analyses do not succeed in avoiding a structuralist and reductionist reading of European integration, (1) because of their focus on structural economic change, and (2) because of the lack of a theoretically informed explanation of the relationship between economic structure and class-based political agency and strategy. I conclude by outlining some general criteria for non-structuralist and non-reductionist CPE of European integration.

Critical political economy

Very generally, political economy is concerned with the nature and interaction of the political and economic aspects of social reality. Different approaches to political economy can be distinguished and categorized along several dimensions or criteria. The most important of these is the conceptualization of the relationship between politics and economy, more specifically 'whether or not they claim to depict a systematic relationship between' the two (Staniland 1985: 5). While one of the central tenets of mainstream approaches to political economy is an ontological (and largely unquestioned) assumption that the 'state' and the 'market' are essentially separate spheres of social reality (e.g. Gilpin 1987: 8–9), critical approaches argue that they are systematically related and that the apparent separation posited and observed by mainstream political economy is itself the product of historical development (Hettne 1995: 6; Mahon 1984: 38; Solomon and Rupert 2002: 292). This critical perspective on the relationship between 'state' and 'market' does not necessarily imply an economic reductionist understanding, where politics is simply reduced to the effects of economic forces, although that position was dominant within Marxist political economy for many years. But it does suggest that major political developments cannot be explained without reference to economic forces (e.g. Holman 1992: 4, 12).

A closely related issue is the stance adopted with regard to 'social reality' and its analysis and conceptualization in the social sciences. The distinction made by Robert Cox between problem-solving and critical theories is useful here and it is worth quoting him at length: 'Problem-solving theory...takes the world as it finds it, with the prevailing social and power relationships and the institutions into which they are organized, as the given framework for action' (Cox 1981: 208). Taking this view of the world makes it difficult to study fundamental transformations, especially when the nature of institutions and the relationship between economics and politics may be changing. But it also tends to limit problem-solving theories to explaining the functioning of existing systems and makes them less useful in raising questions about how they came into existence and are maintained or changing. In contrast to that,

> Critical theory [...] does not take institutions and social and political power relations for granted but calls them into question by concerning itself with their origins and how and whether they might be in the process of changing. It is directed toward an appraisal of the very framework for action, or problematic, which problem-solving theory accepts as its parameters.
>
> (Cox 1981: 208)

These differences are of central importance to the conceptualization of the relationship between politics and economy. While mainstream political economy takes the separation of the economic and political spheres for granted, critical political economy asks how this separation came about, how it has been (re-)produced and by whom, what role it plays in modern capitalist democracies, and why it has become so widely accepted in the social sciences (e.g. Mahon 1984: 38). Critical political economy is, for example, helpful in the analysis of the 'new regionalism' (Hawes 1996) in Europe, where efforts to redefine the relationship between politics and the economy and to 'insulate substantially the new economic institutions from popular scrutiny or democratic accountability' (Gill 1992: 165) have been important aspects of the move towards economic and monetary union.[2] The conceptual separation of politics and economy, together with the related empiricist definition of power employed in mainstream political economy, also results in an inability to achieve what should be fundamental objectives of a political (economy) of the European Union (EU): to understand the nature of power in the EU, including its organization and distribution (Van Apeldoorn *et al.* 2003: 17).

With this in mind, CPE can be defined broadly as a research programme that is based on the following arguments. First, that politics and economy are systematically related. Second, that, while socio-economic power structures and conflict are central to understanding social reality – they represent the traditional domain of Marxist political economy – we should be concerned with social relations of power more generally. Third, that concrete events or phenomena are the outcome of the interaction of different social structures and concrete agency. Explaining events which have been the focus of traditional Marxist analysis – such as class politics or class-based agency and strategies – then, involves examining the interaction of socio-economic with other structures and institutions, as well as discourse or ideology, through agency, which is itself shaped by the interaction of different social structures (Clement and Myles 1994; Clement and Williams 1989; Jenson and Mahon 1993). Political economic agency and strategy must, therefore, be understood as being (potentially) determined by and (re-)producing several parallel, interacting, and/or contradictory structures. Finally, political economy needs to be critical in the sense of scrutinizing existing institutional and other social arrangements, but also in the sense of critiquing the social and discursive parameters within which academic research and theory development takes place.[3]

The structure–agency problem

> [People] make their own history, but they do not make it just as they please; they do not make it under circumstances chosen by themselves, but in circumstances directly found, given, and transmitted from the past.
>
> (Karl Marx[4])

It seems appropriate to begin with this well-known statement of the structure–agency problem, which is perhaps Marx's most important on the issue (Callinicos 1987: 9). Simply put, it suggests that while it is people who make history, while human agents produce society and social change, their agency is constrained – perhaps defined – by existing social structures. Agency cannot occur outside existing social structures and practices, but only through them. At the same time, the social structures and practices that constrain agents are also the product of past agency.

The issue of how much relative importance should be assigned to structures – understood here as 'persistent social practices, made by collective human activity and transformed through collective human activity' (Cox 1987: 4) and agency 'conscious, goal-directed activity' (Anderson 1980: 19, quoted in Callinicos 1987: 11) – in the explanation of social phenomena, and how each should be understood in relation to the other, has been much debated in the social sciences. The position taken has substantially influenced both theories and empirical analysis. Much of the debate about the conceptualization of structure, agency, and their relationship in social theory can be portrayed as one between two opposite standpoints: one advocating the autonomy of individual or collective social actors to act purposefully, the other insisting on the determining effect of social structures (Sztompka 1994: 28ff.; Wendt 1987: 339). A third approach, structuration theory, suggests that structures and agents should be understood 'as mutually constitutive yet ontologically distinct entities', as 'co-determined' (Wendt 1987: 360).

The question of how the structure–agency problem should or can be solved theoretically represents only one side of this issue. The other side, namely how we deal with structures and agents in empirical analysis, is equally important. It is here that many of the structuralist tendencies of contemporary CPE have their roots. As I argue in this chapter, much of the contemporary CPE literature has moved away from a structuralist theorization of the agent–structure problem and social change, and, correspondingly, from a relatively unproblematic base–superstructure understanding.[5] For example, instead of explaining changing state forms or institutional transformations in terms of the needs of certain stages of capitalist development, the trend has been to look at these as more or less contingent outcomes of the interaction of different and possibly contradictory forces. Among these, political, organizational and ideological factors have received greater attention as autonomous factors that are not reducible to structural-economic forces.

Despite these developments in CPE, however, many critical studies of concrete phenomena, such as the emergence of the new regionalism in Europe since the early 1980s, still tend towards structuralist and economic reductionist – and in some cases functionalist – explanation of class-based agency. At least two reasons for this can be identified. First, the goal of most CPE studies continues to be finding explanations or studying social change at the level of social systems. This goal is an important project for CPE scholarship. But while we need to explain ongoing changes at a general, systemic level, doing so only in terms of system-level forces is inadequate. Looking only at the latter implies that we can conceive of socio-economic and political structures and their transformations *without* referring to concrete historical agents (real people and organizations). The structures we seek to analyse are separated from the human agency which (re-)produces them: they are reified. The result is a structuralist reading of these changes.

Second, there is a prevalent underlying assumption that concrete events or phenomena can be explained with the help of a single theory, and, conversely, that, to understand processes like European integration we need only to develop such a theory. This assumption usually leads to a theory-driven analysis in which the need for theoretical cohesion and development becomes paramount at the expense of careful empirical analysis that recognizes the complexity of 'historical events, processes or societies' (Sayer 1987: 10). In the case of approaches which focus on the level of capitalist systems, on modes of regulation and regimes of accumulation, or on the totality of social relations, the result of such theory-determined research is a tendency towards structuralism and functionalism, as well as economic reductionism. Specific events are seen or implied to be logical in terms of the structural (and theoretically defined) characteristics of the system or functionally necessary to the system as a whole, and agency tends to be reduced to the actions of theoretically defined and structurally determined social actors.[6]

This is not to argue that empirical analysis can or should not be shaped by theory, or that social structures do not have a constraining or determining effect on social relations or concrete events, or that all structures are equally important in shaping or producing specific, concrete agency. My point is simply that empirical analysis should not be *subordinated* to the requirements of any *one* theory. Determining which structures and processes are most important, how agents come to act as agents, what kind of social structures they reflect, and what their impact may be on social structures, is a task for empirical analysis. It cannot be adequately dealt with through theoretical conjecture alone.

In Marxist political economy the structure–agent debate has traditionally focused on the relationship between socio-economic structures and the economic system, on the one hand, and the role of classes,[7] as the main historical agents in (re-)producing these structures, on the other. Of particular importance here is the issue of how groups of people who objectively share similar positions in the socio-economic structure come to act as agents. In orthodox Marxism the relationships between economic structure and political, legal, or cultural superstructures, on the one hand, and between objectively defined classes (class in itself) and classes as collective agents (class for itself), on the other, are seen as relatively unproblematic,[8] and socio-economic relations are seen as determining all important historical developments. Other positions within Marxism, however, have emphasized the problematic nature of the process by which classes become agents, the importance of politics – including political strategies and tactics – to class-based agency, or the way in which class struggle and the economic 'base' exist in their pure form only in theory and, in concrete reality, are shaped by other social structures and struggles.

In much of the contemporary CPE literature the debate has moved beyond a concern with the conception and relative importance of structure and agency in a theoretically one-dimensional social reality. It focuses on issues around subjectivity and agency as they are shaped by multiple, intersecting systems of social relations and ideology (or discourse). Even if we continue to conceptualize agency and structure as being mutually determining, we now have to think of agency as potentially being determined by and (re-)producing several parallel, interacting, and/or contradictory structures. The focus therefore shifts to the processes through which concrete agents are constituted, what kind of strategies are developed and implemented, and how these, in turn, shape different social structures (Solomon and Rupert 2002: 293). As I have argued above, this is a task for concrete, empirical analysis and cannot be adequately dealt with through theoretical conjecture alone. With regard to the constitution of a class or class fraction as a concrete agent, this means that empirical analysis must establish whether and how collective agents come to represent or reflect classes and class fractions, what factors shape their ability to act effectively, and how they are affected by other social structures.[9] The following critique of CPE research on European integration will assess the way in which the structure–agent problem and social change are dealt with theoretically, and how this has been translated into empirical analysis.

CPE theories and explanations of European integration

Regulation theory

The regulation approach was developed by a group of French scholars in the 1970s partly in reaction to the structuralism of Althusserian Marxism. Rather than assuming that the reproduction of capitalism is necessarily secured or that there is 'a single objective logic of capitalist development' (Jessop 1990a: 309; Lipietz 1991: 461), they asked 'how capitalism could survive even though the capital relation itself inevitably generated antagonisms and crises which made continuing accumulation improbable' (Jessop 1988: 2, 1990a: 307–8). In answering this question, regulationists moved beyond the conceptual opposition of agency and structure and a reductionist conceptualization of the base–superstructure relationship, and looked to the role played by social norms, organizations, and institutions in regulating social conflict and stabilizing the conditions necessary for a particular economic growth model to succeed (Jessop 1988, 1990a; Hirsch 1992: 203, 219).

Central to regulation theory are two concepts: 'regime of accumulation' and 'mode of regulation'. The former is defined as the 'fairly long-term stabilization of the allocation of social production between consumption and accumulation'. A regime of accumulation must be:

> materialized in the shape of norms, habits, laws and regulating networks which ensure the unity of the process and which guarantee that its agents conform more or less to the schema of reproduction in their day-to-day behavior and struggles.
>
> (Lipietz 1987: 14–15)

That is, the regime must be materialized in a mode of regulation. The emergence of such a mode of regulation together with a given regime of accumulation is, however, not seen as a necessary, 'pre-ordained' part of capitalist development. Nor is the emergence of a mode of regulation that successfully stabilizes a given regime of accumulation viewed as necessarily corresponding to the latter's needs. Instead, they are products of human struggles, only some of which lead to successful regulatory modes or accumulation regimes (Lipietz 1987: 14–15).

Thus, regulationists argue that regulation is necessary to secure the conditions for capital accumulation, but that concrete forms of political, ideological, and institutional regulation cannot be understood as functional to capital accumulation or economic strategies. By doing so, they make it possible to develop a non-reductionist and non-functionalist conceptualization of political practices, institutions, and ideology, which is nevertheless grounded in a Marxist analysis of political economy (Bieling and Deppe 1996: 485; Jessop 1990b; Lipietz 1987), and they open a way for understanding class-based political agency, which does not reduce it to 'objective' interests but takes seriously the ideological and institutional aspects of (class) politics and the contingent and complex effects of agency. To understand the emergence of a particular mode of regulation, therefore, requires analysis of the strategies and practices of real agents, as well as the concrete institutional, economic, and other structural conditions in and through which they operate (Jessop 1990b: 196).

For the purpose of this chapter, the most important problem with regulation theory and with many regulationist studies is the lack of an adequate conceptualization of agency and strategy, both in relation to the existing – political, economic, and ideological – conditions and possibilities for transformative action, and to the development of new regimes of accumulation and modes of regulation (Hirsch 1992: 203).[10] This is perhaps surprising since regulationists emphasize that accumulation regimes and modes of regulation, are products of struggles over strategies, modes of regulation, and accumulation regimes, which are grounded in, but not reducible to, economic structures and conflicts (Bieling and Deppe 1996; Hirsch 1992; Jessop 1990b; Lipietz 1987).

A second problem is that regulationist research has often focused on the relationship between existing regimes of accumulation and modes of regulation, their crisis and transformation, and the possible emergence of new regulatory modes which correspond to emerging regimes of accumulation at the national, regional, or global level. That is, the focus has been on 'structural cohesion', and not on how particular modes of regulation have been – or might be – constituted through the often contradictory activities of class-based and other actors, and which have to be seen as 'historically contingent', if we are to avoid functionalist and structuralist explanations (Hirsch 1992; Jessop 1990b: 154, 186).[11]

Regulationist studies situate the re-launching of European integration in the early 1980s in the context of the crisis of Fordism, seen as a crisis of both the predominant regime of accumulation and the regulatory mode. New integration initiatives – such as the single market initiative and EMU – are explained as products of the search for a response to declining rates of profit and investment, rapidly growing unemployment, and growing government deficits, as well as to a general crisis of legitimation. They are seen as being closely related to new economic strategies that entail changing production paradigms and the internationalization – globally and regionally – of finance and production (Altvater and Mahnkopf 1993: 35–6; Bieling and Deppe 1996: 488–501; Tömmel 1995: 49–53). Consequently integration initiatives cannot be explained simply as effects of structural economic changes, such as changing class structures, the concentration of capital, regional, and global economic integration, and changes in production paradigms and technologies. Instead, they must be seen as non-necessary products of competing strategies pursued by class-based state and other actors with the goal of developing new regulatory norms and institutions at the regional level (Bieling and Deppe 1996: 489; Tömmel 1995: 80). In addition, some scholars argue that incremental changes in policy and governmental decision-making, many of which occurred during the period of 'Eurosclerosis', have also played a role (Tömmel 1995). Finally, it is suggested that the major integration steps taken since the mid-1980s became possible because regionally and globally oriented actors successfully achieved political dominance and built modernization coalitions which became unified through neoliberal hegemonic projects (Bieling and Deppe 1996: 493; Hirsch 1995: 148–55). The following two examples of regulationist scholarship on European integration illustrate these points.[12]

Bieling and Deppe (1996) argue that the success of the new integration initiatives of the 1980s can best be understood as a product of political, economic, and institutional conditions, which allowed new modernization coalitions in different European countries to successfully pursue a neoliberal integration project. These conditions were the result of relatively independent developments and included changing class configurations, the creation of the European Monetary System, and the emergence of a neoliberal ideological consensus which unified different social groups around a hegemonic project (Bieling and Deppe 1996: 488–501).

Bieling and Deppe's analysis demonstrates how regulation theory can contribute to a CPE explanation of European integration. As with other regulationist work, the discussion of agency remains at a general level, without consideration of specific actors. But, unlike many regulation theory scholars, Bieling and Deppe demonstrate how the study of concrete agency and strategies can be made a central part of regulationist integration research.

In contrast to Bieling and Deppe and other regulationist scholars, Röttger argues that 'traditional regulation theory', which focuses on nation-state level regulatory modes and the historical period of Fordism, and which is based on the assumption that 'accumulation and regulation can only find coherence as holistic social projects', has been made redundant by the profound changes in the deep structures of the global political economy (Röttger 1994: 10–17, 1995: 68–75, 1997: 40–6). For Röttger, the emergence of transnational capitalism necessitates a fundamental redefinition of the central regulation-theoretical question, namely 'the problem of the institutional mediation of economy, society and politics' (1995: 75). He suggests that a 'critical theory of global capitalist regulation' (1994) can be developed by making the 'world market the starting point for analysis' (1995: 75). Röttger argues that 'it is possible…to interpret the currently dominant EC integration as a thoroughly successful 'project' [aimed at] tying together competing economic internationalization and regulation strategies and to link them to interests in the periphery' (1995: 72–3).

Röttger's analytical approach is one of starting with the general, deep-structural developments at the global level – explained in relation to changes at the level of production – and of examining how these are manifested in the specific developments of European integration and related projects (Felder *et al.* 1999: 5). The role of national political economies in integration, and its impact on them, is examined at the structural level as well, in terms of their (class) configuration, which, he argues, explains national regulatory modes and European integration strategies. In many ways, this is similar to Gill's approach discussed below and like Gill, Röttger's focus on deep-structural change leads to a structuralist and somewhat reductionist explanation of European integration, which fails to reflect a key argument of many 'traditional' regulationists,[13] namely that modes of regulation are – perhaps accidental – outcomes of social struggles that are grounded in but not reducible to economic structures and conflicts, and thus cannot be explained with reference to them alone (Bieling and Deppe 1996; Hirsch 1992; Jessop 1990b; Lipietz 1987).

To summarize, regulationist studies of European integration offer a way of examining and explaining the political strategies of class-based actors in relation to socio-economic and political structures and processes, without reproducing the structuralism and functionalism of orthodox Marxism. To do this effectively, however, consideration of concrete agency – not socio-economic agency in general – must be brought to the centre of theoretical development and analysis. While recognizing the role of (political) agency or strategies is important, it has little effect if empirical analysis continues to examine agents only at a very general level and to focus on the effects of their actions – the regimes of accumulation and regulatory modes they produce. What we need to look at, and link conceptually to the analysis of modes of regulation and accumulation regimes, is how concrete political strategies are developed, and how they reflect a changing class structure, economic strategies, and political configurations.

The York school of global political economy

The York school emerged in the 1980s as a double critique directed, first, at the positivism and state-centrism of mainstream IPE research and theory and, second, at the structuralism and economic-reductionism of orthodox Marxism (Cox 1981: 6–10; Gill 1993b: 21–6; Payne and Gamble 1996: 6; Sinclair1996: 41). In searching for a critical perspective which would offer a 'structurally grounded explanation' (Germain and Kenny 1998: 5) rooted in a materialist conception of history (Gill 1993b),[14] while avoiding economic reductionism and structuralism, scholars turned to Antonio Gramsci, whose work had been re-discovered in the Anglophone world in the 1970s. The attractiveness of Gramsci, whose main contribution to CPE was a Marxist theory of politics and ideology (e.g. Hobsbawm 1982: 21), lay in 'the historicist and agency-oriented aspects of Gramsci's political sociology' (Murphy 1998: 418) and his methodology (Germain and Kenny 1998: 6).

The York school's central theoretical arguments are that the structures of the global political economy have to be conceptualized in terms of the interaction between three categories of forces – ideas, material capabilities, and institutions – at the levels of social forces, states, and world orders (Cox 1981; Gill 1992: 158). These structures are 'made by people' (Cox 1981: 242, 1987: 4), that is, they are produced and reproduced by human agency.

As a research programme, the York school focuses on the changing global political economy, characterized by economic integration, the internationalization of the state, and the emergence of a transnational or global civil society (Gill 1993a,b; Murphy 1998; Payne and Gamble 1996).[15] Empirical research employs 'the method of historical structures' to identify the configuration of social structures and to determine the possibility of the 'emergence of rival structures expressing alternative possibilities of development' (Cox 1981: 220; Payne and

Gamble 1996: 7; Sinclair 1996: 8–12). Agency, seen as operating primarily through historic blocs, is situated in these structural configurations 'which do not determine actions but nevertheless create opportunities and constraints' (Payne and Gamble 1996: 7).

York school research is characterized by an emphasis on the role of ideas or ideology, sets of intersubjective images through which actors make sense of social reality. This is important for the study of global political economy, because it necessitates a constant critical questioning of the concepts and ideas through which academics and social actors more generally operate, and because it requires careful consideration of the role of ideas in the constitution of collective agents (Cox 1981: 239–49). Ideas (or ideology) are conceptualized as neither reducible to material forces nor entirely autonomous. Instead, Cox argues that 'ideas and material conditions are always bound together, mutually influencing one another and not reducible one to the other' (Cox 1983: 132, quoted in Payne and Gamble 1996: 8).

Ideology is central to the York school's understanding of hegemony. Following Gramsci, Cox argues that hegemony involves both coercion and consent and that it has to be understood 'as a fit between material power, ideology and institutions' (Cox 1981: 225; Gramsci 1971: 52–60, 80, 158–61, 169–70, 175–85, 210–11; Payne and Gamble 1996: 8–9). Hegemony is seen as necessary for the formation of historic blocs, 'coalitions of social forces bound by consent and coercion' (Cox 1981: 132; Sinclair 1996: 9), bound together, in other words, by the hegemony of a class or class fraction and a hegemonic ideology (Simon 1982: 14). While Gramsci analysed the formation of historic blocs at the national level, the York school shifts the focus to the emergence of a transnational historic bloc as a central characteristic of the contemporary global political economy. The formation of this bloc reflects changes in class structure, in particular the emergence and increasing dominance of transnational capital. Neoliberalism represents the hegemonic ideology, the ideological glue that binds together the different elements of the transnational historic bloc. It provides the discursive terrain on which dominant economic and political strategies are explained and pursued, and which provides the structuring principles for the institutionalization of emerging power relations (Gill 1993a, 1995).

As a starting point for analysis this is a useful approach to CPE. Its main strength lies in a non-reductionist conceptualization of ideas. However, the method of historical structures can easily lead to structuralist explanation, when analysis focuses on structural dimensions at the expense of agency, and when 'Gramsci's radical embrace of human subjectivity' (Germain and Kenny 1998: 5) is forgotten.

Stephen Gill is perhaps the best-known York scholar working on European integration. Applying the method of historical structures, Gill situates European integration since the mid-1980s in 'the context of global patterns of power and production, as [a] feature of the political economy of globalization' (1998: 6) and argues that it is a manifestation of the institutionalization of 'disciplinary neo-liberalism' (1995) in Europe. Driving this process is 'the agency of a neoliberal transnational historic bloc and a process of elite international policy formation'

(1998: 11). Expressed in concrete form mainly through the alliance between the European Roundtable of Industrialists (ERT), the Commission, and neoliberal governments (1992: 165), this 'rentier bloc of interests' (1997: 210) 'includes state interests associated with the German-dominated unification project, large-scale finance and productive capital of global reach, as well as European companies, and associated privileged workers and smaller firms' (1998: 12).

Central to Gill's analysis is an emphasis on neoliberalism as the ideology that binds together the elements of the transnational historic bloc and which has provided the rationale for economic and monetary integration over the past two decades (1997: 215). More specifically, he argues that the new regionalism in Europe – specifically the EMU – is a manifestation of the 'new constitutional-ism', which is both the political-institutional dimension of the broader 'discourse of disciplinary neoliberalism' and a strategic project pursued by the transnational historic bloc with the goal of fundamentally redefining discursively and restruc-turing materially the nature of politics and the relationship between economic power and political decision-making (Gill 1998: 5, 1992, 1997).

Gill's analysis of the discursive dimension of European integration strategies, of the efforts of transnational capital and associated forces to restructure the terrain of political struggle, is arguably his most important contribution to a CPE understanding of integration. It is here that the influence of Gramsci is strongest. There are, however, some serious problems with Gill's analysis.

The most obvious weakness in his empirical analysis is the reduction of European integration to economic and monetary integration (Felder *et al.* 1999: 5). This leads him to focus only on the economic forces driving integration and to ignore political dimensions, including the political processes through which both national negotiating positions and regional agreements are arrived at. The focus on the economic aspects of European integration in itself is not problematic, as long as it is recognized as partial. But Gill combines this empirical focus with a methodological and theoretical argument that gives both immediate and ultimate determinacy to economic structures, even though he suggests that their influence is mediated by ideology.

Second, in applying the method of historical structures, Gill does not consider 'the *complex interplay* between ideas, institutions, and material capacities' (Gill 1992: 158). Instead, he prioritizes the influence and changes of economic struc-tures and seeks to show how political institutions are created to respond to these changes, and how ideas facilitate this process by providing ideological unity to socio-economic interests and by legitimating institutional change.[16]

Third, Gill insists that 'we must beware of being misled by the "events history" of the last few years' and that it 'seems more fruitful to emphasize the structural changes that have occurred in the post-war conjuncture' – namely the 'emergence of a larger [transnational] rentier bloc of interests' (Gill 1997: 210). What matters, therefore, are primarily material, socio-economic structures. Ideas and institu-tions are viewed as not just embedded in class structure, but as following logically from it. As a result, Gill's analysis of European integration becomes structuralist, reductionist and functionalist.

These problems are most apparent in Gill's conceptualization of agency and his analysis of the transnational historic bloc that drives European integration. He defines this bloc primarily in class terms, as an alliance of classes or class fractions that share certain structurally defined – and objectively determinable – interests. However, for Gramsci a historic bloc is constituted as a complex of relationships between structure and superstructure (Cox 1983: 131): the central dimensions of bloc formation – how a historic bloc is actually formed, how it relates to class structure, who leads it, and who contests it – are essentially political factors. That is to say, historic blocs are structured ideologically and organizationally, and do not simply represent or reflect the 'objective' interests of the economically dominant classes.

Gill's analysis of the emergence of a transnational historic bloc, and the agency he assigns to it, does not reflect the complex understanding developed by Gramsci. His conceptualization of historical agency as exercised only by dominant classes and their allies, and more narrowly by the elites, resembles instrumentalist theories of the state and ignores Gramsci's emphasis on the importance of ongoing political struggles involving both dominant and subordinate classes and allied forces (Felder *et al.* 1999: 5; Germain and Kenny 1998: 24).[17]

Finally, Gill's empirical focus on the transnational as the main site for 'temporary unifications of the major social relations' (Germain and Kenny 1998: 10) unnecessarily limits the analysis and ignores national political struggles or sites of bloc formation.

The Amsterdam school of international political economy

The Amsterdam school of international political economy shares with regulation theorists the view that the reproduction of capital is not guaranteed and that the conditions for capital accumulation must be secured ideologically and institutionally (Jessop 1990b: 158). What makes this approach different – especially from those regulationists who see no necessary correspondence between class structure and the ideological dimension of a successful mode of regulation – is the argument that the dominant and at times hegemonic ideology, which helps stabilize an economic mode, originates directly in the 'socioeconomic relationships between different fractions of the bourgeoisie, and between (fractions) of the bourgeoisie and (parts of) the working class' (Holman 1992: 12–13; Holman and Van der Pijl 2003: 73–6).The relationship between class structure and structurally determined economic interests, on the one hand, and ideology and political programmes, on the other, is conceptualized by the Amsterdam school in terms of 'comprehensive concepts of control'. These are large-scale political-economic programs...designed to resolve (at least temporarily) manifest conflicts among capitalists and between capitalists and other social forces (Murphy 1998: 194; also see Holman 1992: 12; Van der Wurff 1992: 178–82). To be successful, a comprehensive concept of control must advance 'the interests of the dominant fraction' of capital, respond to the needs of other fractions, and 'secure the needs of capital in general' (Jessop 1990b: 157).

While the Amsterdam school approach in some ways resembles a more traditional Marxist class analysis, it includes methodological and theoretical premises intended to prevent reversion to reductionism and structuralism. First, its proponents argue that comprehensive concepts of control 'must be translated into domestic and foreign policy at the state level to become effective' (Holman 1992: 13, 19). It is here that state institutional structure, the more general configuration of social and political forces, and the relationship between class fractions and the state become important (Holman and Van der Pijl 1996: 56). Second, the Amsterdam school rejects the possibility of determining the content of comprehensive concepts of control abstractly. While the interests and possible strategies of certain class fractions can be deduced from class structure in general, the content of concepts of control is the outcome of struggles between specific class fractions and can be discovered only through empirical analysis. In that sense, class structure and conflicts 'underlie and explain' political-economic strategies and debates but do not determine them (Murphy 1994: 194). Finally, the Amsterdam school insists that an understanding of the transformations of the global political economy can only be developed based on detailed empirical studies of transformations in different locations (Murphy 1994). While some general dynamics of globalization or regional integration may be identified, the struggle over comprehensive concepts of control and the articulation of social forces and the state at the national and local level remains important (Holman and Van der Pijl 1996: 56).

These premises go a long way to countering the structuralist and reductionist tendencies inherent in the class analysis that is at the centre of the Amsterdam school approach. They suggest that government policy and international agreements cannot be understood simply as determined by economic structure; that large-scale (global or regional) developments cannot be explained only in terms of overall structural-economic changes; and that political and ideological forces should be treated in their own right, as having effects, for example, on political-economic strategies and developments.

A central problem of the Amsterdam school approach is not resolved, however, by these premises, namely the reductionist and structuralist explanation of the political-economic strategies pursued by capitalist class fractions. The reasons for this are, in part, methodological. The Amsterdam school approach to empirical research is to start with an analysis of economic structures from which the interests of class fractions are deduced. Political struggle is seen as occurring between different (alliances of) class fractions and their interests. Politics and ideology, then, enter the picture only after class structure, interests and conflicts are established (Holman and Van der Pijl 2003: 76; see also Jessop 1990b: 157–8; Murphy 1998: 196). At least at the economic level, then, class conflict and class-based agency are conceptualized as being outside or prior to politics. This leaves the question of how the agency of capitalist class fractions arises unanswered unless we are willing to assume that it is an unproblematic process, that it emerges quasi-automatically from an objective socio-economic structure.

Otto Holman and Kees van der Pijl, two of the main proponents of the Amsterdam school, situate the relaunch of European integration in the 1980s in the context of the crisis of Fordism, globalization, and the related internationalization of the state, and the changes in the international political system. They explain integration in relation to the concomitant changes in class structure, in particular the emergence of a transnational capitalist class in Europe (Holman 1992; Holman and Van der Pijl 1996). Unlike some CPE analysts, however, they do not reduce European integration to economic integration. Instead, and in critiquing mainstream (especially intergovernmentalist) studies, Holman and Van der Pijl argue that explaining the relaunch in the 1980s is 'not possible without reference to the fundamental changes at the level of production, in the field of power relations, and in the ideological sphere' (Holman 1992: 12, 4), without analysing class structures and strategies. For Amsterdam scholars, therefore, the relaunch of European integration can be explained, in part, as a product of changes in national class configurations, the emergence of a transnational capitalist class, and transformations and a new articulation of comprehensive concepts of control.

Thus Holman examines the capitalist class configurations in EC member countries and in the EC as a whole using an ideal-type categorization of four groups:

1   Import-competing producers of tradable goods for the domestic market.
2   Import-competing producers of tradable goods for the European market.
3   Export-competing producers of tradable goods for the world market.
4   Globally operating financial institutions.

(Holman 1992: 15–16)

He shows how these class configurations determine narrow economic interests and underlie positions on European integration, and how they explain class-based integration strategies at the European level, without reducing these strategies to the more narrowly defined – and structurally determined – interests of class fractions. Holman also insists that class interests and class-based concepts of control must be translated into political strategies and ultimately into state policies to become effective (Holman 1992: 13, 17–20). He therefore avoids the determinism implicit in Gill's analysis.

Holman's commitment to a non-determinist approach is evident in his examination of different and conflicting national and transnational class positions on European integration. While he shows that the position of specific fractions in the class structure, and thus narrowly defined economic interests, have strongly influenced integration strategies and coalition building, their impact on the course of integration – that is, the concrete forms of supranational institutions, economic and monetary policy-making and approaches, and so forth – depends on their successful translation into state policies. This process is never automatic, but must be secured politically and ideologically. At issue, therefore, is 'the development of transnationally effective concepts of control unifying fractions of the ruling class into hegemonic coalitions at the European and global level' (Holman 1992: 15, 16–20).

For Holman and Van der Pijl the ERT is important here. Describing it as a 'novel form of bourgeois domination in Europe' (Holman and Van der Pijl 1996: 58), they argue that it has played a central role in relaunching and driving European integration in the 1980s and early 1990s.[18] But they do not suggest that it simply represents transnational capital, as Gill does. Instead they show how the politics, organization, and ideological dimension of the conflict between different class fractions have all shaped the ability of transnational European capital as a whole to influence European integration. The ability of the ERT to play such a central role in 'mobilizing business interests, governments, and Community institutions' (Holman 1992: 17) is therefore the result not simply of the dominance of transnational, globally oriented capital, but of the processes and strategies that established the ERT as a political agent representing transnational capital, and from which comprehensive concepts of control emerged which successfully unified different fractions of transnational capital behind a common ' "catchall" strategy' (Holman 1992: 17; Holman and Van der Pijl 1996: 69–71).

The ERT is also the focus of research by Bastiaan van Apeldoorn (2000, 2002), who offers a careful, detailed analysis of the ERT's 'political and ideological agency', and more specifically, of the content of its policies and strategies from 1983 to around 1998. Van Apeldoorn shows how this 'elite forum, which mediates the interests and power of the most transnationalized segments of European capital...was of great importance' (Van Apeldoorn 2000: 189) in the relaunch of integration in the 1980s and early 1990s, and in the determination of the governance system that resulted from the relaunch. But this role was not simply a consequence of the structural-economic power of the corporations involved, or their privileged access to political decision-makers. Instead, as Van Apeldoorn shows, it was the ERT's 'ideas' and 'concepts' that profoundly shaped the political discourse on integration when the relaunch agenda was set and implemented (Van Apeldoorn 2000: 189). These ideas and concepts, in turn, were defined by the ERT's increasingly neo-liberal orientation that grew out of internal differences between 'globalist' and 'Europeanist' fractions, which had characterized the round table in its early years (Van Apeldoorn 2002: 9).

Van Apeldoorn sees European integration as systematically connected – but not reducible – to structural economic changes at the global and regional levels. In this context, integration in the 1980s and 1990s was driven by a struggle between competing political-economic strategies aimed at establishing a new European governance system. Capitalist class-based agents play a key role in this struggle. But as Van Apeldoorn shows, integration cannot be understood without the ideas and ideologies through which these agents have made sense of structural changes, and which have shaped the definition of their strategic projects. Here, the growing influence of neoliberalism has been of central importance (Van Apeldoorn 2002: 1–7, chapter 1).

Guiding Van Apeldoorn's analysis is a theoretical approach which he calls 'neo-Gramscian transnationalism'. It incorporates the main elements of the Amsterdam school, but also draws on other CPE approaches discussed in this chapter. Neo-Gramscian transnationalism represents an important contribution to contemporary CPE debates about European integration. First because it successfully elaborates on previous efforts to conceptualize the transnational dimension of the European and global political economy. Second because it offers a more agency-centred and less reductionist conceptualization of capitalist class-based agency, which is based on the recognition that class formation is 'always a polit-ical process', in which ideas and organization play a central role (Van Apeldoorn 2002: 26). Van Apeldoorn's work exemplifies the potential of the Amsterdam school – and contemporary CPE more generally – to contribute to our under-standing of European integration by focusing on the agency of the capitalist class in the context of structural-economic changes. The one weakness of his approach, I would argue, lies in the reductionist understanding of the economic interests and strategies of capitalist class fractions, which he shares with other representatives of the Amsterdam school (see e.g. Van Apeldoorn 2002: 3).

To summarize, the Amsterdam school approach offers a way of explaining European integration as a product, in part, of the strategies pursued by different capitalist class fractions. Its analysis of the emergence of comprehensive concepts of control at the European level, in particular the non-deterministic explanation of the political struggles between different class fractions and of coalition-building between classes, supports an understanding of class-based political agency and strategies as contingent outcomes of political and ideological struggles. However, the conceptualization of how the economic interests and narrower strategies of capitalist class fractions are constituted is less compelling, because the relation-ship between economic structure, on the one hand, and economic interests and strategies, on the other, is seen as direct and unproblematic, and does not involve political and ideological processes or struggles.

Conclusion

The approaches discussed in this chapter represent different but related attempts to develop a critical political economy perspective that is neither structuralist nor economic reductionist. To a lesser extent, they are also critical reactions to main-stream political economy. In their efforts to move towards more agency-centred, non-structuralist and non-reductionist theories that are nevertheless grounded in a conceptualization of economic structures, these schools have drawn extensively on the work of Antonio Gramsci. The main influence here has been Gramsci's position on hegemony and, more generally, on the 'problem of ideology' (see Hall 1996: especially 26–7; also see Van Apeldoorn *et al.* 2003: 36–7).

The three schools have made important contributions to our understanding of the political economy of European integration, in particular with respect to the impact of profound socio-economic changes on integration, the interaction of political and economic change, and the role of ideas and ideology in these processes – although these contributions have been largely ignored by main-stream academia. More generally, they show how *critical* political economy 'can illuminate the interrelated social, political, and economic dynamics of European integration' (Smith 2002: 257). The three schools also demonstrate that key aspects of class-based agency – the structures that produce or make possible class agency, the ideologies through which agents make sense of the world and think of themselves as agents, the strategies they pursue, and the products of their agency – should be central to political-economic analysis.

The explanations of European integration informed by the three approaches share several characteristics. First, the relaunch of integration is situated in the context of fundamental political-economic change (the crisis of Fordism, economic globalization and regionalization), and transformations in class structure, in particular the emergence of a transnational capitalist class. Second, political and ideological factors are examined as part of the process of translating structural economic change into changes at the levels of the national and regional state. Finally, integration in the 1980s and 1990s is explained in relation to the emergence of neoliberalism – seen as a hegemonic ideology – which has served to unify different class-based and other strategies and to redefine political regulation and the relationship between politics and economics more generally. These are important contributions to our understanding of European integration. There are also differences between these three schools, especially with regard to how far the reaction against structuralism, functionalism, and economic reductionism is taken, not just in the general theoretical argument but in empirical analysis.

Four general themes emerge from this review of the CPE literature. First, although theoretically committed to a non-reductionist and non-structuralist conception of social change, political-economic agency and strategies, there is a tendency in the literature to prioritize structural economic forces in ways that reproduce the economic reductionism of orthodox Marxism. In some cases (Gill) this extends throughout the analysis of European integration; in others (Holman, Van der Pijl, Van Apeldoorn) it is limited to the explanation of the economic interests and agency of class fractions. Moving away from economic reductionism, however, can only succeed if it is recognized that we need to look at *both* political and economic forces and struggles at *all* levels, and that political forces shape the economic 'base' (Van Apeldoorn 2000: 191–3; Bieling and Steinhilber 2000a,b). Conversely, political strategies and developments need to be examined with reference to economic forces, if we are to avoid portraying political actors (including the 'state') as operating autonomously from, or in parallel to, economic actors and power structures.

Second, much of the CPE literature discussed here – with the notable exception of Van Apeldoorn (2000, 2002) – can be criticized for an inadequate conceptualization and analysis of concrete class-based agency, in particular with respect to how the structurally defined possibilities of such agency are realized politically, how they are translated into concrete agency and strategies.[19] While the general theoretical frameworks developed by the three schools all offer the possibility of developing a non-reductionist and non-structuralist understanding of agency, most scholars employing these approaches have so far failed to include an analysis of the role concrete class-based agents – other than the European Roundtable of Industrialists – and their strategies might have played in integration, and how they emerged as agents in the first place. What is needed is agency-centred theory and analysis of political-economic *strategy* as the link between economic structure and the goal-oriented activities of class-based agents. Focusing on strategy forces us to examine how agents view and interpret structures, conjunctures, political possibilities, and so on; it forces us to take seriously the role of politics and of ideologies and ideas in shaping political-economy agency, struggles, and structures.[20] Van Apeldoorn's elaboration of a transnational CPE approach represents a significant step towards filling this gap.

Third, most studies of integration focus on the national *or* transnational level. Some authors – regulationists in particular – have been criticized justly for maintaining an almost exclusive focus on the national level. But the single-minded attention of Gill and others to transnational class formation and civil society is equally problematic and partial. While profound changes in the regional and global political economies require us to look beyond the nation state in our analysis of class formation and political-economic agency, the nation state has far from disappeared. Instead of focusing on one level, then, we should ask more generally how politics, economics, geography, and culture/ideology/identity are being articulated in new ways, and what strategies have been pursued by class-based agents in relation to these processes at both the national and transnational levels.

Finally, much of the CPE literature discussed here can be criticized for focusing almost exclusively on political and economic elites as the main agents of European integration. Subordinate classes and class fractions are often ignored, as are the processes and practices through which elites are formed, achieve leadership of classes or coalitions, and come to influence European integration.[21] Little attention is paid to the fact that class struggle involves conflict and cooperation between classes and class fractions; that class strategy should therefore be understood and analysed as reflecting this conflict with other classes and fractions. While it is important to examine the role of political and economic elites in European integration and policy-making, political-economic agency is not restricted to elites. Instead, European integration should be viewed as the outcome of struggles between different agents, including class-based agents, over accumulation regimes and modes of regulation, as well as other objectives. While some outcomes are more likely than others, these struggles have (had) no necessary or logical outcome, and they are ongoing.[22]

Notes

1 This chapter is based on my dissertation entitled 'European Integration as Accumulation Strategy: The European Integration Policy of the Federation of German Industries (BDI) from Eurosclerosis to Economic and Monetary Union'. The Social Sciences and Humanities Research Council of Canada funded the research through a Doctoral Fellowship and a 'Federalism and Federations' supplement, and Queen's University funded part of my research in Germany through the Graduate Dean's Doctoral Field Travel Award. An earlier version of this chapter was presented at the Fifth Biennial Conference of the European Community Studies Association Canada in Toronto, Canada, 31 May to 1 June 2002. I am grateful to Grant Amyot, my thesis supervisor, for his advice and comments on the thesis and that paper, to David Howarth who provided helpful feedback at the conference, and to the editors of this book, for comments on an earlier draft of this chapter.

2 On this issue, the definition of critical political economy, and for a critique of mainstream studies of European integration, see Van Apeldoorn (2002: 'Introduction') and Van Apeldoorn *et al.* (2003).

3 This definition is broader than Marxist definitions, including those associated most often with contemporary historical materialism. For a discussion of historical materialism in the context of contemporary debates about globalization and international political economy, see Rupert and Smith (2002) and other chapters in their volume *Historical Materialism and Globalisation.*

4 In accordance with the German original, which reads 'Menschen machen ihre eigene Geschichte' (Marx 1987: 308), I have adapted this quote from the standard English translation found in Karl Marx, *The Eighteenth Brumaire of Louis Bonaparte,* in Tucker (1978: 595).

5 For an example of a structural-functionalist analysis of European integration see Cocks (1980). Many scholars continue to work within a more traditional Marxist or historical materialist approach (see Rupert and Smith 2002). However, this chapter examines broader, contemporary CPE approaches that have developed partly in reaction to the structuralist and economic reductionist tendencies in traditional Marxism.

6 On this issue see Lipietz (1987), Sayer (1987: 11), and Cox (1981).

7 Classes are defined here as groups of people who are in the same position in the social relations of production and exchange.

8 See Sayer's (1987) excellent critique of this position.

9 On this issue, see Bieling and Steinhilber (2000b: 104).

10 An exception is the work of Jessop and others on accumulation strategies and hegemonic projects (Jessop 1990a: 196–219; Leys 1985).

11 Part of the problem here seems to be the assumption that historical agency, which constructs and transforms accumulation regimes and modes of regulation, must operate through 'holistic societal projects' (Röttger 1995: 71–2; unless noted otherwise, all translations from German texts are my own). This leads to a conception of agency as defined by the economic structures of the emerging accumulation regime and limited to a macro-level, and which links specific agency directly to outcome.

12 Given the scope of this chapter and the need to discuss a number of different approaches, it is impossible to do justice to the full range of theoretical arguments and studies of European integration, which fall under the regulation theory label. I have addressed these in greater detail in Chapter 2 of my dissertation (Pistor 2002).

13 See Röttger's critique of Jessop (Röttger 1995: 71–2).

14 There is some disagreement among scholars that subscribe to this approach about whether this characteristics (i.e. 'structurally grounded explanation' rooted in a materialist conception of history) are central to the approach, and how much it brings the York school into Marxist debates more generally (see e.g. Murphy 1998: 417, 420).

15 While there are some differences between York school representatives, there is a core of shared methodological and theoretical arguments, which are most commonly identified with the pioneering work of Robert Cox (especially 1981, 1983b), as well as with Stephen Gill (Gill 1993a; Germain and Kenny 1998: 3; Payne and Gamble 1996: 6–7).

16 Cox has also been criticized 'for consistently stressing the importance of ideas in his theoretical work and yet falling back on more straightforward class analysis in his empirical work' (Payne and Gamble 1996: 9).

17 For a critique of Gill's 'top–down perspective' and his reification of 'transnational ruling class agency', see Colas (2002).

18 This is the period covered by Holman's research.

19 See Solomon and Rupert (2002: 293), who argue that 'the class-based relations of production under capitalism create the *possibility* of particular kinds of agency, but these possibilities can only be realized through the political practices of concretely situated social actors'.

20 If it can be argued that there is no given interest of capital in general but only constructed interests of historically situated capitalists, and that the construction of an interest of 'capital in general' is itself an important part of the process by which capital becomes a collective agent and secures political class domination, then the elaboration of a general economic strategy under some form of political leadership and involving an ideology which can unify different capitalist class fractions and other social forces, must be at the centre of our analysis. Bob Jessop's 'accumulation strategy' is a useful concept for this purpose: 'An "accumulation strategy" defines a specific economic "growth model" complete with its various extra-economic preconditions and also outlines a general strategy appropriate to its realization' (Jessop 1990a: 156, 159, 160, 166, 198–9).

21 With regard to the ERT, this kind of analysis is done for example by Cowles (1995). The ERT's role and policies are analysed in detail by Van Apeldoorn (2002).

22 This interpretation in similar to that proposed by Bieling and Steinhilber (2000a: 14, 2000b: 104), Cafruny and Ryner (2003a: viii), and Van Apeldoorn (2002: 6).

8   The EU and inter-regional cooperation

In search of global presence?

Mary Farrell

Abstract: Many have observed that the lack of a European Union common foreign policy and a common defence and security policy has prevented the EU from acting as a political heavyweight in the international arena. Instead of pursuing a more traditional 'hard power' approach to international political relations the EU has engaged in inter-regional cooperation with other supranational regional entities representing a community of states to achieve its goals internationally. In an effort to explain why regions of this kind do cooperate and why this strategy is favoured by the EU this chapter suggests that cooperative hegemony fills in the gaps left by traditional theories of liberalism and realism. Cooperative hegemony's emphasis on the role of ideas, the importance of state actors, and the necessity of institutions for cooperative actions, the chapter argues, best explains how the EU is able to translate its significant global economic power into cooperative efforts with other regions and thereby increase its global political influence.

Introduction

The European Union (EU) has for long been regarded as a political lightweight in international relations, explained in large part by the absence of a common foreign policy and a common defence and security policy. As a political community of sovereign member states, it remains reluctant to mobilize the financial resources and indeed the political commitment to launch even the most basic defence force. Months after the US–Iraq war ended in spring 2003, the EU was still struggling with the establishment of the promised Rapid Reaction Force, a unit intended for peace-keeping and humanitarian efforts in trouble spots around the world.

Yet in the economic arena, the EU is considered to be a major player in the global economy, and the volume of trade, investment, and financial flows stand as testament to the economic strength of the bloc. A significant aspect of the EU policy emerged in the past decade with the signing of many regional cooperation agreements, and the enhancement of inter-regional relations (Panagariya 2002; Sapir 2000; Tharakan 2002). The question often asked in international relations, 'why do states cooperate', is modified in this chapter to become 'why do regions cooperate?'

Regions are understood here as supranational regions, encompassing sovereign states in some form of cooperation or integration arrangement – such as EU,

Mercosur, Association of South East Asian Nations (ASEAN). The particular question to be addressed in the chapter is how and why the EU engages in institutionalized cooperation with other regional blocs. In answering the question, one can of course consider the explanatory power of the traditional approaches to international relations. Realism and liberalism still have much to offer by way of explaining the interests of the state actors, and the importance of institutions in structuring international relations (Jackson and Sørensen 2003). Yet these two well-worn sets of lenses through which we view the behaviour of states in the international system fail to capture the nuances of behaviour and the motivations that drive cooperation between states, and even less so the phenomenon of EU cooperation with other regional groupings such as Mercosur, ASEAN, and the African, Caribbean, and Pacific (ACP) states.

The chapter develops the argument in the following sections, starting with a brief review and comment upon the theoretical literature and a subsequent consideration of the empirical evidence. It presents a possible alternative theoretical explanation for regional cooperation, in the cooperative hegemony approach developed by Pedersen (2002). Subsequent sections examine the nature and scope of existing policy towards inter-regional relations, examining a selected number of inter-regional agreements with Asia, Africa, Eastern Europe, and Latin America. Limitations of space prevent a detailed examination of each agreement, so the aim will be to highlight differences and common elements with respect to such issues as institutional arrangements, objectives, processes, and scope.

The cooperative hegemony approach is complementary to existing theoretical perspectives on European integration, but it goes further to answer the question why states (as a collective entity) engage in cooperation (Pollack 2001; Rosamond 2000; Vayrynen 2003). Pedersen makes the claim that cooperative hegemony constitutes a partial theory of regionalism (Pedersen 2002: 687). However, instead of seeing this as a limitation to the approach, it may more properly be considered as an acknowledgement of the complexities that characterize the international system, requiring a multi-faceted analysis of the driving forces and elements that combine to shape the system (Geyer 2003).

In this chapter the concern is not with the motivation of a state to engage in regional cooperation. Instead, we are interested in the motivation of the community of states that is represented by the EU. So we can assume that there are collective benefits for the political community over and above the advantages to be gained by an individual state.

Why cooperate? Theoretical pluralism

The realist perspective retains its relevance for understanding the broader motivations behind the EU's actions in the international system (Jackson and Sørensen 2003). In particular, the realist view of the self-interested and power-seeking state remains true also for the group of states acting collectively through the EU. We can extend the perspective to allow for the possibility that the pursuit of power is conducted through the exploitation of economic means and strength, rather than by war and aggression, or other coercive means. This view of the EU can be seen as an extension of the rationale for its creation, and ultimately as the goal of its founding fathers.

The successive attempts to deepen integration over the past two decades, notably through the Single Market programme and the introduction of the euro, have served to consolidate the internal strength and dynamic of the EU. However, it requires larger markets outside the EU-15 in order to extract the maximum economic benefit from deeper integration. With increased interdependence and an intensified competition at the global level, and against the background of an international system with a dominant power, the EU must fight to defend and extend its position internationally. One way of securing these economic interests and ultimately the power of the EU is through inter-regional cooperation.

Liberalism shares with the realists the view of individuals (and states) as self-interested and competitive. But there is also a willingness to cooperate across international boundaries on the basis of shared interests in the pursuit of prosperity and increased welfare. Interdependence is both a causal factor in international cooperation and also the result of political cooperation among sovereign states, international organizations, and non-state actors.

States and other actors may be willing to cooperate in the international system. Yet even powerful states require some framework to facilitate international cooperation, given the fact that risk, insecurity, or lack of knowledge can make decision-making difficult. Institutional liberals claim that international institutions help to promote cooperation. A high level of institutionalization significantly reduces the instability of the system (Keohane 1989; Lake 2001; Oye 1986).

Institutions may be regarded as more than simply a-political actors facilitating international cooperation by providing information, reducing transaction costs, and playing an enforcing or monitoring role. Institutions, the EU in particular, can be considered as political actors motivated by self-interest and influenced by considerations of position and power in the international system. In the pursuit of both absolute and relative gains, regional cooperation and inter-regional relations in particular may be heavily influenced by geopolitical and security considerations.

Geopolitical and security considerations are given particular attention in much of the international political economy literature (Strange 1988). The history of regional cooperation in Europe, Asia, and Latin America suggests that states initiated cooperation in order to foster the emergence of binding security communities or as a response to external threats either affecting military or economic security (Solingen 1998). More recently, the existence of a hegemonic power has been recognized as a driving force for regional cooperation by way of a counter-hegemonic response (Hurrell 1995).

The past decade witnessed many, often contradictory, views regarding hegemonic influence and the possible nature and scope of hegemonic power itself (Kupchan 2002). Some analysts considered the possible decline of the United States as the world's sole hegemon (Kennedy 1988). However, the declinist literature generated widespread rebuttals, which were backed up by the consolidation of the US position as the dominant power in the 1990s (Cox 2001; Nye 1990). In the absence of any direct challenge to hegemonic rule, inter-regional cooperation remains an indirect reaction to the pervasive influence and might of the world's super-power.

For the realist the question is how the international power distribution can benefit the individual states within the system. For the institutionalist the key question is how power politics can be mediated through cooperation within the framework of international institutions, thereby taking for granted that the growing material interdependence among states and societies makes such cooperation not only necessary but also inevitable (Keohane 1989). International institutions can shape both the context in which states decide and the actual behaviour of states and non-state actors. It is by creating international norms, rules, routines, and expectations defining appropriate behaviour that international institutions exert a positive influence on state behaviour. They manage or prevent conflict and frame the context within which power politics operate.

Hegemony is not always conceived of as requiring support for cooperation or needing the legitimacy that cooperation might bring. It is viewed differently by the elites who gain directly from hegemonic practice and those groups (inside the hegemonic state and outside it) who regard the existence of hegemonic policies as detrimental to their interests. These conflicting perspectives stem from the different ways in which hegemonic power can be exercised: (1) to create a transnational order, underpinned by rules and laws (the benign hegemon); (2) to ignore or misuse the international rules and laws; and (3) to use hegemony in order to gain structural power within the international system (Palan *et al.* 1996). The question to be considered here is, how can inter-regional cooperation be interpreted under these conditions?

Cooperative hegemony: a strategy for cooperation?

While the EU cannot claim the degree of power and influence that the United States has in the international system, it has an increasing degree of influence through the economic power that it has aggregated for itself (Keohane 2002). Overall, its capacity lies in the use of 'soft power' (such as cultural and ideological/ideational assets), rather than the 'hard power' (in the form of military and economic capabilities) that gives the US its crucial advantage and leading edge.

For the political economist what is of interest is the way in which the EU uses economic power to secure political ends and in doing so extends its economic power base even more. As we will see in the following section, inter-regional cooperation is pursued through the exploitation of soft power for greater economic gain. The example of Eastern Europe will show that issues of security are seen in terms of the possible impact upon this pursuit of economic power. Insecurity is regarded as an obstacle to be removed along the pathway if it could directly hinge upon economic interests. The question is whether the exercise of soft power in the particular context of the EU's inter-regional relations can constitute an exercise of 'cooperative hegemony' and a gradual extension of European influence in the international system.

The cooperative hegemony approach involves the use of soft power through engagement in cooperative arrangements linked to a long-term strategy (Pedersen 2002). Implicit in the strategy is the notion that states have freedom to devise strategies, to incorporate new ideas, and to revise strategies. Under cooperative hegemony, institutions and ideas are combined to offer a framework through which a regional order is constructed. While it is a strategy that is open to militarily weak powers, or to powers in search of global reach, it is also a viable counter-strategy in an international system where a dominant state holds power. In this case, the model is proposed as a useful explanatory approach in understanding the EU strategy of inter-regional cooperation.

Realist approaches fail to capture the dynamic of cooperation among states, and in this particular context the greater emphasis upon the state as the unitary actor makes the theory less plausible for understanding the behaviour of supra-national/international entities. Similarly, the liberalist perspective does not capture adequately the complex intermingling of ideas, institutions, and power that are combined together in coherent and long-term strategies by a regional (supranational) political actor.

The question is, when can cooperative hegemony be useful, and under what conditions can such a strategy be developed? Here, I explain what is envisaged in cooperative hegemony before going on to consider the approach as a way of understanding inter-regional cooperation among groups of sovereign states. Pedersen proposes the cooperative hegemony approach as a strategy for regional cooperation that could be used by a large state in the region, with three crucial preconditions:

- the large country in the region must be able to harness the support of the neighbouring states for its political project – a 'power aggregation' strategy;
- the large country must be able/willing to share power with the smaller states – 'power-sharing' capacity;
- there should be a commitment among all the states in the region to a long-term regionalist strategy.

These are the essential requirements for regional cooperation to develop. It is clear that these conditions call for a high degree of institutionalization in order to facilitate the power-sharing capacity. In the case of asymmetrical regionalism, where there is a large state and many smaller states, a strategy of cooperative hegemony may require compensatory and redistributive mechanisms, at least in the early stages of cooperation. The use of these mechanisms, which Pedersen refers to as side-payments, enables the larger state to win over the political support of the other states.[1]

A cooperative hegemony approach has certain advantages that make it an attractive strategy for both large and smaller countries in the region, since it can embrace the interests of all the countries while facilitating the strategic considerations of the large country. For one thing, there are advantages in coop-eration to create a larger and more integrated regional market. Hence, the larger country/bloc in a regional/inter-regional cooperation arrangement will seek to pursue power aggregation strategies linked to economic advantages. In the case of a large, economically efficient country, there are major benefits to be derived from an integrated regional market.

A second advantage concerns the possibility of generating stability and security externalities through regional cooperation based upon extensive extra-territorial economic presence. Whenever stability is important to a large state, there is a high level of motivation to develop cooperative strategies. The case of EU eastward enlargement is an example of using cooperative hegemony to secure security externalities. The current EU policy towards the countries on the eastern border of the future EU-25 – Russia, Ukraine, Belarus, and Moldova – is in large part driven by the need to ensure stability on the enlarged Community's eastern, often volatile frontier.

A strategy of cooperative hegemony can also have inclusion advantages, whereby the large state can access resources, raw materials, and markets directly through the incorporation of other states into the regional cooperation arrangement. Equally, there may be an inclusion advantage associated with the possibility of integrating dispersed interests through regional institutionalization. The principle of inclusion allows for the possibility of creating regional order and stability without the need to resort to coercive influence and extra-territorial control.

The fourth advantage relates to the possibility for diffusion of ideas, norms, and rules. It is here that the central feature of cooperative hegemony, regional institutionalization, plays a key role in locking in the other states to the ideas and values of the hegemon. As the next section shows, the EU plays a major role in diffusing its own particular set of ideas and intrinsic values respecting human rights, the rule of law, and good governance in the conduct of inter-regional cooperation. The question is, what makes cooperative hegemony work?

It is important to have one large country (regional power) with the capability and the credibility to persuade and convince its neighbours that there are gains to be had from participating in and supporting the political project of the hegemon. Persuasiveness in this case is closely aligned with leadership skills, and crucial to the project is the willingness to exercise leadership on an ongoing basis. Cooperative hegemony differs from the traditional hegemony in that the latter describes the unipolarity of one dominant state with the capacity to influence the behavior and the environment of other states, without needing to resort to cooperation or other institutional arrangements and power-sharing.

Cooperative hegemony does require power-sharing, but it also requires an asymmetrical distribution of power in the region, favouring the large state. Pedersen (2002) warns, however, against a power distribution that is too asymmetrical, with the consequent risk of alienating the smaller states. Where there is an extreme asymmetry of power, the large state might consider that power-sharing was not in fact necessary to secure its goals. Such unwillingness to cooperate with smaller neighbours could result in the alienation of the other states and the ultimate failure of regional cooperation.

Regional asymmetrical relations can pale into insignificance in the face of external threats, leaving smaller states more willing to accept a regional power distribution than they might not otherwise be willing to countenance. The existence of large powerful and aggressive states outside the region can have its own effect in shifting the power balance within a region. These external threat considerations are particularly relevant in the context of Latin American countries within Mercosur, against the backdrop of the proposed Free Trade Area of the Americas (Klom 2003; Patomäki and Teivainen 2003).

Why would a regional power want to share power through the medium of institutions? Obviously, if the costs of not sharing are higher than the benefits of keeping power unilaterally, then the rational decision is to share power. Most important is the willingness of the big state to share power. This willingness may be determined by historical, cultural, and political traditions. The EU has a history of internal and external cooperation, so the existence of domestic coalitional interests with a culture of power-sharing will most likely produce regional strategies of cooperative hegemony. There is a greater guarantee of regional power-sharing where the domestic group or groups share a discourse that is supportive of power-sharing as a way to serve their interests.

The foregoing discussion suggests that we can assess the possibility for cooperative hegemony through the possible existence and interaction among a set of indicators:

- asymmetry of power
- credible regional actor
- commitment to leadership over the long-term
- power-sharing arrangements
- regional institutions
- the use of soft power (ideas, ideology).

How will the cooperative hegemon act? There are a number of possible strategies, all intended to secure the support and ongoing commitment of the other states for the political project. It is possible to co-opt smaller states through the offer of side-payments and economic incentives for collaboration, while states of all sizes can be co-opted through locking-in strategies linked to trade and investment. Of particular importance are regional integration strategies that emphasize common interests and a common identity in relation to the 'outsider' big power. The next section examines the EU's inter-regional cooperation against the above set of indicators.

The empirical evidence

From its inception integration in the EU was based upon internal liberalization combined with protectionism against non-members. In recent decades the EU has adopted an outward orientation with the rise of international interdependence. Possessing a dominant share of global trade, the EU is also one of the largest sources of foreign investment and contributes the largest amount of the inward investment in the United States. In addition it attracts significant foreign investment from the United States, Japan, and the rest of Asia. Contrary to fears that the European Single Market would create a 'fortress' Europe, the EU has gone on to extend its global economic reach.

The lack of a common foreign policy, in direct contrast to the success of the common commercial policy, has inhibited the evolution of the EU as an international political actor. Nonetheless, the EU has developed a comprehensive set of cooperation agreements, bilateral arrangements, and inter-regional relations that define the international political role of the Community, using economic channels just as the founding fathers set out to build a political community through economic integration. The issue we need to consider is to what extent this international community, based on the portfolio of EU inter-regional arrangements, was co-opted by the strategies of cooperative hegemony.

EU and ASEAN

The ten-member ASEAN originated in the 1960s as an organization whose main task was managing security in the region. The member countries relied on the gradual development of cooperation and trust among themselves as the principal method of preserving security. Consequently they avoided the kind of substantive binding agreements that have characterized the EU (Bowles and MacLean 1996). In this sense ASEAN constituted a 'soft security' organization, without any desire to use military resources to deal with conflict, whether internal to a member state, or throughout the region and its close environs. In fact ASEAN was little concerned with economic integration until the early 1990s when the countries agreed to set up a free trade area.

Internally ASEAN favoured a looser approach to integration and fostered the principle of non-interference in the domestic affairs of the member states, a position they held throughout the Asian financial crisis (Dieter and Higgott 2003). After the Asian financial crisis in 1998 there was much discussion about the possibility of monetary cooperation (Ahmad and Ghoshal 1999; Bowles 2002). In general ASEAN maintained a low degree of institutionalization and remained an inter-governmental organization. It is therefore not surprising that in the inter-regional relations with the EU, the same low degree of institutionalization is evident (Rüland 2001). Instead the EU gives great emphasis to the ideational factors, to the transfer of norms, principles, and rules as part of the dialogue with policy-makers, and through the consultations with experts and bureaucrats.

From the beginning of the 1980s EU–ASEAN inter-regional dialogue began in earnest and was conducted largely on an informal basis in dialogue and meetings at ministerial level. The Asia–Europe Meeting (ASEM) began in 1996 as an informal process of dialogue and cooperation, covering political, economic, and cultural issues. It brought together the EU-15, the European Commission, and the ten Asian states (Brunei, China, Indonesia, Japan, South Korea, Malaysia, the Philippines, Singapore, Thailand, and Vietnam). ASEM, like the Asia Pacific

Economic Cooperation (APEC) forum, incorporates as members some countries that belong to no regional organization, so the weak culture of cooperation through regional institutionalist frameworks is reflected in the way inter-regional relations with the EU are managed (Forster 1999; Richards and Kirkpatrick 1999).

The degree of informality in the inter-regional framework meant no binding arrangements were made, although cooperation did serve the purpose of stimulating agenda-setting across a variety of issues (concerning such issues as refugees, Cambodia, Afghanistan). It can be said that this approach to inter-regional cooperation served a useful purpose in developing the profile of the EU and of ASEAN as international actors. With international profile comes prestige and a strengthening of the legitimacy of the regional actor.

From the beginning of the 1990s the dialogue between the EU and ASEAN was strained by political differences over such issues as human rights and democracy, marking the clash of values between the two regions. At times the Asian states also adopted a strategy of balancing the EU with APEC, so that negotiations with the EU were often shaped by the weight of external political factors. The EU was anxious to retain cooperative ties with the dynamic (at least until 1997) economic region, but after the financial crisis the normative considerations returned to the inter-regional dialogue, generating a more value-based political dialogue.

ASEM has taken over many of the functions of the ASEAN–EU dialogue and offers greater significance for the EU since it includes China, Japan, and South Korea as members. It can be considered a counter-weight to APEC and a way to reduce the American influence in the region. Like ASEAN, ASEM is non-binding, informal, and consensual, but the weak institutionalization has limited the capacity of the framework to arrive at substantial decisions (Hamilton-Hart 2003). Despite the common interests of the two regions in areas such as trade and investment, the framework could not facilitate agreements on common positions nor agenda-setting for the global institutions. But the weak institutional framework was only one constraint limiting the cooperative relations. A more substantive limitation to deeper cooperation rested on the fact that the ideational aspects of the cooperative strategy failed to address the question of the different values and principles in the two regions.

In 2001 the EU sought to redefine its relations with Asia, announcing a new strategic partnership for the region. The new strategy signalled what amounted to a declaration of intent, to strengthen the EU's political and economic presence in the region, 'raising this to a level commensurate with the growing global weight of an enlarged EU'. The new Asia strategy also embraced ideational considerations, with human rights protection, democracy, good governance, and the rule of law given prominence (CEC 2001b: 18).

The new strategic partnership is still at an early phase as far as substantive inter-regional cooperation is concerned. However, the geographic scope is much broader than before, since it extends to include Australia, a country with which many of the Asian countries have close economic ties. The strategy rejects the idea of focusing exclusively on the regional organization and opts for trans-regional rather than inter-regional cooperation. In recognizing the regional diversity within and across Asia, the EU proposes to develop a web of relations extending to the regional power that is China, with India as another regional power, while also addressing the security concerns of South-East Asia, and the different interests of Japan.

A cooperative hegemony approach needs to engender support for the project among the other states if it is to be successful. In the case of the new strategic partnership with Asia, the EU proposes a shared political project based on promoting peace and security at the global level, enhancing the effectiveness of the UN, and managing the global environment. This partnership extends to shared responsibility for dealing with trans-border issues such as crime, illegal immigration, drugs, and terrorism.

Economic issues occupy an important place in the EU strategy towards Asia. At the heart of the matter is the EU's desire to enhance liberalization within the framework of the WTO system of rules. The EU also favours a stronger institutional framework in order to 'allow for a more coherent approach' to Asia–EU relations, on the basis that it would 'give a clear public signal of the commitment of both parties to raise our relationship to a new level' (CEC 2001b: 12). The overall strategy envisages extending the reach of the EU across issue areas in which previous engagement was limited. One such issue area is social policy, where the EU proposes to engage in further dialogue on social policy issues by presenting the 'European model' as an exemplar of best practice with the 'links between trade and social development, including the promotion of core labour standards'.

Certain elements of the new strategy for Asia suggest that the EU has adopted a cooperative hegemony approach in inter-regional relations. The EU discourse surrounding the Asia strategy is firmly linked to concepts such as partnership and the sharing of power. At the same time the discourse reflects the ideas and normative framework that is the hallmark of the European system (Nicolaïdis and Howse 2002). The EU wants to simultaneously diffuse its ideational-institutional model within and across Asia, while co-opting the Asian countries to support the EU position in the international fora, at the UN, the WTO, and on the global stage.

EU and Latin America

As with Asia, regional cooperation with Latin America reflected the recognition of diversity in the region. The result was a series of agreements and policy statements by the EU directed at the region as a whole and at the sub-regions within the continent, including Mercosur, Central America, and the Andean Community. Initially, the roots of this policy were to be found in the EU's development programmes and based upon Article 177 of the treaty establishing the European Community. By the start of the millennium, a new strategy with Latin America announced a partnership to 'place human development and the civil society at the heart of the relationship between the two regions'. Three priority areas of cooperation were identified by the European Commission: (1) the promotion and protection of human rights; (2) the promotion of the information society; and (3) the reduction of social imbalances by means of a global approach to the campaign against poverty. In more concrete terms the new Latin American strategy focused upon monetary and financial stability, the support for the peace process in Colombia, immigration, drugs-trafficking, and the WTO rules (Hurrell 1998).

The current EU strategy paper for Latin America marks a shift away from traditional development policy and must be seen against the failure of the development models of the 1970s and 1980s. It can also be seen in the context of the proposal to create a Free Trade Area of the Americas (Wrobel 1998). Both of these facts lend a sense of urgency to the regional political agenda. There are normative considerations driving the EU position, in the stated concerns with poverty, democracy, and the rule of law. But there are also strong political economy forces behind the EU support for Mercosur (Naillant and Ons 2002). While the EU supports the Mercosur integration process and the creation of a 'strategic inter-regional partnership', an over-riding motivation for the EU is to counter-balance the likely influence of the proposed FTAA (Mercosur–European Community Regional Strategy paper 2002–2006).

As the fourth largest economic group in the world after the EU, NAFTA, and Japan, with a GDP of $1100 billion and a population of 220 million people, the Latin American region has enormous economic significance for an economic bloc such as the EU. In this regard a major focus of EU efforts is support for the completion of the Mercosur internal market, the external liberalization of the community, and the enhancement of the institutional structure. Current EU strategy towards Mercosur has entered a new phase with the negotiations for the Inter-Regional Association Agreement. The focus of this agreement is economic cooperation, largely dealing with trade and aimed at securing bilateral, gradual, and reciprocal trade liberalization in accordance with WTO rules. The EU is therefore endeavouring to prise open what it regards as a potentially lucrative market.

The EU has sought to legitimize and justify cooperation by referring to common political values and shared interests and common agendas in the international community (Manners 2002). From its inception Mercosur adopted a similar (although more limited) institutional design to that of the EU. It proposed to deepen the institutional arrangements, to create a dispute settlement system, establish a common competition policy and eliminate non-tariff barriers. These proposals reflect the continued influence of the EU model (Kanner 2002; Sanchez Bajo 1999). Despite these similarities it remains an intergovernmental organization (Mecham 2003). Parallel to this intergovernmentalism there continues to be a weak institutionalization of the inter-regional cooperation framework for the EU and the Latin American region.

For Mercosur, and for Latin America in general, there are possible gains associated with inter-regional cooperation. Collaboration with the EU may serve to raise the profile in the international geopolitical arena, an aim that is particularly relevant for Brazil. But there is also the possibility for Mercosur to engage in balancing strategies, not least in the context of the negotiations around the proposed

Free Trade Area of the Americas (FTAA). Inter-regional cooperation with the EU could also be a way for Latin America to secure greater autonomy outside the US sphere of influence.

From the perspective of the EU the strategy is part of the quest for greater international presence and 'international actorness' (Ginsberg 1999). The model of strategic partnership between the EU and Mercosur bears some of the hallmarks of the cooperative hegemon. It reflects an ideational/institutional structure although at the moment the ideational aspects are more prominent. It is a model that allows the EU to pursue political goals largely through economic means and at the same time to transmit certain normative values and ideas such as good governance, the importance of human rights, and the necessity of democracy.

EU and Africa

Inter-regional cooperation between the EU and the African continent has its origins in the former colonial ties between certain member states and the African region. The Lomé agreement came about as certain European countries preferred to retain the relations with former colonies after the European Community got underway. Successive Lomé agreements were devised as instruments under the European development policy. The agreements offered duty-free access to the European market to the African, Caribbean, and Pacific (ACP) producers in the area of primary products, without the requirement of reciprocal access in return.

The Lomé agreements promised a radical departure in development policy, going beyond the offer of market access to include a declaration of the equal partnership between Europe and the ACP states and were hailed as innovative in terms of relations between developed and developing countries (Holland 2002). Nowadays, EU policy statements abound with references to partnership. However, as the Lomé agreements have shown, there was a mismatch between the rhetoric and the reality.

Despite the creation of an institutional framework for the conduct of political dialogue and implementation of policies, the partnership singularly failed to produce concrete results in terms of development or the reduction of dependency. The ACP economic bargaining power was instead much weakened and the group had to accept the imposition of conditionality clauses by the EU. These conditionality clauses were added in the negotiations for the fourth agreement which took effect in 1990 for a ten-year period. Under conditionality provisions the ACP states were required to adopt clauses on good governance, democracy, and the rule of law. Any ACP state that failed to meet the criteria and standards became subject to censure and the suspension of financial assistance. With the move towards conditionality the EU shifted its policy stance from partnership towards paternalism; the ACP countries could no longer rely upon privileged access and financial assistance.

The Cotonou agreement of 2000 was the successor to the Lomé agreements. The new agreement retained the notion of partnership, but now extended to include the participation by all sectors of society. It also brought two new elements: local ownership and differentiation among the ACP states. In the new agreement the earlier notion of equality of partnership was set against the requirement for a local ownership of development strategies. In other words the developing countries should set their own development programmes and targets. The second element of the Cotonou agreement was the decision to follow a strategy based upon differentiation in the arrangements for ACP countries and regions, which allowed for bilateral and sub-regional agreements below the ACP-bloc level.

Noteworthy in the Cotonou agreement is the replacement of the non-reciprocal agreements with the reciprocal Economic Partnership Agreements (EPAs) between the EU and selected groups of countries within the ACP bloc. These new agreements are intended to be reciprocal and in addition to be compatible with the GATT/WTO rules. Negotiations have already begun with the European Commission and it is envisaged that the EPAs should take effect by 1 January 2008, with a period of transition to full liberal trade spread over twelve years.

Cotonou is itself a new model of partnership in inter-regional cooperation between the EU and ACP. It recognizes the different levels of development among the countries, and proposes a multi-speed approach to development and regional cooperation. Under the Cotonou agreement development and economic growth are premised upon free trade and bilateral regional integration based upon economic liberalization.

Does the cooperative hegemony approach explain the evolving EU policy towards the ACP group of states? From the beginning the concept of partnership was central to the conduct of EU/ACP inter-regional cooperation. Implicit in the agreement was the notion of power-sharing. Until the Cotonou agreement the EU favored power-sharing strategies over power aggregation strategies in its relations with the ACP group of countries. However, the relationship was highly asymmetrical and the power-sharing was more illusory than substantive. Despite the offer of market access to the ACP producers under the various Lomé agreements, the ACP group actually lost significant share of the European market over the period of these agreements.

The Cotonou agreement marked a shift in EU policy towards the ACP group of countries in the direction of greater focus on power aggregation strategies. Development policy also changed to emphasize the links between trade and development (CEC 2000). In fact regional integration may be seen as a new form of conditionality clause in the current policy towards the ACP group where bilateral agreements between the EU and selected (not yet identified) groups of African countries, intra-regional cooperation agreements among groups of African countries, and inter-regional relations between the EU and regional organizations are all part of the new framework for cooperation.

More than ever before the EU is relying on an ideational realism in shaping its strategy towards the African region. The dialogue reflects support for liberalization and endorsement of the values and principles that are to be found in EU strategies elsewhere – support for governance, the rule of law, respect for human rights. Although the strategy recognizes the existence of wide regional diversity among the developing countries as far as capability to integrate into the global economy is concerned (as we saw with Asia and Latin America), the EU has largely opted for the policy of comprehensive trade liberalization and regional integration agreements that conform to the WTO rules. This approach serves the economic interests of the EU in particular since the strategy is based upon securing market access for European producers while selling the concept of the European 'model' of regional integration.

The question remains whether the African countries will buy into this trade liberalization under the guise of regional integration strategy. Concerns have already been raised by many of these countries over the continued viability and relevance of the ACP bloc, given the European Commission's intention to negotiate bilateral agreements at the sub-regional level. The EU bilateral strategy of negotiating with groups of countries rather than the ACP bloc impinges on the cohesiveness and unity of the regional grouping. Further fragmentation is a possibility as the gap between the poorest developing countries and those gradually integrating with the global economy widens. The recent European initiative on 'Everything But Arms' (EBA), which gives market access for every product except military hardware and armaments to the forty-nine poorest countries is a separate element under development policy. The poorest countries are party to both the EBA initiative and to the Cotonou agreement. However, the EBA offers the best conditions for the poorest countries (non-reciprocal market access for all products) and if they opt for the EBA it could undermine the market access guaranteed by Cotonou and, ultimately impact upon the viability of the ACP group.

EU and Eastern Europe

Inter-regional cooperation between the EU and the Central and Eastern European countries (CEECs) has evolved over a number of phases since the collapse of communism in the late 1980s culminating in the accession of eight new Eastern European states in 2004.[2] With this latest stage of East–West relations inter-regional cooperation metamorphoses into full integration as the accession states meet the specified criteria regarding their eligibility for membership.

Prior to 1989 the relations between the EU and the CEECs were extremely limited and confined mainly to initiatives by individual European countries (e.g. Germany's *Ostpolitik*) and to occasional trade policy initiatives aimed at individual CEECs, with the intention to divert trade westwards rather than towards the Soviet Union. After 1989 the EU was somewhat uncertain how to react to the political changes taking place following the collapse of the Soviet Union. While Western Europe responded with aid and with macroeconomic and technical assistance, the response was in general *ad hoc* and uncoordinated, lacking any strategic long-term focus.

The overwhelming concern of the EU as a whole was with the potential destabilizing forces on its eastern borders. Eventually the EU decided on the Association (Europe) Agreements with Poland, Hungary, and Czechoslovakia in 1991, and two years later with Romania and Bulgaria (Mayhew 1998). These agreements involved trade liberalization and also imposed EU competition and state-aid rules on the signatory countries. But the agreements went further than trade liberalization, to include multi-faceted, preferential agreements of unlimited duration containing clauses on human rights, democracy, and the principles of the market economy. In addition the agreements provided for political dialogue on all topics of 'common interest' at the highest level, with an institutional framework to facilitate cooperation. Although not initially offering membership, the agreements with the Eastern European states were subsequently modified in the wake of the Copenhagen Council meeting in 1993 when the EU member states agreed to accept the membership of the countries that met the eligibility requirements.

The Copenhagen declaration on the criteria for eventual membership marked an important change in EU policy towards the CEECs. The criteria set out the benchmarks for the Eastern European countries to follow in order to be eligible for accession to the EU:

- stable institutions (guarantee of democracy, rule of law, human rights and minority rights);
- functioning market economy, and the ability to compete inside EU;
- ability to adopt the *acquis communautaire*, the body of EU legislation, and to accept the aims of political, economic, and monetary union.

A further condition in the Copenhagen declaration referred to the capacity of the EU to absorb new members without any adverse impact upon the momentum of European integration. Although the European Commission has made light of this condition, the inclusion of a provision on internal cohesion in the EU-15 suggested a degree of caution on the part of the member states. The implicit concern that enlargement should not adversely affect the momentum of European integration seems prescient in the light of the difficulties in reaching agreement on the draft constitutional treaty at the December 2003 European Council meeting in Brussels.

The shift in policy towards the CEECs characterized two of the elements to be found in the cooperative hegemony approach. First, the ideational orientation of policy, with the EU insisting that the applicant states should accept and incorporate the core European values as a precondition of membership. Joining the club was conditional on the observance of the rules, and the acceptance of the ethos of its existing members. Second, the inter-regional relations were structured around a deep institutionalization that facilitated political dialogue and involved the political actors of the CEECs at the highest level. The institutionalized processes also helped to broaden the scope of dialogue by bringing in new actors and also new issue areas.

The pre-accession strategy was the conduit through which European values were to be transferred. In essence, it contained the following elements:

- preparation of the associated countries for joining the European internal market – setting up a competition policy in each country, in conformity with EU competition rules; limiting the use of state aids to domestic firms; adopting the internal market body of legislation;

- promotion of economic integration – by creating a physically integrated region, trade and commercial policy, and the adoption of law on rules of origin;
- cooperation between the applicant countries themselves;
- cooperation in the three pillars of the Maastricht Treaty – in such areas as education and training, environment policy, justice and home affairs, and foreign policy.

The implementation of the pre-accession strategy was conducted on the basis of further institutionalization, with the European Commission playing a prominent leadership role in a top–down approach to monitoring the progress of the accession states towards meeting the criteria. As part of this monitoring the Commission produced annual reports on the progress of each candidate country, which in itself served to rally the political institutional systems in the applicant states around the political project of enlargement (CEC 2002). The annual reports were the markers along the road to accession, benchmarks against which each country was assessed and its progress compared against that of the other candidates in the path towards the ultimate prize – entry to the rich club that is the EU.

The countries that showed progress as measured by how well they could adopt and adapt to the European model – based on a market economy, rule of law, respect for human rights, and a system of 'good governance' – were rewarded for their capability to imbibe the values, norms, and principles and ultimately their ability to converge to the model (Pridham 2002). The pre-accession strategy therefore determined that the accession states would conform to the hegemonic 'state', that is, the EU, rather than the applicants having the opportunity to transform the identity of the EU. Thus the EU shaped the candidates in the image of the 'European model' even before these countries became full members.

In sum the pre-accession strategy had both psychological effects and political/behavioural effects. It created a set of expectations around the future of accession to the EU (Sjursen 2002). It also suggested the inevitability of accession and the responsibility and accountability of the governments and political actors in each state to ensure that the accession strategy would be adhered to, at least to the extent necessary to secure entry to the EU. In line with the psychological effects, the strategy had a parallel and linked effect on the behaviour of the authorities and actors in the applicant states. Since membership of the EU required changes to the legislation in each country, to the administrative and legal structures, and to the policy mix therein, the overall outcome of the pre-accession strategy was a transformation of the entire institutional framework.

In this regard one of the pre-conditions for cooperative hegemony – the power-sharing capacity of the hegemon – was met at best by 'encapsulated power-sharing' (Pedersen 2002: 689). This conclusion is qualified because a careful examination of the Pedersen approach suggests that the degree of power-sharing will be influenced by a number of factors – the balance of fear directed at the biggest state in the region; the willingness of the large state to share power; and the nature of the political system as far as how much power-sharing actually took place at the domestic level. Strategic considerations may prompt the large state in a region to share power as part of a larger recompense to be gained by pursuing its power aggregation strategy – if there is a greater gain to be had from a power aggregation strategy. In the case of the CEECs political and practical considerations around the absorption of so many countries with diverse political, economic, and social conditions meant that the logical strategy was to prepare them beforehand. In practice the CEECs had very little influence in the processes and the Copenhagen criteria were essentially decided upon by the EU-15.

Indeed the criteria and the conditions set out in the pre-accession strategy imposed their own sense of urgency. This was compounded by the turmoil and social crises surrounding the transition to democracy. Governments were left with the unmistakable conclusion they needed to produce some workable solutions to retain the support of their citizens. With few options available to them, it is perhaps not surprising that the states were willing to accede to the programme produced by the European Commission on behalf of the EU-15.

Already weakened politically and institutionally as a result of the transition to democracy, they were unable to shape the power-sharing capacity of the EU. The result was that the EU power-aggregation capacity was enhanced, and ultimately dominated the other two pre-conditions for cooperative hegemony identified by Pedersen: the sharing of power in common institutions with broad competences; and the EU's (as large regional power) capacity to commit to a long-term policy of regional institutionalization.

The EU and the wider Europe

The latest enlargement of the EU has enormous implications both for the internal structure and also for the external relations of the community. With a new set of borders, the EU-25 will be required to review and adapt relations with neighbouring countries that are not members of the EU (White *et al.* 2002). How these new sets of relations will develop is yet to be determined. It is clear nonetheless that the enlarged EU may face insecurity and instability on its borders with the risk of internal repercussions.

Geo-strategic considerations highlight the need for the EU to develop a coherent and substantive policy for the conduct of relations with its neighbours on the eastern borders. Romania and Bulgaria are tentatively scheduled to become members of the EU in 2007. Russia has not declared an interest in joining the EU. Nevertheless it remains an influential actor in the region with an interest in closer relations with its western neighbour. Ukraine and Moldova are not currently considered ready to be candidates for EU accession.

Common interests abound for both the EU and these neighbouring states on the borders of the future EU-25. Not least is a shared interest in the provision of security, sustainable development, and cooperation for the management of cross-border problems such as drugs, illegal human trafficking, and migration flows. For the EU the over-riding consideration is security and stability on its borders. It is this interest that has dominated the wider Europe strategy programme introduced by the European Commission in 2003 (CEC 2003).

The strategy itself suggests many of the elements in the cooperative hegemony approach. Emphasizing shared values, the European Commission highlights notions of partnership and cooperation, stressing the interdependence and need for collective decision-making by the EU and its neighbours on the new eastern frontier. The 'ring of friends' strategy offers the eastern countries sharing borders with EU-25 the prospect of a stake in the EU's internal market in return for their commitment to adopt the values and norms of the EU. It is envisaged that political and economic relations between the EU and its neighbours should become as close as relations within the European Economic Area, while maintaining a strategy of differentiation among those Eastern European border countries. In concrete terms the EU is presenting a carrot-and-stick policy by offering the benefits of closer economic and political ties in exchange for progress by the Eastern partners in political and economic reform.

The 'wider Europe' strategy represents a radical step forward from the previous cooperative and partnership arrangements with Russia and other Eastern European countries. Current policy offers the promise of preferential treatment for trade, and calls in return for the partners to accept a timetable for extensive regulatory approximation. The neighbours are asked to adopt much of the *acquis communautaire*, to embrace the values and norms of the EU, and to commit to political reform towards the goal of creating a system that is a mirror image of the EU in its normative design and value systems.

At the moment 'the ring of friends' strategy is in a formative phase and so it is difficult to assess how well it may work. Both the EU and Russia have common interests and not least for both is the question of security. In addition for the EU there is the wish for greater political involvement in conflict prevention and crisis management. Russia is interested in closer economic ties with the EU and in adopting the rules and standards of the European Single Market it sends a signal to the foreign investors that the country is a competitive partner. Nevertheless, Russia is still searching for an identity in post-USSR and is still involved in state- and nation-building. The country's leadership is seeking to establish a leading role in global affairs and the international security frameworks, and to carve out new relationships with the EU, with the United States, and the neighbouring countries in the region.

Conclusion

We are witnessing the emergence of the EU as an international actor in a manner that plays upon its strength as an economic giant, while implicitly acknowledging its weakness as an international political actor (Nye 2000). It is worth recalling the origins of the EU and in particular the aim of the founders to create a political community by economic means (Haas 1958). The premise of this chapter is that the EU is replicating its internal success at the international level and pursuing the goal of becoming an international political actor by extending its economic reach through inter-regional cooperation (Hennis 2001). This is essentially the political project that is inherent in the current European strategy of inter-regional relations.

Since the EU is not a military power and is constrained by the lack of common foreign and security policy, it must act on the basis of the strengths that it already has. These strengths relate to its influential position as an economic power in the global economy, a power that is generally recognized and accepted. Hence the EU can use its global economic strength in the pursuit of inter-regional cooperation, with the ultimate goal of increased international political presence (Ginsberg 2001).

A major part of this inter-regional cooperation strategy is based upon the support for regional integration, as is the case with policy towards Latin America and Africa. In this respect the EU is taking advantage of the growing interest in regional integration and cooperation, even among countries such as America or Japan that have not pursued such policies in the past. There is currently a competitive wave of regional integration on a global scale (Radtke and Wiesebron 2002). European policy-makers have harnessed this wave of cooperative endeavour to build support for their own project of establishing an international and global presence.

There are other advantages of a more immediate nature that inter-regional cooperation can elicit for the EU. In the case of the EU and Eastern Europe there are clear advantages of scale from the enlarged market and advantages of stability from the strategy towards the Eastern neighbours, Russia, Ukraine, and Moldova. Relations with the African, Caribbean, and Pacific (ACP) group of countries were developed out of the colonial ties of member states that wanted to retain economic links, and preserve sources of raw materials – cooperation that resulted in advantages of inclusion for the EU.

Following the Cotonou agreement the EU is pursuing a distinctly different strategy with the ACP, based upon free trade and regional cooperation and integration. Under this new framework there is a shift from securing advantages of inclusion to advantages of diffusion. In other words the EU is making use of the evolving institutional framework for EU–ACP cooperation to diffuse its ideas and values – economic liberalism, human rights, democracy, and the rule of law. The proposed Economic Partnership Agreements are intended to lock in the ACP states into a system with a set of rules determined by the EU.

Regional cooperation within Asia has evolved slowly and often in very different ways (Higgott and Stubbs 1995). With the new strategy towards Asia the EU has proclaimed the direct aim of increasing its presence in the region (CEC 2001b). The strategy combines a number of distinct advantages for the EU, advantages that will become even more important for the future in the context of strengthening the EU as a global actor. There are clear advantages of scale in terms of expanding market share in a dynamic region, particularly with China which has been targeted as an important partner for the EU.[3] Perhaps more importantly there are advantages of diffusion in the spreading of European values and norms, and the enhancement of mutual awareness and understanding. Ultimately the aim is to build a basis for future cooperation on issues of common concern and create a possible ally in international negotiations. However, these are long-term strategies. Cooperation with Asia could also be relevant to the strategy of developing a counter-weight to US hegemonic influence.

How well does the cooperative hegemony approach serve as an explanation for the EU approach to inter-regionalism? In its emphasis on the role of ideas, the importance of state actors and the necessity of creating institutions as a framework for cooperative action, the cooperative hegemony approach encapsulates a coherent explanation for regional cooperation. The three pre-conditions for cooperative hegemony put forward by Pedersen – power aggregation capacity, power-sharing capacity, and commitment capacity – do not necessarily have equal importance in a regional cooperation strategy. In the case of the EU it is possible that a particular pre-condition or combination of conditions may have significance in a given region, but a different combination is relevant for another region. In the inter-regional cooperation between the EU and Eastern European countries, power-aggregation strategies were more in evidence than power-sharing strategies. With the ACP countries the EU adopted power-sharing strategies from the beginning. However, given the enormous asymmetrical distribution of power between the two regions, there was little regard for power-sharing and the ACP found itself reacting to agendas rather than setting the agenda.

In addition the ideational-institutional framework varies from region to region in the context of European inter-regional cooperation. ASEAN–EU relations rest on a very week institutionalization, whilst EU–Eastern Europe has perhaps the strongest degree of institutionalization. The analysis of EU cooperative relations suggests that the degree of institutionalization varies with the commitment of the large state to that region, and the culture with respect to institutionalization. ASEAN, for instance, has a low degree of institutionalization, and cooperation is very much intergovernmental. Nevertheless there is a strong interest in regional and inter-regional cooperation on the part of political and economic actors (Hamilton-Hart 2003).

For the EU as a global actor with 'soft power', the cooperative hegemony strategy is reasonable and ultimately essential to retaining its position of influence. Given its strength in areas such as economics, technology, culture and ideology, and institution-building, the EU is therefore well placed to pursue a cooperative hegemony approach. The EU has the internal cohesion and political unity that is needed to harness commitment from the member states and the supranational institutions for what is ultimately a long-term strategy. Furthermore, the leadership skills and the policy-making capacity of the European Commission are prerequisites for the conduct of such a strategy over a sustained period. The effective use of soft power depends upon such influence being exercised in a coherent way across a number of areas and issues simultaneously. While it is more difficult to assess the outcomes of soft power compared to 'hard power', where the impact can be easily and readily identifiable, it is a strategy that retains the commitment and support of the European societies to whom all the member states must ultimately be accountable. However, it remains doubtful whether such a strategy can be pursued in the long term without a common foreign policy in the EU, given the growing complexity and the challenges in international relations generally.

Notes

1 Within the EU, a similar strategy was adopted when the member states agreed to the doubling of the Structural Funds budget in the late 1980s, coinciding with the launch of the Single Market liberalization programme. Later on, the Cohesion Fund was introduced to support the four poorest countries of the EU in their preparations for monetary union.

2 Poland, Hungary, Czech Republic, Slovenia, Slovakia, Lithuania, Latvia, Estonia – the other two accession states being Cyprus and Malta.

3 EU exports to China increased fourfold between 1990 and 2000. China has now replaced the United States as the largest recipient of foreign direct investment. The Chinese financial authorities hold significant foreign exchange reserves, while the countries of east Asia now account for 70 per cent of global foreign exchange reserves compared with only 30 per cent in 1990. However, it is noteworthy that most Asian central banks keep 80 to 90 per cent of their reserves in dollars, rather than euros (*Financial Times*, 29 August 2003).

9 Understanding new forms of European integration

A study in competing political economy explanations

Waltraud Schelkle[1]

Abstract: Just as European integration itself has changed and evolved, so too must the ways in which we understand this process. The traditional Community Method of integration has been theorized using equally traditional theories of functionalism and realism. While not without virtue, these theories are no longer sufficient as a means by which to understand integration in Europe as they presume integration to be about preserving domestic policies. This chapter argues that a better explanation for current trends in integration is to induce change in contentious policy spheres. The new 'Open Method' Coordination (OMC) is most significant in this respect and when placed within the framework of the political economy of reform, able to fill the gaps left by previous modes of understanding. In order to illustrate OMC's explanatory potential an empirical analysis of social welfare policy is used, given that this has been one of the areas most resistant to integration in the past and illustrates the stark difference between fundamental interpretations of what EU policy coordination is about – preservation or reform of domestic policies. It is argued that by considering OMC and applying it to national and EU policy processes we are better able to comprehend several features that have puzzled observers, such as the intergovernmental nature of this integration method or the opportunistic handling of non-state actor participation.

Introduction

The time-honoured Community Method is no longer without alternative. Students of European integration wonder how significant it is that other modes of integration are gaining terrain. The Community Method endowed the Commission with the exclusive authority to initiate policy harmonization. Yet, flexible and soft methods of policy coordination have been developed recently to provide a potential alternative. The Nice Treaty sanctioned flexible integration which had been going on for some time, for example, with respect to border controls under the Schengen Agreement or monetary policy in Economic and Monetary Union. What is now called Enhanced Cooperation takes place when a selection of member states decides to integrate policy areas more closely than others. Another integration method, 'Open Method' Coordination (OMC), has been introduced since 1994 to integrate various economic policies (Broad Economic Policy Guidelines, BEPGs), labour market policies (European

Employment Strategy or Open Method on Employment) and basic safety nets (Open Method on Social Inclusion and on Pensions). The coordination of these areas is 'soft' since commitments and recommendations are politically binding but not legally enforceable (Directorate-General for Economic and Financial Affairs 2002: 10).

The debate on the Open Method is so vivid because it is more generally about the nature of European integration.[2] To some observers, it is a quantum leap as regards the creation of that conspicuously absent social union of Europe (Rhodes 2000; Atkinson 2002) and even an experimentation site for a new form of postnational democracy and participatory policymaking (Mosher and Trubek 2003; Sabel and Zeitlinger 2003). However, these high hopes face a simple question: how do we know that soft integration makes a difference to what governments do anyway? I will provide some evidence suggesting that OMC has an effect on the ongoing reforms of social policy in member states.

Others see the Open Method as too vague and non-binding (Scharpf 2002), a mere fig leaf for the barely dressed Empress called 'Social Europe' but simultaneously an unwarranted evasion of commitment and accountability that characterizes the Community Method (Chalmers and Lodge 2003). But if so, why did governments raise expectations in the first place and engage in 'cheap talk' which may prove politically costly when disappointment sets in? I will argue that OMC of economic and social policies is unlikely to revolutionize the operation of the EU but is a new method of integration that tells students of European integration something about the significance of that process for national policymaking which has not been fully absorbed in our theories yet.

In this chapter I critically explore two integration theories, functionalism and realism, to find explanations of OMC. While not without merit, these two established approaches assume that European integration is about preserving domestic policies, even if that requires sharing or transfer of sovereignty over their implementation. In contrast, a political economy of reform approach suggests that it is more plausible to see this new method of integration as an instrument to change domestic policies after national attempts have failed. The stark difference between these fundamental interpretations of what EU policy coordination is about – preservation or reform of domestic policies – can best be illustrated in the area of social welfare, which is why the empirical part of the chapter concentrates on this area.

The next section outlines why OMC may, in principle, constitute a new form of integration,[3] distinct from the Community Method and from Enhanced Cooperation. The second section explores what difficulties established theories of integration have in coming to terms with OMC. These explanations do not fully grasp that ever since the 1980s European integration has become a lever for large-scale institutional change in memberstates. The third section proposes an institutionalist political economy of reform approach. The fourth section then tries to give an alternative explanation for OMC. Evidence for this interpretation will be provided in the fifth section.

In what ways is OMC a new form of integration?

Open Method Coordination is officially applied to a whole list of policy areas (Radaelli 2003: 14–15): economic policy coordination (BEPGs, direct taxation), social welfare (employment, inclusion, pensions, health care), policies to foster the 'knowledge society' (innovation and R&D, education, information technology), environment and immigration. The Lisbon Council proclaimed that the coordination of these areas should make the EU the technologically most developed knowledge society in the world within a decade. In its fully developed form, however, it is at present applied in four areas only, namely the BEPGs, employment, social inclusion and pensions.[4] To this end, the Lisbon Conclusions spell out what OMC implies if fully developed (Council 2000, point 37):

- European guidelines: the use of guidelines, specifying timetables for the achievement of goals;
- benchmarking: the use of quantitative and qualitative indicators and benchmarks (best, good or worst practice) to assess and compare change over time, with due regard to national circumstances;
- National Action Plans (NAP): translation of the guidelines into national and regional policies;
- multilateral surveillance: periodic evaluation and peer review of the achievements, measured as improvement of indicators and convergence to good practice.

The following analysis takes OMC as being defined by these four elements, rejecting the tendency of EU officials and some of the literature to regard any consultation about policies between governments an instance of OMC. Such a broad understanding would make this possibly new method of integration virtually indistinguishable from what, for instance, G8 summits do. This specification is also suggested by the Council conclusions on 'streamlining' in spring 2003. The Council concluded that BEPGs coordination of the different processes should be streamlined, which means to follow a timetable that matches the different stages of coordination between policy areas (Council 2003: points 17–19). Streamlining presupposes that policy areas are softly coordinated in this well-defined sense of the Lisbon strategy.

Flexible integration differs from soft integration in that not all member states are supposed to take part.[5] Presumably it realizes a 'generalized subsidiarity principle', popularly dubbed 'Europe à la carte' (Dewatripont *et al.* 1995: ch. 3). Member state governments, not the EU, ultimately determine how closely certain national policies become integrated. Thus the method of Enhanced Cooperation allows those with stronger preferences for deepening to go ahead, yet tries to ensure that the front-runners keep their arrangement open and take possible negative consequences for outsiders into account by stipulating the latter's consent.

In contrast to this shifting involvement that flexible integration allows, soft integration includes all present EU member states and may even include candidate countries before full membership (Council 2003: point 11). The BEPGs make this difference between flexible and soft but inclusive integration obvious. They extend the stipulations of the Stability and Growth Pact (SGP) to the outsiders of Economic and Monetary Union insofar as they require them to observe the three per cent budget deficit-criterion but exempt them from the pecuniary sanctions of the Pact. That is, the BEPGs integrate 'softly' in the sense that the Excessive Deficit Procedure will not apply to Denmark, Sweden, the UK, and from 2004 onwards the accession countries. They can get a Council reprimand, however, should they (be about to) violate this fiscal criterion. The 'blame and shame' mechanism of multilateral surveillance can be activated to prevent fiscal profligacy of non-members leading, for instance, to large devaluations of their currencies vis-à-vis the euro and thus to trade distortions (Dewatripont *et al.* 1995: 71). The soft extension of the SGP is thus meant to ensure that flexibly integrated EU members devise their economic policies as a matter of common concern.

The deviations from the Classic Community Method are even more noticeable, as is widely discussed in the literature. OMC does not endow the Commission with an exclusive right to propose policy initiatives to the Council. The supranational body is responsible only for proposing meaningful indicators and distilling best or, more modestly, 'good' practices out of NAPs (Rhodes 2000: 3; Mosher and Trubek 2003: fn. 4). From a legal perspective, one may interpret the spread of OMC as a redress of the EU's constitutional architecture 'by placing the European Council at the heart of the Union's policymaking' (Chalmers and Lodge 2003: 3).

Open Method Coordination is also different from the Community Method in that a government's failure to implement what it has committed to in a NAP will not be sanctioned. A formal legal reason is that OMC in the Lisbon specification is so far applied to macroeconomic and redistributive policies only, that is, 'policy areas where, in all jurisdictions, law, classically understood, has a less direct role' (Chalmers and Lodge 2003: 3). Soft coordination is thus unlikely to lead to policy harmonization. Both sets of policies are constitutive elements of different 'worlds of welfare capitalism' (Esping-Andersen 1990). These elements are highly complementary. For instance, minimum wage regulations, the generosity of social assistance and the scope of wage bargains between unions and employers are characteristically linked to determine the wage floor of economies and make them more or less prone to deflationary and inflationary pressures. This complementarity makes each one resistant to change so that legal enforcement would be required to modify the entrenched functioning of welfare institutions and their stabilizing role. This stylized fact of institutional inertia, that comparative research of welfare state reforms established time and again,[6] is a challenge for any explanation of OMC and I will argue below that this challenge above all recommends a political economy of reform approach.

Why is the Open Method difficult to explain for established theories of integration?

Established theories of integration struggle to come to terms with OMC, which is not to deny that they have some explanatory power. For the purpose of the following analysis, it suffices to differentiate broadly between functionalist and realist explanations.[7]

Functionalist explanations such as supranationalism see spillovers or externalities between policy areas, across governance levels and borders as the driving force behind ever closer integration. In the presence of such interdependence, communitarization and policy supervision by a supranational agency helps national policies to (better) achieve the intended goals for the domestic political economy. The Commission acts as a policy entrepreneur that assumes the competencies which governments and their constituencies are willing to give up in order to gain in problem-solving capacity. How does OMC of economic policies (BEPGs) and of social policies (employment, inclusion, pensions) fit into this explanatory framework?

Monetary unification calls for coordination of other economic policies both to make markets of members more flexible when exchange rate adjustments are no longer viable and to avoid spillovers on the euro from profligate fiscal and exchange rate policies. In this view, the BEPGs provide a comprehensive framework to internalize these spillovers, for all economically relevant policies and for all members of the EU economy even if they are not members of the euro area and therefore not subject to the club rules of EMU. The soft method also allows for consensus building through deliberation (Hodson and Maher 2001), that is, problem-solving should conflict arise. In contrast, the EMU members should have reached that consensus upon entry, which is why hard sanctions are required should governments still be tempted to free-ride on the agreement. A vexing question for this functionalist explanation is why the BEPGs constitute an intergovernmentalist mode of integration, with the Council and not the Commission at the helm of coordination.

There are a variety of explanations for OMC of social (including labour market) policies. A long-standing argument has been that negative externality from market integration, namely higher factor mobility, puts pressure on more generous welfare states, possibly leading to a 'rush to the bottom' of social welfare provision (Scharpf 2002: 656–8, 662–5). However, this negative externality calls for Community Method integration, that is, hard law measures to ensure minimum standards. Thus OMC in social policies must be explained as making up for the lagging behind of 'Social Europe' (e.g. Falkner 2000; Rhodes 2000) while simultaneously taking into account that welfare states in the EU belong to different 'worlds of welfare capitalism' (de la Porte 2002; Esping-Andersen 1990). At other times OMC of these so far neglected policy areas is explained as addressing the participatory 'deficit' that an ever closer economic union creates (e.g. Mosher and Trubek 2003; Pochet 2003). It is interpreted as a new mode of governance, with the potential to become constitutionalized as the overarching integration framework. Therefore it is hoped to solve the problem of the EU democratic deficit through 'deliberative supranationalism'.

Again, one problem with this set of functionalist explanations for OMC of social policies is the intergovernmentalist mode of integration or governance that it represents compared to the Community Method. A functionalist explanation would expect that policies would be transferred to the supranational level and pursued by supranational actors to preserve or improve incrementally the outcome of domestic policies. With OMC the policies are still conducted by national governments albeit in a European intergovernmental arena. Pointing out that participation of non-state actors, one of the stated goals of OMC, makes up for this lack of supranationalism does not necessarily help. As the proponents themselves notice with some disappointment (Mosher and Trubek 2003; Pochet 2003), participation of social partners and other NGOs is very uneven, and generally much less than one would expect if OMC is 'deliberative supranationalism' or 'polyarchic democracy' in practice.

Realist explanations such as intergovernmentalism identify the various interests of governments (and sometimes non-state actors) behind integration. In this view, integration is contested and proceeds in discontinuous steps, depending on the preferences, political-economic weight and bargaining skills of the actors involved. The EU agencies, including Commission and Court, are granted competencies only when governments perceive a need to fill an agency slack, but are typically kept on a tight leash; the Council keeps its prerogative. How is OMC explained in this conceptualization of EU integration?

Monetary unification made it necessary to take care of the effective veto right of the German government and the Bundesbank. The stipulations in the Maastricht Treaty, (such as the independence of central banks), and the subsequent Stability and Growth Pact (SGP); written down in secondary legislation, which prolonged its stipulation of fiscal prudence into EMU, were obvious concessions to this effect. The BEPGs can be seen as a follow-up on the subsequent 'neo-liberal turn' of macro-policymaking under 'German hegemony' (de la Porte *et al.* 2001: 5–6). It is explained as a form of economic diplomacy exempt from majoritarian scrutiny. It either satisfies the inherent drive of power-seeking politicians and bureaucrats, as public choice theorists contend (Rieger 2001; Sinn 1992: 178–80), or it is symptomatic of a more general trend in member states. The latter may be seen as a shift away from parliamentary control towards expertocratic forms of scrutiny (Moravcsik 2002: 613). Still the question remains why member state governments devote resources to meetings for BEPGs' coordination if these meetings are non-committal talking shops at best and courts to condemn domestic fiscal policies at worst.

Open Method Coordination of social policies, in particular their participatory pretensions, is not easily explained through a realist theoretical lens. It is seen as a smoke-screen that has little to do with a new form of policy integration. In this view, either it has come about because the EU is seeking a role for itself in this policy area even if that is unlikely to have much practical effect (Moravcsik 2002: 607n.), or it is due to the hijacking of the agenda by a coalition of member states with rather problematic long-term consequences for the legitimacy of EU institutions (Chalmers and Lodge 2003: 24). The few authors who give a realist explanation for the emergence of OMC of social policies hardly conceal that they are puzzled by this new form of integration.

In sum, functionalist explanations make a good case for why integration of these policy areas has become necessary for economic or political reasons. Yet they struggle with the question why an intergovernmentalist mode of governance has been chosen instead of supranational governance, which would be more effective at performing functions, such as effective redistribution and efficient allocation of public resources. Realist theories, by contrast, help to understand what triggered the genesis of that particular intergovernmentalist integration method, but they seem to have been taken by surprise by the sheer dynamic with which soft integration is propagated, sustained and applied to ever more policy areas.

A common source of explanatory power *and* shortcomings seems to be that functionalist and realist theories of integration assume policy integration to be a way to protect or preserve the substance of national policies. They just diverge in their view of how much loss of national control over the policy agenda this involves. Given this intention of policy-makers and interest groups, the ensuing changes in the substance of policies after they have been integrated must then be interpreted as unintended consequences, as necessary adjustments beyond what was anticipated to be the price for protection. It is here that the OMC makes little sense. OMC is not about delegation and coordination of *existing* national policies to preserve them but about fostering change, with the help of timetables, indicators and benchmarks, and the exertion of the soft pressure of peer review.

Why an institutionalist political economy of reform approach?

A political economy of reform approach turns the underlying assumption of functionalist and realist views on its head: change, not preservation of national policies is the very goal of integration. OMC then makes sense in an institutionalist view of integration, namely as an attempt to institutionalize a sustained effort to reform, in particular of domestic welfare states. In that perspective, it is the conservation of policies that is the consequence, feared or unintended of institutional inertia, with integration being instrumentalized to give the appearance of mere reform activism.

This points to the fact that, *ex ante*, an institutionalist explanation does not naturally lend itself to a political economy of reform approach. Institutions serve, above all, to stabilize expectations. This rationale allows institutionalist theories – in contrast to functionalism – to explain why policies may survive long after the original constellation of interests or structures that fostered them has dissolved. This focus on stabilizing inertia and path dependency tends to give institutionalism a deterministic bias. Fundamental change, leaving the trodden path of institutional evolution, is the rare exception begging for explanation.[8] The theoretical problem that OMC poses is thus to explain in line with an institutionalist account of policymaking that governments seek potentially profound institutional change. A coherent explanation is to interpret OMC as an intergovernmental institution to tackle the inertia of domestic institutions.[9]

Seen as a lever for domestic reform agendas, OMC is hardly new. It has predecessors in the Exchange Rate Mechanism (ERM), the Internal Market Programme and the monetary union. Some time after the late 1970s, it dawned on governments that what is nostalgically called a 'Golden Age' of post-war growth had come to an end. Ever since this time the political economy of the EU has been characterized by the attempt to use integration as a lever for reform. The Internal Market Programme and the Maastricht strategy of monetary integration were implemented deliberately as signals to domestic actors, at a time when the abusive term 'Eurosclerosis' put pressure on policymakers (Scharpf 2002: 647–8).

The seminal article in political economy that noted this change was Giavazzi and Pagano (1988), which gave a rationale for the Italian government's effort to stay in the ERM despite high inflation. It hoped to change the inflation expectations of domestic price and wage-setters by pegging the exchange rate. While the success of this strategy was a notoriously limited, the idea of 'the advantage of tying one's hands' has subsequently been generalized. Integration may be used as a 'commitment device' to enforce domestic reforms. In the run-up to EMU, governments presumably committed to privatize and re-regulate without the support of accommodating fiscal and monetary policies. Again, the evidence for the rationale having worked is mixed and other political economy accounts of that shift in EU governments' policy stance seem more convincing, in particular McNamara (1998).[10] Yet the political economy strand of the literature on European integration grasped that something fundamental had changed in the way governments use the EU for their political agenda and EU organizations not only adjust but are keen to assume a new role. By contrast, the political science debates on *neo*functionalism and *neo*realism, stimulated by the revival of institution building with the Single European Act of 1987 and the subsequent emergence of 'New Europe', seem not to reflect fully this change (Rosamond 2000: chs 5–6).

More specifically, OMC of economic and social policies has taken up when it could be presented as part of a renewed effort to modernize the European economy. It will be argued in more detail below that OMC of social policies makes a difference in that it gives welfare state reform a unifying theme. The Lisbon agenda redefines the problems in terms of employment and economic reform. The prioritizing of the BEPGs over the OMC of social policies as well as the stated goals of the Lisbon conclusions mark a watershed to what officially motivated the Social Protocol of the Maastricht Treaty. As Falkner (1998: chs 2–3, explicitly 73, 88) amply documents, this first initiative to become serious about 'Social Europe' was defensive, meant to cushion the effects of market integration. The goal then was to agree on social minima, that is, on 'market-correcting' legislation to prevent social dumping (Falkner 1998: 154). In 2000 social policy was proclaimed as a 'productive factor' and soft integration is meant to organize mutual learning how to realize this potential for economic modernization (Council 2000: point 5).

The political economy of economic reform and transition, which for obvious reasons flourished in the last decade, studies processes of large-scale institutional change.[11] Large-scale and not piecemeal reform is what EU policy-makers perceive as lying ahead. If so, that literature gives tentative answers on two questions that will be crucial for an institutionalist explanation of OMC. First, when is gradualism more likely than a 'big bang' to further the adoption of a reform package?

Second, what role does participation of non-government actors like social partners or charities in formulating the agenda play in comprehensive reform processes?

Whether gradualism furthers or hinders large-scale reform depends on the nature of the uncertainty (Roland 2000: ch. 2). If uncertainty is of the idiosyncratic sort, the identity of winners and losers is unknown even if all believe that reform will produce a net benefit overall. In this case, gradualism may hinder the full implementation of the package. It creates an interim status quo bias because the losers from the first round oppose it, while the winners of the second round (who may be the initial losers) are not in favour yet. If uncertainty is of the aggregate variety, that is a reform package with an expected net benefit may turn out well or badly, then gradualism can actually help to implement the whole package. The sequencing creates an option to reverse the reforms if the first wave has a bad out-turn. Paradoxically, this option value of reversal – assuring voters that one may always go back – helps to overcome the status quo bias of uncertainty. The value of that option is the higher, the lower reversal costs are to begin with, the more complementary reforms are, and the more formative one reform step is for the likely outcome of the next.

The evidence on participation or 'social consensus' as a lever or barrier to reform is mixed (Rodrik 1996: 33–8; Williamson and Haggard 1994). Prominent economists like Leszek Balcerowicz or Jeffrey Sachs maintain that large-scale reform needs a strong and autonomous executive to push a package through or at least a 'honeymoon period' to lock in reform. As Rodrik notes, this widely held view that good economics needs voodoo politics is rather ironic. It implies that *homo oeconomicus* becomes myopic or outright irrational whenever he turns into *homo politicus*. Even from a hard-nosed economic point of view, participation may not be such a bad thing, if losers can be compensated or if we allow for organizational learning thanks to formal consultation procedures. The evidence on the instrumental role of social consensus is mixed. Sometimes it was a prerequisite for reform, sometimes a result of success. In addition, there are valid non-instrumental reasons for participation, namely if social consensus is seen as a value in itself or as a precautionary measure against the risks of social engineering, given that in large-scale reforms mistakes have correspondingly large devastating effects. Again, and underlining the thrust of the argument in this section, soft coordination make sense if we see it as a reflective mode of policy coordination, taking into account the many uncertainties that structural and large-scale reforms encounter or themselves create.

How can the OMC be explained by this political economy of reform approach?

The institutionalist explanation of OMC makes sense of two characteristics that the functionalist and the realist type of explanations have difficulties with: that it is a soft method and that it is an intergovernmentalist mode of integration. Moreover, it suggests that participation in OMC is bound to have a mixed record; it may have an impact in some policy areas but will not take place in others.

Why soft integration? After all, the earlier instances of using integration as leverage for reform applied hard law measures. The Internal Market Programme was brought about by the classic Community Method of policy harmonization initiated by the Commission and enforced by law. The Maastricht strategy followed a carrot-and-stick logic to enforce strict convergence and thus achieved the same goal of policy harmonization, if more by the ultimate sanction of being refused admission to EMU than by law as such. The most popular reason for 'softness' seems to be that the policies integrated by OMC are too diverse and 'politically sensitive' to be harmonized by hard law measures (e.g. Sabel and Zeitlin 2003: 23). Yet, in the heydays of overt Keynesianism, monetary and fiscal policies were diverse and considered sensitive areas in which self-determination was the profoundest expression of economic and ultimately political sovereignty. Experience of the arrival of EMU suggests that there is nothing that makes policies and thus national prerogatives inherently idiosyncratic. Political decisions and market forces determine how immune a policy area is to outside interference or spillovers.

It is less the inherent 'sensitiveness' of a policy area uncertainty that can account for the softness of OMC. Policy harmonization cannot be enforced when there is widespread uncertainty about the economic policy framework in the EU and welfare state reforms in member states, that is, uncertainty that to an unknown extent results from the process of integration itself. This situation is basically shared by all member states.[12]

Uncertainty starts with identifying the exact source of the need for reform. As regards economic policy coordination, how much does the EU need by way of additional institutions and how much can be left to spontaneous adjustment to signals from monetary policy? Regarding social policies, is it market integration, technological change, or socio-economic and demographic change that calls for welfare state reforms (Esping-Andersen 1999; Iversen and Cusack 2000)? Is there only one major source? If not, do measures that diminish pressure in some areas, for instance fiscal ones, lead to fewer or even more problems for reform efforts in other areas, for instance child poverty? Empirical cases do not provide the answer. There are economies which are admired for their employment record in the 1990s, like the US, the UK and Ireland, that persistently have high rates of poverty, especially of working poverty. Thus, are the quantity and the quality of jobs related by a trade-off or can the tax and transfer system make them complementary – up to a point, perhaps? And then there is uncertainty about the *finalité* of it all. Do we need a full-fledged fiscal federation in EMU in the long run or just more effective policy coordination? In social policy, do governments need to find reforms that suit their small worlds of welfare capitalism, or is there now only one Third Way to go in an integrated EU? In sum, there is uncertainty at every stage of the impending reform process, beginning with the identification of the problem and ending with the scope and depth of required changes. While these questions concern first and foremost domestic reform measures, they are also a matter of common concern, both triggered by integration and shaping that process. It is a situation of policymaking under 'deep uncertainty' (Lohmann 2000).

In such a situation, OMC can serve to organize learning of a particular sort.[13] If it is 'deep' uncertainty that EU governments face, it is unlikely that OMC will lead to policy transfer, which is a form of policy harmonization. Generally, an institutionalist approach cautions against the optimism of the policy transfer literature that a configuration of rules and practices can be 'exported' at all. Institutions such as wage bargaining arrangements or the networks of policy-making are deeply embedded in the social fabric and have created formal and informal entitlements to consultation or transfers. They have to become evidently dysfunctional before they become seriously challenged. Even if tried, because of institutional complementarity any transfer is likely to be partial and thus the same policy operates in a different way (Chalmers and Lodge 2003; Ferrera 1998). In a context of deep uncertainty, the interest in the experience of others is rather to narrow down the set of one's own possible responses along the lines: 'others faced comparable difficulties but did not go for that solution, so it's probably not a good idea.' Learning then is not about copying, but a screening device for ruling out untested options and observing available options tested elsewhere. Open Method Coordination ensures that this screening is memorized by a supranational organization and is therefore less likely to be forgotten when national governments change (cf. Rodrik 1996: 25).

Thus OMC of social policies allows for the simulation of a gradualist reform strategy by comparison. Member states need not implement a large-scale reform themselves but can analyse what this involves in a comparative exercise involving welfare states of similar development and/or institutional setting. That welfare states, even if similar, may choose different speeds can be explained by basically three factors (Roland 2000: ch. 2). Each highlights the potential value of OMC, in particular for reluctant reformers:

1   The nature of uncertainty that voters perceive to be generated by a particular reform. A status quo bias is created by idiosyncratic uncertainty, in particular reforms concerning directly redistributive policies. OMC of these social policies allows governments to wait for results of similar reforms in other countries and then go for it or propose a modified version to make it more acceptable to prospective losers.[14]

2   The effective heterogeneity of voters, which is determined by the significance of any opposition to change and the available opportunities to buy off this opposition. Open Method Coordination allows mobilization of the potential beneficiaries against domestic opposition, namely giving them international backing if weak at home, and identification of what it takes (or has taken in early reformer countries) to compensate the prospective losers.

3   The level of estimated reversal costs. These depend, for instance, on how vocal stakeholders of reform are or on how profound the required administrative changes will be – the higher these anticipated costs, the more status quo bias there is. OMC allows a country to 'free-ride' on the experience of other countries with lower reversal costs, that is, to observe what backtracking potentially implies without actually incurring reversal costs.

Open Method Coordination of social policies can thus overcome the status quo bias against reform by raising the option value of reversal through comparison and by allowing for selective participation to overcome inertia caused by idiosyncratic uncertainty. The comparative exercise may transform a situation of idiosyncratic uncertainty about the identity of winners and losers into one of aggregate uncertainty about the lucky or unlucky realization (namely in other countries), given that it is seen as a beneficial reform at all.

The BEPGs, by contrast, seem to respond more to aggregate uncertainty since they are concerned with macroeconomic and structural policies. The success of the supply-side reforms that OMC on economic policies organizes depends to a large extent on aggregate demand conditions, for instance the stage of the business cycle and the national fiscal stance. Faced with a bad outcome of domestic reforms that have been implemented elsewhere, a government may point to the payoff of these reforms if they have a good realization. Slow reformers win additional time, and in that sense the BEPGs allow for even more gradualism than aggregate uncertainty favours in any case.

Moreover, the BEPGs deal with the large-scale problem of ongoing reform processes by imposing a consistency constraint on each single sub-process – Cardiff, Cologne etc.[15] For social policies, this means that the envisaged reforms have to be justified as part of a comprehensive economic modernization effort. The primacy of the BEPGs also discriminates against certain reform options, for example, purely redistributive ones trying to achieve more equity at the cost of efficiency, since that would conflict with the goals of other processes. Or, positively stated, the constraint asks for reforms to be informative as regards their contribution to 'activation', making the reform of each country possibly a step in an ongoing process of economic modernization which, technically speaking, is equivalent to increasing the option value of reversal. The next section provides examples for this difference that the BEPGs make for the thrust of social policy reforms.

The explanation of its characteristic 'softness' entails why OMC is an intergovernmentalist mode of integration. It has been suggested that soft integration deals with the uncertainty that surrounds *domestic* reforms, be it the restructuring of the welfare state or adjustments to a new economic policy framework in EMU. Soft integration is thus a vehicle for these reforms, partly because it lends itself to portray these reforms as a 'matter of common concern' in line with a functionalist argument, partly because it is a flexible instrument that increases governments' room for manoeuvre in line with a realist account. In contrast to both, however, an institutionalist account makes us aware of the fact that the intergovernmentalist mode is not necessarily a – deplorable or welcome – triumph of member states over the Commission.[16] In a situation of policymaking under deep uncertainty, the Council at the helm protects 'Brussels' against the charge of 'dictating retrenchment' or 'imposing Social Europe', whatever the political orientation of the Eurosceptics is. Compared to the Community Method, the intergovernmental mode is less susceptible to campaigns against European integration launched by welfare organizations, trade unions or employers' associations if disappointed with the outcome. In this sense, the locus of control in OMC, the Council, acts as a kind of '*Sollbruchstelle*' or 'locus of planned breakdown' (Lohmann 2000). The Council is the part of a machine that takes the hit when it comes under stress to prevent greater and possibly irreparable damage to the machine at large. In this case, the machine is called 'European integration'. The Council can do so because it is ultimately the EU organization that is democratically legitimate and accountable (Hix 1999: 45–8, 180–7).

If this institutionalist explanation of OMC is plausible, observers should not be surprised that participation varies in the different areas where OMC is applied. If OMC is predominantly concerned with domestic reforms in a situation of deep uncertainty, the participation of non-state actors – and thus a stronger EU leverage – is sometimes but not always appreciated by governments. As noted above, if uncertainty is idiosyncratic, governments can take a wait-and-see attitude that may be productive to convince fearful potential losers by pointing to others' experiences. In contrast, if uncertainty is aggregate, the instrumental value of participation is not necessarily obvious to reform-minded governments with a technocratic leaning.

The subordination of OMC on social policies to the BEPGs also means that another consideration may play a role, namely the fiscal salience of the reform area involved. After all, the ageing of society and high rates of unemployment create budgetary pressures for reform. One would expect that, *ceteris paribus*, governments want to see less participation if large fiscal sums are at stake (cf. Moravcsik 2002: 608). They would welcome the participation of social partners or welfare organizations with a non-economic agenda, if the respective reform area is less driven by fiscal considerations than by concerns about social cohesion.

What is the evidence for this political economy explanation?

Any evidence on the alleged role of OMC for domestic reform processes needs to be preliminary at this stage. There is a particular difficulty for the institutionalist interpretation to show that OMC makes a difference. It was argued above that the exercise in 'comparative gradualism' which soft integration under idiosyncratic uncertainty allows is of particular value for slow or reluctant reformers. Conversely, we should also not be surprised if governments that are active in reforming a particular policy area at home, may not bother to coordinate that with – or ascribe that to – the EU-level exercise.[17] If that rationale of OMC holds, soft integration cannot have had much discernible impact yet.

Thus I will provide indirect evidence for the elements of my explanation that differentiate it from the two competing types of explanation. The first element is meant to motivate the soft and intergovernmental character of OMC. Member state governments seek to reform despite deep uncertainty about the depth and scope of their task. The second is the proposition that soft integration of policies is instrumental for economic reform. Finally, the third element is that participation in OMC is bound to have a mixed record across the different policy areas that are softly integrated.

Domestic reforms under conditions of deep uncertainty

The first element of my institutionalist explanation shows up in considerable reform activism of member states even before OMC was introduced but with no discernible impact of these reforms on the levels or the composition of social expenditure. Taken together, this suggests a preoccupation with domestic social welfare but a lack of direction in these atomistic efforts.

Boeri (2001) explores the intensity and direction of reforms in the area of employment protection legislation, non-employment benefits (including social assistance)[18] and pensions from 1986 to 1997. This is a time period before an OMC on employment was seriously implemented. Table 9.1 summarizes his findings in a crude quantitative way, namely by consolidating values of ±1 for marginal reforms and ±2 for 'radical' reforms, + if the reform increases the generosity of the system, − if it reduces it.[19]

Two results stand out; first the fourteen countries have undertaken roughly 200 reforms in a decade, that is, more than one reform per year and country. Such

Table 9.1 Welfare state reform intensity[a] and direction[b] before the Lisbon Council, 1986–1997

	Employment protection	*Non-employment benefits*	*Pension systems*	*No. of reforms[c]: restrictive (−), expansionary (+)*
Austria	−2	0	+5	(−): 7; (+): 11
Belgium	−1	−3	+1	(−): 8; (+): 6
Denmark	0	−3	−1	(−): 6; (+): 4
Finland	+1	−2.5[d]	−3	(−): 9; (+): 5
France	−5	−2	+1	(−): 10; (+): 5
Germany	+2	−1.5[d]	+1	(−): 9; (+): 11
Greece	+2	+2	−1	(−): 2; (+): 5
Ireland	−1	0	−1	(−): 7; (+): 5
Italy	0	+1.5[d]	−6	(−): 11; (+): 8
Netherlands	+3	−4	−2	(−): 8; (+): 12
Portugal	+4	+3	+3	(−): 2; (+): 10
Spain	+3	−3	0	(−): 6; (+): 5
Sweden	+2	−2	0	(−): 7; (+): 9
United Kingdom	+1	−5	−3	(−): 6; (+): 3
No. of reforms[c]	restrictive (−): 20 expansionary (+): 24	restrictive (−): 44 expansionary (+): 34	restrictive (−): 39 expansionary (+): 37	(−): 103; (+): 95

Source: Based on Bertola, Boeri and Nicoletti (2001: Appendix).

Notes
a ±1 for 'marginal' reforms, ±2 for 'radical' reforms.
b − for reducing, + for increasing the generosity of the system.
c Irrespective of the intensity of reform.
d ±0.5 for minor (marginal or radical) countervailing reforms.

activism hardly justifies the diagnosis of 'Eurosclerosis' as the notorious inability of the EU and its member states to change outdated arrangements. Second, most countries have undertaken reforms that are balanced as regards a restrictive and an expansionary stance. Only with respect to non-employment benefits, that is, expenditures on social inclusion, did most countries try to make the systems less generous.

Ditch and Oldfield (1999) support this latter finding for the narrower category of social assistance. Most countries were tightening 'consolidators', that is, they undertook marginal reforms that made existing eligibility criteria like work tests more stringent (e.g. France and Germany) or lowered benefit levels (e.g. Finland and Sweden) without changing the system. Of all EU countries, only Portugal sought to extend the provision of social assistance, starting from a very low base in 1993. Until the late 1990s, the UK was the sole 'innovator' in the EU, introducing a Family Credit, a New Deal for Lone Parents and a Jobseeker's Allowance, which together amounted to a coherent 'welfare to work' package.

The instrumental role for economic reform

As regards the second element of the explanation for OMC presented here. The difference that OMC makes is discernible. From its beginnings in the late 1990s soft social policy coordination has been constrained by fiscal considerations and the Lisbon strategy entails a deliberate thrust in favour of economic modernization.

Even before OMC came into practice, a levelling off of welfare spending can be observed as Figure 9.1 indicates.[20] The range of spending levels has slightly shifted upwards, from below 15 per cent of GDP (Portugal) and 30 per cent

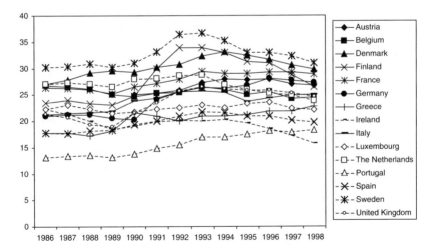

Figure 9.1 Changes in the level of social expenditure, 1986–1998 (percentage of GDP); Austrian data from 1990 only.

Source: OECD Social Expenditure Database, 2001.

(Sweden) to about 16 (Ireland) and 31 per cent (Sweden), respectively. With the exception of Portugal, we also observe little convergence of spending levels.

Thus governments tightened the fiscal constraint, presumably in the run-up to EMU, before soft integration started. This sequence suggests that OMC of social policies is not only formally, through Article 99 of the Treaty, subordinated to economic policy coordination by the BEPGs but has been effectively subordinated ever since its inception.

Other qualitative evidence supports this interpretation. The Lisbon strategy stresses that social policy has to be seen as a 'productive factor' which allegedly contributes to making 'the European economy the most competitive and dynamic knowledge-based economy in the world', including more and better jobs and social cohesion.[21] This wish-list should not distract from the apparent attempt to make social policies contribute to economic modernization (cf. de la Porte 2002; Pochet 2003).

- The Lisbon strategy pushes the 'activation' paradigm in the employment strategy, in particular urges discouraging early retirement or lowering marginal taxes for entrants into the labour market.[22]
- It pushes the 'welfare to work' paradigm in social inclusion policies, that is to condition the payment of transfers to able-bodied recipients on taking part in retraining programmes or working at low wages.
- In pensions it emphasizes the aspect of fiscal sustainability rather than considerations of, for instance, closing the gaps in old age security for citizens with irregular employment biographies.

All this indicates that economic reform lies at the heart of OMC. These shifts in emphasis were contested and not an inherent tendency of welfare states in the late twentieth century (Hemerijck and Schludi 2000; Schmidt 2000a). Unions and classical social democrats were not convinced easily that this is more than neo-liberalism with a human face, namely 'modernization' of the Third Way variety (Mosher and Trubek 2003: 71–3).

These results seem to indicate that OMC of both economic and social policies made a difference. First, it defined the main problem that reforms are supposed to tackle, namely unemployment or low employment intensity. Second, it gave a general thrust to welfare state reforms, namely 'activation'. While it would obviously require a monograph to prove, this interpretation has all the elements of McNamara's account of the evolution of the ERM (McNamara 1998: 64–71). The reform activism indicates that there was a perception of policy failure ('Eurosclerosis' or inability to reform) and governments felt a need for reform; to overcome the inertia of institutions and further sustained reform, an 'ideational turn' was required. An alternative paradigm of activation and inclusion, or 'Third Way', became available in the mid-1990s. This paradigm drew attention when some countries (Denmark, the Netherlands, the UK) were doing better in the area of employment, although in very different ways.

The case of the UK underlines how selective this perception and contrived the problem definition in the Lisbon strategy is. While the Beveridge system is indeed a role model for well-targeted, moderate social expenditure and high employment intensity, the UK does not do well on most other indicators such as poverty, income inequality or old age security (Hemerijck and Schludi 2000: 202–5). Thus it is not said that the UK can be considered to be among the so-called 'best pupils in class'.

Mixed record of participation

The third element of the explanation offered above shows up in that, for the time being, participation seems to vary positively with the relevance of status quo bias and negatively with the strength of fiscal motives for the reform effort. The stylized facts about participation, that is, consultation on or even involvement in formulating the reform agenda across the four policy areas, are as follows (de la Porte 2002; Pochet 2003):

• Participation is most intense in the Open Method on inclusion.
• In OMC of employment policies, participation is less intense but improving, owing to rising interest of social partners.
• No broad participation has been foreseen in the Open Method on pensions but there seem to be some successful attempts by interested organizations to get access.
• Economic policy coordination along the BPEG is virtually closed to non-state actors.

This ranking of participation corresponds with the importance of idiosyncratic uncertainty and thus the relevance of any status quo bias. Reforms of non-employment and employment benefits are least predictable as regards the identity of winners and losers, except that they are likely to affect lower to middle income, wage dependent households disproportionately. Open Method Coordination of inclusion and employment policies allows governments facing vocal opposition to these policies to free-ride on the experience of front-runners and adjust their proposals without risking getting stuck after the first wave of reforms. Pension reforms are fairly predictable as regards the distribution of gains and losses between young, middle-aged and retired citizens. Since the intended effects will show up only in the long term, aggregate uncertainty is of less relevance and can do little to recommend the gradualism that OMC provides for. The status quo bias here is not generated by uncertainty but by opposing interests. Finally, the BEPGs try to align reforms of redistributive, structural and macroeconomic policies, each of which will have winners and losers. The technical and complex nature of this exercise makes it unlikely; however, that idiosyncratic uncertainty of voters is a big obstacle to implementation.

The ranking of participation is negatively correlated with the fiscal significance of the respective policy area as Figure 9.2 indicates. Overall economic policy coordination is virtually closed, with only weak consultation of labour market parties. Participation is allowed and encouraged where there is little at stake in

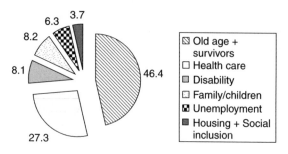

Figure 9.2 Social benefits by group of functions, in EU-15 2000.

Source: Eurostat – ESSPROS.

Note
As percentage of total social benefits. Eurostat reports social benefits in gross terms; that is, taxes or other compulsory levies payable by beneficiaries are not deducted.

fiscal terms, above all unemployment benefits (6.3 per cent of total social benefits in EU-15 countries) and social inclusion (smallest share with 3.7 per cent). Pensions, along with health and disability, are the most expensive social welfare programme (46.4 per cent of all social benefits); consequently the soft integration of reforms is not very open.[23] Other factors may determine how open the respective Open Method is. An institutionalist explanation cautions against the expectation that OMC is the hallmark of a new form of inclusionary policy-making. Nor does it dismiss any significance of interest group mobilization at the EU level.

Conclusion

Integration once served to preserve the substance of national policies in the presence of interdependence (Milward 2000: ch. 1). This is what functionalist and realist theories grasp. They have difficulties, however, making sense of soft coordination that has been expanded to a number of policy areas, in particular in the area of social welfare which was notoriously resistant to European integration. This chapter argued that this points to a profound change in the underlying motivation for policy integration and has called for a different method to achieve it.

Integration has become a device to foster *change* of national policies by *creating* interdependencies. The latter dynamic is not fully reflected in the study of European integration yet. The pretext of economic reform is what drives recent advances in the integration of economic and social policies. If political economy approaches were once seen to be enlightening because economic integration was perceived to lie at the heart of European integration (Jones and Verdun in this volume), they are now relevant to understand this twist in its dynamic. The political economy explanation given in this chapter proposes that economic modernization now lies at the heart of recent attempts at social policy integration in the EU. Economic modernization gives a direction to profound changes that governments have tried to bring about in their respective welfare states for some time before they eventually agreed to softly coordinate these domestic reform efforts.

Profound and interdependent reforms of various social policies amounts to policymaking under 'deep uncertainty' (Lohmann 2000). Applying insights of a recent political economy literature on large-scale institutional reform (e.g. Roland 2000), the chapter argues that in such a situation OMC provides an instrument to emulate 'gradualism by comparison'. Gradualism is able to overcome a status quo bias against domestic reforms created by uncertainty about the identity of those who gain or lose in the process. Participation may or may not be helpful to overcome this bias, which is why OMC handles participation variably and opportunistically. The difference that OMC has already made to welfare state reforms is that it recasts the tasks ahead in terms of employment-intensive economic modernization and the thrust of ongoing reforms as one of 'activation'. It is an intergovernmentalist mode of integration but as such protects the Commission against blame-shifting by member states. Thus, as long as member states need to reform national welfare systems fundamentally, we are likely to see OMC being applied to instrumentalize integration for these domestic agendas as well as the Commission to be proactive in making soft integration work. This would amount to a sea change indeed, given how long it took member states to overcome their resistance to social policy integration and given the Commission's scepticism against the Open Method until very recently.

Notes

1 I am most grateful for constructive comments from the editors, as well as from colleagues at the LSE, notably Damian Chalmers, Kevin Featherstone, Martin Lodge and Imelda Maher.
2 The website of the European Union Center at the University of Madison-Wisconsin lists at the time of finalizing this paper (October 2003) some 90 papers (URL: http://eucenter.wisc.edu/OMC/).
3 Following Chalmers and Lodge (2003), OMC is here used as a generic term since there is no such thing as *the* Open Method *of* Coordination.
4 As regards pensions, OMC is in the process of being fully developed. A first joint report, accepted by the Spring Council in 2003, did not contain common indicators; another report is scheduled for late 2004 (Pochet 2003: 12).
5 Cf. TEC Art.128 for the European Employment Strategy which so far is the only OMC of social policies with a treaty base. The BEPG is a particularly telling example for this difference, discussed below.
6 Cf. Esping-Andersen (1990), Ferrera (1998), Pierson (2001), Scharpf and Schmidt (2001a).
7 See Verdun and Cowles in this volume, chs 1 and 2 and Rosamond (2000) for a comprehensive discussion of integration theories in political science. The authors quoted below are not necessarily general proponents of either approach but their particular explanations for OMC fall into one of these two admittedly broad categories.
8 Consequently, the institutionalist analysis of Pierson (1994) found that Thatcherism and Reagonomics achieved precious little welfare state retrenchment, which was not due to a lack of resolve.

9 In this endeavour to find a theoretically consistent explanation, my analysis obviously follows a general social science or 'American' approach and refuses an area studies or 'European' methodology (cf. Verdun in this volume, ch. 1).

10 For a critique of this logic at work in fiscal policy coordination under the SGP, see Schelkle (2002).

11 Very accessible are Rodrik (1996) and the contributions in Williamson (1994), while two textbook treatments require more literacy in reading economic models (Drazen 2000: ch. 13; Roland 2000: ch. 2). This literature is truly impressive, analysing phenomena considered to be beyond the reach of rigorous study and empirical generalization until recently. Yet it is based on the assumption that policy-makers know the optimal or at least welfare-improving reforms (Drazen 2000: 403). The analysis can thus concentrate on the question why Pareto-superior reforms may not be adopted. This helps to establish an academic division of labour with economists but, as I argue below, is an assumption that presumes too much certainty for the reforms that motivate OMC.

12 Sabel and Zeitlin (2003) document how this has thrown 'left' and 'right' positions on the welfare state into disarray. In contrast, Margaret Thatcher went for flexible integration and opted out of the Social Protocol of the Maastricht Treaty because she was convinced that this was bad for UK employment, while all other member states had expressed interest in taking a social chapter into the treaty (Falkner 1998: ch. 3).

13 The objective of learning is itself mentioned in the Lisbon Conclusions on the Open Method and most authors who write on OMC mention it. Some concentrate on this aspect, for example, de la Porte *et al.* (2001) and Radaelli (2003). Bulmer and Padget (2003) explore how OMC may contribute to policy transfer.

14 The existing welfare administration is naturally also affected by idiosyncratic uncertainty, and OMC, in particular the bureaucratic reporting exercise that it is above all, can also be seen as an instrument to tackle institutional inertia of domestic administrations (cf. Ross 2000: 17–18 on the importance of bureaucratic politics).

15 The Cardiff process coordinates policy implementation and reforms in product and capital markets to complete the internal market. The Cologne process provides a consultative forum to observe wage developments and the policy mix between the monetary stance and fiscal policies. Cf. Directorate-General Economic and Financial Affairs (2002: 8–11) for the treaty base of this statement and Atkinson (2002: 626–7, 633–5) on the effective coupling of social policy with economic goals since Lisbon.

16 It is interesting to note that the Commission has cautioned against further extension of Enhanced Cooperation in a communication to the Constitutional Convention (Scharpf 2002: fn. 18), while it has apparently overcome its initial reluctance with respect to the Open Method, as documented in the White Book on Governance, and is now active in propagating OMC (Pochet 2003).

17 Cf. Atkinson (2002: 629) on Ireland's and Germany's poverty strategy. More generally, Ross (2000: 15 and fn. 20) suggests that it is not clear how much effective change there is; Mosher and Trubek (2003: 73–6) conclude from the finding of impact studies of the European Employment Strategy that the officially acknowledged or observable impact on national policies varies widely, say between countries like the Netherlands (none but good performance), Italy (some) and France (considerable and acknowledged).

18 Non-employment benefits include unemployment benefits but also transfers in cases of early retirement, disability or maternity leave.

19 Reforms are classified 'radical' if they increase/decrease a subsidy by more than 10 per cent or if they change the structure of the system for permanent workers ('insiders'). For details, see Boeri (2001: 11–13). The measurement is crude because countervailing reforms can offset each other *numerically*. Thus an entry of 0 may hide the fact that the country has undertaken a number of reforms but in opposite directions. Luxembourg has been left out because information on this small city state was available only for employment protection.

20 A look at the composition of social expenditures reveals that spending on old age cash and health plus sickness benefits has gone up in a majority of countries. The balance is roughly even for expenditures on family benefits and social inclusion, the latter covering most 'non-employment benefits' in Table 9.1.

21 A key sentence in the Lisbon conclusions reads: 'The Union possesses...social protection systems able to provide, beyond their intrinsic value, the stable framework required for managing the structural changes involved in moving towards a knowledge-based society' (Council 2000: point 3).

22 The German government, for instance, did just the opposite after German unification and is now reversing this in its 'Agenda 2010'.

23 Health care reforms are about to be softly integrated in the Lisbon specification and that will be an interesting case to watch: fiscal salience suggests that participation will be rather selective, as with pensions; but idiosyncratic uncertainty surrounding health care reforms suggest an important role for the 'gradualism by comparison' that OMC provides.

10 The political economy of European integration in a spatial model

Robert Pahre[1]

Abstract: While most of the other contributors to this volume argue for combining research broadly across paradigms, this chapter argues that modest syntheses are likely to be more productive. To demonstrate this, I develop a synthesis of two distinct research traditions within the rational choice paradigm, endogenous policy theory and spatial theory. The resulting theory helps explain the domestic political foundations of European integration, many of which are familiar to the literature. Second, and less familiar, the theory generates hypotheses about some ways that European integration transforms domestic politics. In particular, I show that European integration makes governing parties more likely to exclude Eurosceptic or Europhobic parties. European integration also fosters elite-mass divisions in Eurosceptic parties and movements, with elites favouring greater integration than the rank-and-file in their parties.

Introduction

> He saw distinctly now that though Metrov's ideas might perhaps have value, his own ideas had value too, and their ideas could be made clear and lead to something only if each worked separately in his chosen path, and that nothing would be gained by putting their ideas together.
>
> (Leo Tolstoy, *Anna Karenina*)

The study of the European Union (EU) seems doomed to fall between two stools. As an intergovernmental organization, the EU originally belonged to the field of international relations. However, more than half of all legislation in domestic parliaments now stems from EU politics in one way or another, making the EU a central part of domestic politics best studied in comparative politics. Making the choice to deepen European integration is often grounded in domestic political economy, but at the same time deeper integration reshapes that domestic political economy, thereby transforming domestic politics in Europe.

The EU also sprawls across disciplinary divides. Its centrepiece has been political economy, with a customs union, common agricultural policy, and competition policy as the longest-standing elements of union. Understanding these policies requires study of political economy, an interdisciplinary hybrid that – whatever its challenges – at least has the advantage of being familiar.

More recently EU studies have also been buffeted by interparadigmatic divides. Though political economy provides its policy foundations, much of the motor force for integration can be traced to idealistic proponents of the European idea. These dual forces produce tensions between the largely rationalist paradigms dominating political economy, such as Marxism and public choice, and non-rationalist paradigms such as constructivism or post-structuralism.

Given these persistent divisions, it is natural for scholars to be sensitive to the methodological pluralism of the field and to argue for greater communication across these divisions. In this volume, for example, Jones and Cowles both argue for convergence of approaches and for bridging gaps between paradigms. Many other contributors agree that scholars should work to synthesize apparently incompatible research traditions. Since any research tradition must be incomplete, it is always tempting to take two such traditions and try to merge them, filling in some of the holes left by each.[2]

The most obvious problem with this approach is that the resulting synthetic tradition will also be incomplete, as any logical system must be. By trying to combine statements from two distinct traditions, this synthesis will also face the challenge of identifying and then resolving inconsistencies between the two traditions. Synthesizing neoliberal institutionalist and constructivist explanations, for example, may appear attractive at the surface for explaining (say) creation of the euro, but it leaves unresolved deep conflicts about ontology and epistemology, among others. Even if the interparadigmatic synthesis seems plausible and consistent in its surface claims, it is very hard to verify that all the assumptions underlying each paradigm (see Kuhn 1996) are consistent with each other. The resulting study is likely to be superficial and to abandon the analytic power available within either well-developed tradition.

This is not to say that synthesis is impossible. However, synthesis is most likely to succeed not at the level of metatheory or even a full paradigm, but in narrow subfields whose very concreteness allows scholars to set aside many larger questions (see *inter alia* Dogan and Pahre 1990). These narrow areas need not be related, as the application of Newton's law of gravity to international trade theory illustrates (Pahre 1996). I maintain only that the advantages of specialization apply not only to a single field but also to synthesis across boundaries (Dogan and Pahre 1989). Narrowness, not interparadigmatic metasynthesis, is key for scientific advance.

In this chapter, I argue for such a narrow synthesis and then develop the synthesis that I advocate. My objects are two distinct traditions within rational choice theory, endogenous policy theory (EPT) and spatial theory. To outsiders these probably seem very similar to one another. Their origins are very different, however, as is their use by scholars today. Endogenous policy theory is a product of economics, found especially among international economists who examine the politics of tariffs (endogenous tariff theory). EPT has not really been used to study the EU. Spatial theory has been developed by Americanists in political science, though it dates to the economist Anthony Downs's application of the Hotelling problem to party competition. It has also provided the foundation for the theory of two-level games in international relations (Putnam 1988), which scholars have successfully applied to both the European Union and the United States, among other countries.

The reasons for seeking synthesis are straightforward. Spatial theory takes politicians' preferences as given. As a result, it is plagued by indeterminacy whenever we analyse more than two or three actors bargaining over more than one or two policy dimensions – the number of possible preference configurations to analyse simply grows too large. In contrast, EPT provides a solid foundation for understanding politicians' preferences but it has a weak conceptualization of political interaction (Nelson 1988), an issue at the heart of spatial theory. Spatial theory is also independent of political economy, while EPT is a theory political economy *par excellence*. Developing political economy foundations for spatial theory therefore holds substantial promise for a political economy of the EU.

I apply the synthesis to two problems, one old and one new. The old problem is the political economy foundations of cooperation in the EU. In that section I also briefly discuss the delegation problem by which the member states delegate some tasks to the European Commission or other organs. Though the theoretical form of my argument may be unconventional, the underlying logic will be familiar to scholars of the EU. This familiarity helps make the overall argument more plausible.

The newer problem is the question of how membership in the EU affects domestic politics. I am particularly interested in how domestic opposition to European integration becomes manifest in Euroscepticism, and how Eurosceptics may or may not be represented in government. This section uses illustrations from several EU countries, but I give special attention to the cases of Austria and Slovakia. These are understudied countries in the field of EU studies, though each has attracted significant attention in recent years due to the demagogic politics of charismatic politicians, Jörg Haider and Vladimír Mečiar. Slovakia is also interesting because it is the only Central or Eastern European country ever to have had Europhobic parties as part of a government coalition (Kopecký and Mudde 2002: 317). These two countries provide a congenial focus for comparative study because they are neighbours, one a member and the other a candidate member,[3] both with multiparty parliamentary systems and one or more strong Eurosceptic parties. Both held elections in fall 2002, with politics exhibiting many of the features that I predict. The way in which Haider and Mečiar have tried to reconcile their underlying hostility to the EU with the needs of coalition politics will provide a central focus for the final sections of this chapter.

Spatial models

Spatial models of policy have become an increasingly common way to examine politics of the EU. These models treat policy as the choice of a point in space, with the point usually defined by its coordinates in a small number of dimensions. For example, one might treat the Left–Right policy dimension in Europe as a line, with social democratic positions to the left of the origin and Christian democratic positions to the right, and other party positions arrayed around and between these points. A second common policy dimension in EU studies is European integration, with policies and parties arrayed on a dimension from Euroscepticism to enthusiastic integrationists. Interestingly, parties' positions on integration are not monotonically related to their Left–Right position, since it is generally true that centrists favour more integration than more extreme parties on either the Left or Right (Aspinwall 2002; Sitter 2001; Taggart 1998). Specific policy areas, such as strict/relaxed environmental protection or tight/loose money, could also be modelled in this way.

Strongly discontinuous policies fit this framework less easily. However, many seemingly discontinuous policies may be less discontinuous than they seem. For example, legal sovereignty seems dichotomous and therefore discontinuous: a state is either sovereign or it is not. Sometimes people mobilize against any diminution of their country's sovereignty. Such views may be found among Eurosceptics. Yet every state has its effective sovereignty diminished to a greater or lesser degree: some decisions about the polity are effectively made outside it. Eurosceptics who appreciate this point argue that the cost of further reductions of sovereignty may be more than they are willing to pay. This kind of reasoning acknowledges that sovereignty is effectively a continuous policy dimension.

Spatial theories of politics are largely rationalist (relaxed somewhat in Hinich and Munger 1994, among others). Every actor has an ideal policy and evaluates other policies in terms of the distance from this point. Each actor prefers policies closer to its ideal point over policies farther away. *In such a model, actors must decide whether to change policy away from the status quo (or reversion point).* With some simplifying assumptions, applying the model can be a matter of basic geometry.

The field of EU studies has seen two major uses of the spatial model idea. The first is largely empirical. For example, scholars have tried to uncover the major policy dimensions over which members of the European Parliament or other decision-makers struggle (Aspinwall 2002; Noury 2002). The emerging consensus seems to be that both Left–Right and integrationist dimensions play a significant role, with other dimensions important only idiosyncratically for certain countries, parties, or periods. This contrasts with similar analyses of US politics over two centuries, where a single dimension dominates, supplemented only occasionally by a second dimension (Poole and Rosenthal 1985).

Other empirical studies in the spatial tradition have examined the policy positions of national parties and/or publics in order to understand the ratification of certain EU treaties or decisions in national legislatures or referenda (Hug and König 1999; König and Hug 2000; König and Pöter 2001). These studies have demonstrated the usefulness of spatial theory for explaining decisions and could easily (and confidently) be used for predicting referenda results.

The second major use of spatial theory has been theoretical, especially in the study of 'two-level games' (Putnam 1988). Two-level theory views governments as positioned between domestic society and the international system, and interacting with other actors in both of these realms. The major application of two-level theory to the EU has been the study of how governments obtain domestic ratification of their agreements with other governments (Milner 1997; Moyer 1993; Pahre 2001; Schneider 2000; Schneider and Cederman 1993). As one would expect, there has been significant overlap with the empiricists discussed above who are also interested in the ratification problem. Research has now begun to move into other areas, such as domestic implementation of European commitments (Martin 2000), or the formation of governing coalitions that anticipate negotiations over EU affairs (Pahre 1997).

A second area of theoretical research has been the interaction between national-level governments and supranational actors such as the European Commission. Garrett and Tsebelis (1996, Tsebelis 1994, Tsebelis and Garrett 2001) have given substantial attention to the legislative process in EU bodies, with their theories attracting both substantial criticism and refinement (Crombez 1996, 1997, 2002; Hösli 1993, 1995, 1996; Moser 1996a,b). These theories have elaborated the conditions under which actors such as the European Parliament or the European Commission may affect policy outcomes.

These more theoretical works face a challenge in that models become indeterminate very quickly when there are several policy dimensions, and become complicated very quickly when there are more than a few actors. One debate, between 'intergovernmentalists' represented by Madeleine Hösli (1993, 1995, 1996), and 'supranationalists' led by Geoffrey Garrett and George Tsebelis 1996, Tsebelis 1994, Tsebelis and Garrett 2001, hinges in part on whether any given distribution of preferences is as likely as any other. The agenda-setting powers of the European Parliament are also highly contingent and depend on how frequently we find particular constellations of preferences in the real world (Kreppel 2002). It would be helpful to show theoretically that actors and their preferences tend to be constrained in some way.

The next section pursues this agenda. I argue that in many political economy applications the preferences of any two states will indeed be structured in a particular way. Legislative and executive preferences may also be patterned in a predictable way, though the dependence of the executive on parliamentary majorities in most European systems complicates this claim somewhat.

The spatial model of policy in two countries

The political economy of institutions, whatever the perspective, routinely emphasizes how institutions privilege some interests at the expense of others. For example, upper houses in many countries over-represent rural interests and therefore give greater weight to conservative values, right-of-centre parties and agricultural interests than do lower houses.

It is easy to overlook the fact that political boundaries have a similar effect, biasing some interests over others. People who live outside a boundary do not vote, so any interests they have are ignored in the political system within those boundaries. For example, American cities routinely impose hotel taxes on guests far in excess of local sales taxes – which hotel guests also pay – because hotel guests do not vote. Visitors to a city receive discriminatory treatment because it is in the interests of residents to tax them more harshly.

Such political discrimination plays a fundamental role in the political economy of the EU. Pre-integration policies have all been chosen at the national level by political processes limited to those people living within the boundaries of a single nation-state. Each nation-state routinely ignores the effects of its economic policies on foreigners. For example, tariffs impose costs on both foreigners and domestic consumers, while providing benefits to domestic producers and taxpayers. Because they ignore foreign producers' interests in low tariffs, politicians set tariffs higher than the globally optimal level.[4]

This tariff problem has been well analysed in the spatial theory of policy and provides a point of departure for other policy problems. Figure 10.1 follows other presentations of trade policy problems in two dimensions (Mansfield *et al.* 2000; Milner 1997; Milner and Rosendorff 1995; Pahre 1998, 2001). In this case, two countries (A and B) each choose an autonomous trade policy. Each actor's ideal foreign tariff is zero and each favours a positive home tariff because of protectionist lobbying. Country A has the ideal point $\{t_A, 0\}$ and B has the ideal point $\{0, t_B\}$. A and B each choose their ideal domestic tariff, yielding a status quo or non-cooperative outcome at $\{t_A, t_B\}$.

For simplicity, I will assume that utility is a negative function of the distance from the outcome of the game to this ideal point, so that indifference curves are circles around each player's ideal point. In a more elaborate model, the indifference curves would be ellipses because home tariffs are more important than foreign tariffs to each government.

Each country's tariff imposes externalities on the other because the costs of the tariff are paid in part by foreign exporters. This economic fact has political significance in that foreign governments will want to negotiate home tariffs downwards, since these foreign governments' constituents receive no benefit,

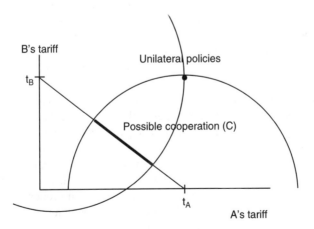

Figure 10.1 The tariff problem.

either economic or political, from these home tariffs. The home government will have a similar interest in negotiating foreign tariffs down. Because of this shared interest in removing the political externalities of domestically set tariffs, A and B can always negotiate some cooperative agreement C (Pahre 1998). The possible outcomes of this game make up the 'win-set', agreements that A and B could rationally make.

In summary, this analysis establishes the basic political economy of foreign economic policy in a spatial model. Two countries each choose a policy that harms the other, and have an incentive to negotiate that policy in a direction conducive to both. Domestic political economy creates an incentive for European integration.

Though I have used tariffs as an illustration, the same pattern of preferences is found in most areas of economic policy. If Ireland and France set corporate tax rates at dramatically different levels, neither considers the interests of voters in the other country. Irish politicians are not concerned that low taxes may reduce the tax base of the French welfare state, to the detriment of French pensioners. For their part, French politicians do not consider the interests of Irish workers in attracting higher-paid manufacturing jobs and raising the country's standard of living to French levels.

In tax policy as in trade policy both countries benefit from at least some mutual policy adjustment. This mutual adjustment (or political convergence) takes into account the interests of Irish citizens in French taxes and French citizens in Irish taxes, even if differences of opinion remain. Indeed, because of differences in preferences between French and Irish voters, we would expect different tax rates even after some convergence.[5]

This analysis can easily be translated into the spatial theory of policy. Consider a policy that is under national control in countries A and B (policy P and regulation R, respectively). Country A will set P 'too high' in global terms because it does not consider B's interests.[6] Equivalently, country B's ideal value of P will be lower than A's ideal. Similarly, B's policy R will be set too high unilaterally, and A's ideal value of R will be lower than B's on that dimension. We can illustrate this situation in a generic spatial model of political economy, shown in Figure 10.2. This figure bears an obvious similarity to Figure 10.1, showing the similar logic of the familiar tariff game and a variety of other political economy problems in a spatial model.

Applied to these other policy issues, the model captures well one of the core reasons for European integration. Before political integration, the countries of Europe would choose policies that had economic and political externalities for other countries. Now these policies can be addressed, and externalities reduced or eliminated, within a framework of European cooperation and political integration. For example, such concerns were written into Article 99, paragraph 1, of the Amsterdam Treaty, which states that 'Member States shall regard their economic policies as a matter of common concern and shall coordinate them within the Council.'

The framework may also translate to other, non-economic issues. Jones and Verdun's introduction argues that political economy offers useful tools not only in

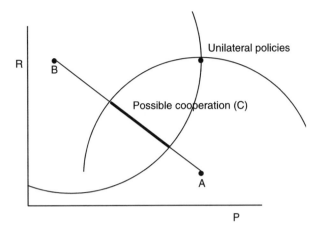

Figure 10.2 The generic policy problem.

the typical political economy fields of study, such as trade or monetary integration, but also for areas in which the political and economic overlap is less obvious, such as foreign policy or social policy. The spatial model here requires only some negative externalities of each country's policy on another, such that everyone in the home country cares less about those externalities than do people in the other country.[7] For example, French cultural policy may have negative externalities on the cultural development of other Francophone countries (Belgium and Luxembourg), creating some incentive for cultural integration.

This simple model also accounts for the logic behind the principle of subsidiarity that is supposed to guide European integration (de Búrca 1999). Though far from consistently honoured in practice, subsidiarity does establish the principle that the Union should act only when policy has effects across national boundaries that can be addressed through common action. In terms of the framework here, cooperation should occur only when there are externalities of one country's policy on others. These are essentially the same conditions.

Implications for politics in Brussels

Though this theory of political economy helps understand both European economic integration and the principle of subsidiarity, many questions remain. For example, the framework does not explain why the member states chose to delegate powers to the Commission instead of setting policy themselves. Presumably principal–agent theory (Garrett 1992; Kassim and Menon, ch. 3 this volume; Pollack 1999) can provide an explanation within this framework. This section will speculate about what a principal–agent model might produce in this framework.

Let us accept the claim that the member states have chosen to delegate policy to the Commission. This delegation makes sense only if the members would expect the

Commission to implement some policy close to the cooperative point C in the model of the previous section. Granting these assumptions, several points follow.

Proposition 1. The European Commission will favour general interests over the particular interests of individual nations.   Delegating power to the European Commission makes sense only if its preferences are close to the cooperative point C. This point entails dropping some policies that favour national-level groups at the expense of people in other countries. The European Commission should not have this bias and should favour policies that do not discriminate between persons of different countries.

Proposition 2. The European Commission will favour eliminating national rules that impose costs (negative externalities) on the citizens of other member states.   This proposition follows from the first one and has several implications for particular policy areas. First, the European Commission will want to eliminate tariffs and non-tariff barriers to trade between member states. The logic behind this proposition should be familiar from the political economy of tariffs analysed above. Second, the European Commission will favour a strong competition policy. A domestic monopoly or oligopoly benefits home producers and harms both home and foreign consumers. While these costs and benefits may be politically beneficial for a home government, foreign governments do not benefit from the rents earned by the uncompetitive practices of home firms. Cases of imperfect competition should therefore attract the Commission's ire. Third, the European Commission will oppose regional and industrial subsidies from member nations to their own regions and firms, even if the Commission favours making its own regional and industrial subsidies. Quite simply, the Commission does not (and should not) trust the political economy of member states to intervene in markets in ways that do not harm people in other member states. However, the Commission will see itself as capable of making the proper trade-offs between (say) French and German interests.

Proposition 3. Notwithstanding Proposition 2, the European Commission will favour European interests over outsider interests.   The Commission is not a philosopher-king looking out for global welfare, but an actor firmly embedded in the political economy of the EU. Like any other political actor, it privileges those persons inside its boundaries over those outside. For example, we should *not* expect the Commission to take a generally free-trade stance, since this position would give weight to the interests of foreign exporters – even though the Commission takes a free-trade stance with respect to the internal market. Political economy, and not ideology, drives the Commission in this framework.

These claims seem reasonably falsifiable and yet generally consistent with the behaviour we observe in the EU. For some people, these claims may even seem hopelessly obvious. After all, the European Commission was created as guardian of the treaties and thus as a representative of the collective interest. The propositions simply clarify some ways in which the Commission should view that collective interest.

Viewed differently, however, it is not obvious *why* the Commission should have been created in this way. The Commission could have been a partisan actor, with preferences systematically on the Left or the Right, or it could have been a delegate of powerful actors such as the Franco-German condominium, or it could have been a neutral mediator between national interests such as the Secretary-General of the United Nations and the executives of many other international organizations. These options still seem plausible to many. For example, Tsebelis and Garrett (2000) discuss a variety of constellations of preferences for EU actors in which some of these roles can be seen.

My argument is different and stronger. The role and preferences of the Commission are grounded in the political economy of integration and are thus *systematically biased* in a certain direction. Specifically, the Commission will want to reduce policies with cross-border effects within the EU because those effects were not considered in the political process when those policies were made at the national level. These preferences are not an idiosyncratic feature of the EU and are not simply one preference ordering among many other possible orderings. Instead, the biases of the Commission are a natural result of the structure of preferences in any such situation.

Whatever their use, these claims about the Commission are secondary to the main goal of this chapter. These claims should establish the plausibility of the spatial model of political economy that I advance here. My central focus, however, is the relationship between domestic political economy and the politics of the EU. Having established the domestic political foundations of the EU, I now turn to some ways in which this political economy also shapes domestic politics in the member states.

Implications for eurosceptic parties and coalition government formation

Though the model so far assumes that domestic political actors care more about the political economy within their borders than outside them, it does not require that all these actors value them in the same way. In fact, we would expect people to have different valuations of the same outcomes. These differences in utility provide one of the reasons why political parties have different policy preferences. The differences that provide the foundation for my analysis are between parties that value European integration highly ('Europhile') and those that value it slightly ('Eurosceptic') or not at all ('Europhobe'), categories that I will define later.

This section examines the politics of government coalition formation in an environment dominated by cooperation with other member states of the EU.[8] It applies best to that majority of European countries with parliamentary forms of government and without single-party majority governments. The analysis here should not apply to politics in Great Britain, Malta, or other countries with majoritarian politics.

Consider three parties with different evaluations of the EU. Figure 10.3 retains the same illustrative policy dimensions as in Figure 10.2 but allows people in

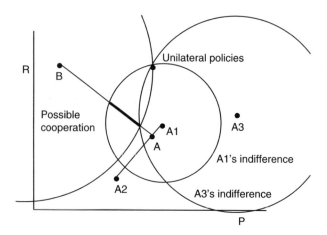

Figure 10.3 Eurosceptic parties and European integration.

country A to disagree over these policies. All three parties in A want higher levels of home policy (P) than does B, so all their ideal points are to the right of B's ideal point. In addition, all three parties want fewer foreign regulations (R) than does B, so their ideal points lie below B's.

For example, country A may want higher barriers to asylum seekers at home: that is, higher P. Yet everyone in A would like lower barriers in B (lower R), so that foreigners seek asylum in B instead of in A. Despite this common national interest, the three parties in A have very different ideal policies, which means that they disagree about which asylum rules the country should have. Party A3's ideal points are most distant from everyone else's, and we would recognize that party as facing greater difficulties in agreeing with others. Let us call A3 a Eurosceptic party. In terms of the current terminology of the field (Taggart and Szczerbiak 2002, among others), it would be a 'soft' Eurosceptic party that would reject many but not all forms of integration that other parties would accept.

Suppose that two Europhile parties form a coalition, which then negotiates deeper integration with the EU. Figure 10.3 shows such a case, with pro-EU parties A1 and A2 forming a coalition government at A that negotiates integration with B along the heavily shaded contract curve.[9] I have drawn the figure so that A3 would reject all but one point on this contract curve, though A3 would accept some agreements in the lens extending to the south of the unilateral equilibrium. In such an environment, either all three parties in A prefer the cooperative point C to the unilateral policy Q, or A3 prefers Q to C while A1 and A2 prefer C to Q.

Now consider negotiations over a new government, after elections for example. If A1 and A2 form a coalition, European integration does not present any issue, since both prefer C to Q. European integration is also not an issue if A3 prefers C to Q, much as A3 might prefer a lower degree of integration (that is, in the lens

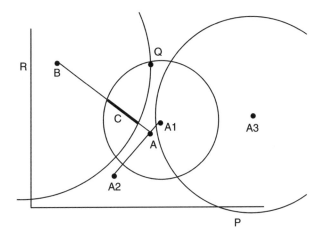

Figure 10.4 Eurosceptics that reject existing integration.

in Figure 10.3). In these cases, the Euroscepticism in A3's party platform would not affect its coalition behaviour.

The negotiations are more complicated if A3 prefers Q to C, as shown in Figure 10.4. Suppose that it wants to negotiate a possible new government with either A1 or A2. I assume that there are some benefits available to coalitions outside this figure, such as other issues or the benefits of office-holding. If A3 wants a coalition to reject C in favour of the unilateral policy Q, it will have to offer either A1 or A2 some additional gains in these other non-EU issues, since A1 and A2 can always form a coalition with one another in which they would not have to forgo the utility gains of C. By raising the cost of a coalition with A3, this logic makes A3's entry into the government less likely than it otherwise would be. This means that

Proposition 4. Eurosceptic parties are less likely to join governing coalitions than are Europhile parties. European integration offers utility gains to political actors above and beyond those available from domestic politics, since European integration also affects the policy of other member states. Parties that forgo these utility gains are more expensive coalition partners and are therefore less likely to be invited to join a government.[10]

We see these forces at work in both Austria and Slovakia. Austria's most Eurosceptic party is the Freedom Party (Freiheitliche Partei Österreichs, FPÖ). It has traditionally included a centrist, market-oriented wing and a xenophobic right wing that traces its intellectual heritage to the Nazis and other German national-ist parties before them (Bailer *et al.* 2000; Manoschek 2002; Ötsch 2000: ch. 3; Schorske 1961; Wodak 2000). The right wing has dominated the party since Jörg Haider took over the leadership of the party in 1986, and this leadership has also moved the party against the EU in 1993 (Plasser and Ulam 2000; Rauscher 2000; Zöchling 1999).

For over a decade, Haider was unacceptable as a coalition partner (*regierungsunfähig*[11]) for both the People's Party (Österreichische Volkspartei, ÖVP) and the social democratic SPÖ (Sozialistische, later Sozialdemokratische Partei Österreichs). This unacceptability stemmed from several considerations, notably the racism of the Nazi past and the issue of European integration. Though immigration into Austria comes mostly from post-Communist countries, Austrians associate it with the EU – with some reason, since the accession process certainly helped encourage this flow and these post-Communist countries' membership in the EU will make these migrations unstoppable after a transition period. The EU is therefore very much entwined with the issues of xenophobia and racism in Austrian political life. Haider himself has linked foreigners in Austria to the EU (Ötsch 2000), so that the Euroscepticism that I emphasize is intimately connected to the xenophobia that attracts foreign media attention.

The ÖVP later relaxed its opposition to forming a coalition with the FPÖ. Its chairman, Wolfgang Schüssel, came to believe that working with Haider was the only way that the ÖVP could escape being a permanently junior partner in SPÖ governments. The ÖVP nonetheless expected the FPÖ to make major policy concessions on the EU and human rights as a precondition to forming a coalition.

In the elections of 1999, the FPÖ managed to earn barely more votes than the ÖVP, becoming the second-largest party in the country for the first (and only) time. The ÖVP and FPÖ eventually agreed on a government in which the ÖVP would serve as the senior member though it was marginally the smaller party. Schüssel became Chancellor, and Haider remained formally outside the cabinet though the FPÖ's members tended to be close associates of his (for the time being).[12]

Given widespread concern over this government, President Thomas Klestil – a member of the ÖVP with a long-standing dislike of both Schüssel and Haider – required that the coalition treaty include a preamble reaffirming core principles of Austria's political order. Alongside democracy, human rights, and non-discrimination, the preamble committed both parties to continued membership of the EU and support for enlargement (Tancsits 2001). While other issues such as racism have also affected the politics here, the FPÖ's difficulties in joining coalitions is clearly consistent with the logic of Proposition 4, as is Klestil's requirement that the FPÖ affirm its support for the EU.

Debates over the EU have also been central to coalition politics in Slovakia, presenting a fundamental cleavage between government and opposition.[13] The government of 1998–2002, essentially re-elected in 2002, is a broad coalition of many pro-democracy parties from across the political spectrum. These governing parties can be classified easily on the conventional Left–Right dimension found in Europe and elsewhere, and these parties are generally members of the corresponding international party federations such as the Socialist or Liberal International (Pridham 1999).[14] They were joined in 2002 by ANO (Alliance of the New Citizen), a new and somewhat unconventional media-based party of the centre-right.

The opposition consists of right-wing parties: HZDS (Hnutie za demokratické Slovensko, Movement for a Democratic Slovakia), led by former Prime Minister Vladimír Mečiar, and the SNS (Slovenská narodná strana, Slovak Nationalist Party). Robert Fico, currently the most popular politician in the country, leads another unconventional party, Smer ('Direction'). Though often labelled rightist, Smer includes elements from the ex-Communist Party of the Democratic Left (Strana demokratickej l'avice, SDL). These three unconventional parties employ rhetoric contemptuous of 'politics as usual' and often use demagogic techniques of political mobilization that rely heavily on nationalistic appeals. However, Smer fits somewhat uneasily here, less nationalistic than the other two, more willing to take concrete policy stances (see http://www.strana-smer.sk/program), and much more acceptable as a coalition partner to the conventional parties.

All parties except for SNS officially support Slovak membership in both the EU and NATO, and all give much stronger support for the EU than for NATO (see Kopecký and Mudde 2002: 313–15). However, it is not clear how sincere this official position is in the case of HZDS, especially for NATO. The different attitude towards NATO reflects lingering anti-NATO sentiment from the Communist period, groups that find neutrality on the Austrian model attractive, and close ties between some groups and the Russian Federation and/or its petroleum sector. Both the multiparty government coalition and international observers have clearly acted as though HZDS (much less SNS) membership in a government would be tantamount to rejection of the European and Atlanticist lines of recent Slovak foreign policy. Even in the public euphoria after the 2003 Slovak referendum favouring EU membership, Prime Minister Dzurinda accused some parties who had supported membership, such of the HZDS, of having done so insincerely ('Dzurinda vyhlásil').

In Slovakia, much of the politics around the election of 2002 concerned which parties were acceptable to the governing parties and to the EU. Robert Fico invested significant time in presenting himself to the West so that outsiders would not label him unacceptable before the elections. During the campaign, he categorically excluded a coalition with the HZDS under Mečiar, saying that this leadership has 'no coalition potential' (Haughton 2002). Fico also emphasized this position in visits with American congressmen, and with Slovak President Rudolf Schuster.

After the doubts of the mid-1990s, re-election of the Dzurinda coalition government in 2002 confirmed Slovakia's position in the mainstream of post-Communist democracies. The division between government-eligible, pro-EU parties seems likely to persist. Smer will probably remain in an ambiguous position, theoretically acceptable as a potential coalition partner at the elite level, despite its Euroscepticism, but also a magnet for opposition to the EU at the mass level. More overtly nationalist opponents of the EU, especially the SNS and (ambiguously) the HZDS, will be condemned to opposition roles.

In both Austria and Slovakia, then, opposing the EU imposes a heavy cost in terms of a party's coalition possibilities. These costs are not an absolute bar, as the FPÖ's participation in government shows, but it is instructive that the FPÖ had to affirm support for the EU in order to join the 2000 government. Smer and perhaps an HZDS without Mečiar may also be coalitionable, but at a significant policy cost. Certainly HZDS will have to decide how to play the EU and NATO issues now that Slovakia will be joining both organizations.

My explanation of why anti-EU parties tend to be out of government differs significantly from others, which treat the relationship as a spurious result of centrist politics. For example, Aspinwall (2002: 106) argues that pro-integration centrists are elected more often, and are more likely to form governments because consensus (PR) systems are biased toward centrist parties. The literature divides on this question, but many associate centrism with Europhilia, extremism with Europhobia and Euroscepticism (see among others Martin and Stevenson 2001). This alternative claim would be unable to explain why a centrist Eurosceptic party, such as Denmark's 'Radical Left' (Radikalt Venstre, RV), would typically find itself outside government in the 1970s and 1980s (Pahre 1997).

Other key evidence for my framework is the fact that centrism and Europhilia do not necessarily go together in countries lacking parliamentary coalition dynamics, such as the United Kingdom or Malta (and perhaps France). These countries fall outside the theory here, since coalition formation is central to the model. Aside from Malta, these majoritarian countries would be anomalous for theories linking the Left–Right spectrum to Euroscepticism. As far as I know, no one has yet identified the presence or absence of parliamentary coalitions as a variable affecting Eurosceptic party behaviour.

The elite-mass cleavage in Eurosceptic parties

The politics of coalition formation may stretch beyond the interparty negotiations sketched out in the previous section. The analysis above assumes some benefits outside the integration policy dimensions from joining a coalition government. These benefits could lie in other policy areas, or they could stem from the benefits of office-holding to the party's elite. This section examines how the benefits of office-holding combine with the political economy of integration in a spatial model to produce elite-mass cleavages of a certain type. I argue that we will observe parties with a pro-integration leadership and anti-integration mass membership, but will not observe the reverse type of party, with anti-integration leaders of pro-integration masses.

This argument rests on the assumption that the leadership and the masses have different preferences over government membership even if they have the same preferences over policy. The rank-and-file in a party will receive any policy benefits that the elite obtain in a coalition treaty, but only the elite receive the benefits of office-holding.[15] Presumably the party leadership considers both policy and office-holding gains when it decides to enter a coalition.

This analysis of the preferences of the leadership versus the masses helps explain an otherwise puzzling regularity in elite attitudes across Europe. If only policy mattered, both ordinary members and the leadership of a party should have a similar distribution of preferences on policy matters. Disagreements over policy will naturally occur within the leadership as in the membership at large, but there is no a priori reason to expect different ranges or distributions of policy preferences. However, only the leadership can enjoy the non-policy perks of office, so it will value joining the governing coalition more than the membership does. If faced with a choice between joining a pro-integration government and remaining hostile to the EU in opposition, it is entirely possible that the leadership will find the utility of coalition greater than that of opposition, while the rank-and-file prefers opposition, *even if they have the same preferences over policy.* In other words,

Proposition 5. We may observe parties in government with a pro-European leadership and Eurosceptic membership, but will not find parties with a Eurosceptic leadership and pro-Europe mass membership in parliamentary coalition systems. This claim depends on the argument in the previous section that Eurosceptic parties are less likely to join government coalitions, combined with the assumption that leaderships are more likely to value joining the government for personal, office-holding reasons.

We find this pattern most frequently among the Social Democratic parties in Europe. In Sweden, for example, 40 to 50 per cent of the Swedish Workers' Party (Svenska Arbeiderpartiet, SAP) are Eurosceptic despite the pro-European orientation of the leadership. About two-fifths of the party electorate may defect in elections to the European Parliament, voting mostly for the Eurosceptic Left (Vänstra) instead. Austria's Denmark's, and Germany's Social Democratic Parties, among others, exhibit a similar, if smaller, cleavage.

In Austria, the SPÖ includes a sizeable wing that suspects that labour mobility in the EU will threaten Austrian jobs, especially after enlargement. Not surprisingly, this wing is often associated with the trade unions and with the chambers of labour. In contrast to these mass reservations, the leadership has been consistently pro-European.

The FPÖ faces similar divisions between its electorate and some of its leadership. These divisions have racked the party internally because Haider remained outside the government and formally renounced the leadership of the party, while more pragmatic elites took over important roles in the government. Ironically, these divisions mirror those in the SPÖ, from which the FPÖ seems to have taken many of its more fickle voters in the 1999 election.

The FPÖ's cabinet members seem to have 'gone native' while in government, moving toward many of the establishment policies that their party had long decried out of office. From his position as prime minister of Carinthia (Kärnten), Haider has been free to criticize his own ministers as sell-outs on many issues, and the EU became an arch-enemy for him (Ötsch 2000: ch. 5). If we assume, quite reasonably, that these cabinet members valued office-holding to some degree, it is not surprising that a cleavage would emerge between them and non-office-holders such as Haider and much of the mass electorate. Even a strong Haider loyalist such as Vice-Chancellor Susanne Riess-Passer found that she had differences of opinion with her good friend 'Jörgi' when she was in office. These internal FPÖ divisions eventually drove the government apart in 2002, as Schüssel decided it would be propitious to humble the FPÖ in new elections.

We find similar splits in Slovakia's less stable polity. In a young party system such as Slovakia, dissidents regularly defect from parties to form new parties. Much of the factionalization revolves around personalities and EU policy does not seem to be any more or less important than any other issue in generating party divisions.

When the EU is an issue, however, it always has effects in the direction that we would expect. As the HZDS leadership tried to convince Slovaks and outsiders of the party's support for the EU in the lead-up to the 2002 elections, it stirred up domestic Euroscepticism and Europhobia. Party leaders such as Mečiar have been willing to take a more European line since it has become clear that support for the EU is a precondition for joining the government. The mass membership of the party has been much less likely to change its views in response to such considerations. HZDS's efforts to become acceptable for participation in government therefore came at heavy internal cost, ultimately producing a split in the party during the run-up to the 2002 elections.

Smer has a similar split. Though favouring EU membership, Smer's opposition role and 'alternative' rhetoric allow it to appeal to Eurosceptics. Like many opposition politicians in other accession countries (cf. Szczerbiak 2001 for Poland), Fico argued for a harder bargaining stance, with a list of 'untouchable national interests' (Meseznikov 2002: 88). As a result, Smer includes many Eurosceptic masses despite a pro-EU leadership.

Fico's former party, the SDL, also appeals to a substantial number of Eurosceptic voters. SDL supports EU membership and is an attractive coalition partner in the centre-left of the political spectrum, but it has significant Eurosceptic voters (Henderson 2001: 21). In short, even the more confused and factionalized politics of Slovakia is consistent with the proposition.

Throughout Europe, the reverse cleavage, with a Eurosceptic leadership and pro-integration mass membership, is not found in countries with regular parliamentary coalitions.[16] Britain would be an exception because both Eurosceptic and Europhile leaders have appeared at the head of each of the two major parties since membership. However, Britain does not fit the assumptions of the theory here because it is a majoritarian system that does not face the problems of coalition formation found in most other parliamentary democracies.[17] Government membership therefore does not depend on an EU litmus test in these countries. The same kind of Eurosceptic leadership with more Europhile mass is found in Malta, where coalition governments are also mostly unknown. The Maltese Labour Party attracted many fewer votes than usual in 2003 when it campaigned on an explicitly anti-membership platform. The fact that Eurosceptic leaderships of pro-integration parties occur only where the assumptions of the model do not apply is strong circumstantial evidence in favour of the logic identified here.

Euroscepticism and opposition electoral appeals

In a liberal democracy, elites who consistently pursue policies contrary to the wishes of a large share of their electorate risk the wrath of that electorate. This seems to be the case for those parties with the elite-mass cleavage, especially as European integration becomes more important to the public. As a result, we should expect

Proposition 6. Governing parties with a split between leadership and masses on the EU the EU will lose votes to anti-EU parties who are excluded from the government. When voters have alternatives, especially opposition parties that have chosen not to compromise their Eurosceptic principles in order to join the government, they will eventually choose those alternatives. The EU therefore provides a particularly salient issue for opposition parties. It allows them to exploit a natural division between elites and masses, in hopes of attracting disaffected members away from the pro-integration policies of their leadership (Sitter 2001; Taggart 1998).

In the late 1990s, Austrian workers who opposed the EU had to turn to one of two non-governing parties, the Greens or the FPÖ. The SPÖ lost votes to the FPÖ in particular, who could exploit themes of opposition. Indeed, the FPÖ campaign in 1999 emphasized the need for '*Reform*' and '*Wende*' (a change of direction) in Austria. The change was possible because, when out of government, the FPÖ could criticize a series of policies associated with the EU, including immigration.

The Austrian case is particularly instructive since any interpretation of politics on a purely Left–Right dimension would expect SPÖ dissidents to register their protests by voting for the Greens instead of leaping rightward over the ÖVP and landing on the FPÖ. This vote for the Greens did not happen because the Austrian Greens generally support European integration (see http://www.gruene.at/pdfs/wahlprogramm.pdf). On this matter, they resemble the German Greens but differ from the Nordic Greens. In the analysis here, this pro-European stance made the Greens unattractive for Eurosceptic masses in the SPÖ electorate, who voted for the FPÖ instead.[18] In this respect, the Austrian Social Democrats face a challenge very different than that found in Denmark or Sweden.

The importance of this protest vote became especially visible in the 2002 elections. After fighting a mistake-prone campaign,[19] in which it emphasized its hostility to foreigners, immigrants, and the Czech Republic, the FPÖ lost well over half its support. Its protest voters left the FPÖ once it joined the government. Having compromised its principles on Europe (and other issues), the FPÖ could no longer appeal to SPÖ working-class voters on that issue. Out of government, the SPÖ also gained some flexibility on the EU issue, which helped paper over its internal divisions. As a result FPÖ support moved most of the way back to its base level of under 10 per cent. The ÖVP leaped past both of its major rivals to become the largest party in Austria for the first time in decades.

The new government represents a significant humbling of the FPÖ, with an 'unacceptable' turncoat as Finance Minister and FPÖ ministers relegated to minor ministries such as culture or sport. *The Economist* ('The same peculiar team', 1 March 2003) describes FPÖ participation in terms that treat office-holding and the EU issue as two different issues:

> with his [Haider's] influence down, the main aim of his disgruntled colleagues is, it seems, to cling to whatever jobs in government they may be offered. Moreover, though many Freedom Party voters remain xenophobic and hostile to the EU, the party itself no longer threatens to veto the EU's enlargement to the east, nor could it do so if it tried.

Of course, the theory here links the office-holding motive to the leadership's changed position on the EU, at least in part. Interestingly, history seems to be repeating itself. As I write this in 2003, divisions over the EU may have contributed to the split between Haupt, the formal party leader and deputy prime minister for about a year, and his mentor Haider.

The arguments in this section follow from the fact that the EU is different from other issues. Elites might ignore mass preferences on any issue in order to join the government and obtain the benefits of office-holding. Leaders compromise beliefs all the time as part of the coalition formation process. What makes the politics of the EU different is the systematic bias in favour of pro-integration parties joining the government. This stems from the fact that a pro-European position gives a domestic party some leverage not only over domestic policy but also over the policies chosen by other European countries. Party leaderships who wish to join the government therefore face systematic pressure to adopt a certain kind of policy (pro-European) and systematic pressure against other kinds of (Eurosceptic) policies. This means that mass-elite cleavages do not appear haphazardly, as they do on the EU issue in Britain. Instead, mass-elite cleavages on the EU issue in parliamentary democracies will always have leaderships more integrationist than their followers.

Conclusions

This chapter has presented a synthesis of political-economy and spatial approaches within the rationalist paradigm. For those outside rationalist traditions, it presents a cautionary tale. Any serious effort to 'bridge gaps' requires that scholars go beyond picking a few claims from incompatible traditions and juxtaposing them inside a simple narrative on the EU. Instead, it requires some attention to fundamentals and theoretical synthesis from the ground up.

My chapter is self-consciously 'American' in Amy Verdun's terms (see Verdun, Ch. 1 this volume). I place EU studies solidly within general theories of IPE and show how political economy concerns convert to a spatial model. However, the positive political economy approach here allows for variety in preferences, specificity in institutions, complexity as far as one wants it, and uniqueness. It insists on using a common method to examine unique institutions and processes, but I would argue that this use of a common method is preferable to using induction to study unique events. It is impossible to generalize to other events from inductive study of an allegedly unique topic and just as impossible to bring in insights from the study of other issues.

The narrow synthesis here is clearly progressive in a Lakatosian (1970) sense, predicting new facts without (apparently) losing insights of the two underlying perspectives. Of course, its very narrowness leaves many questions unanswered. Like many rationalist accounts of politics, this chapter has focused on institutions and institutionally governed areas of politics. Following most political economy models, I have emphasized distributional questions over informational issues. This means that I have neglected institutions with primarily oversight functions such as the European Court of Justice or the European Court of Auditors. Symbolic issues are similarly excluded.

I have also downplayed other factors. For example, corporatism in Austria and elsewhere breeds the growth of protest parties. These protest parties often find Euroscepticism congenial, using it to attack the Europhile establishment. The consensus politics of corporatism lie outside the model, except insofar as the model requires parliamentary coalitions.

Though the theory illuminates the basic logic behind integration in general, I have emphasized several propositions about how European integration changes domestic politics. The bulk of my propositions focus on the growing divide between pro-integration governing elites and dissidents both in the governing parties and in the opposition. The result is a narrowing of political perspectives within government and within the spectrum of political parties in opposition. This narrowing highlights differences with the broader range of views among the public and doubtless contributes to public alienation from the political establishment.

One could criticize this effect of the EU as undemocratic in shutting out certain mainstream political views – namely, scepticism about the European project – from participating in government. Viewed differently, the familiar 'democratic deficit' of the EU appears not only in Brussels but in stifling certain aspects of national-level politics.

Notes

1 I would like to thank Doug Dion and the editors for comments on this chapter. Of course, any errors are my responsibility.
2 Indeed, any logically consistent set of statements must be incomplete by Gödel's Theorem. For fuller analysis of communication between two scholarly fields, each conceptualized as a system of propositions incompletely describing the world, see Pahre (1996).
3 Slovakia became a member of the EU as of May 2004.
4 Economists routinely assert that the globally optimal tariff level is zero, but my reasoning suggests that tariffs will be too high even if the globally efficient tariff were nonzero for some reason.
5 Phrased differently, neither competitive pressures nor convergence should produce a 'race to the bottom' as long as preferences differ (see among others Rodrik 1997).
6 I label the unilateral policy as 'too high' for convenience and by analogy to tariffs. As the corporate tax illustration shows, some policies may be 'too low'. In such cases, we can just reverse the direction of the axis so that the unilateral policy again looks 'too high'.
7 The framework does not work in the case of positive externalities, in which France's unilateral policy has beneficial side effects for Germany. Such cases do not create much of an incentive for policy coordination, since the non-coordinated set of policies are already mutually beneficial.

8 Because I do not model the process formally, this section does not draw explicitly from the literature on coalition formation in parliamentary democracies, but is certainly informed by it (Laver and Shepsle 1990; Martin and Siverson 2001; Pahre 1997; Strom 1990).

9 I assume that the coalition government negotiates as a unitary actor with an ideal point A, which we may think of as the policy of the coalition treaty; however, parties A1 and A2 must also prefer the agreement to the unilateral policy, so that their indifference curves also constrain the agreement. With the preferences shown, A1's preferences are constraining while A2's are not, so I do not show A2's indifference curve.

10 Note that any hard Eurosceptic party that refuses to compromise with country B on principle would completely forgo these utility gains. As a result, it is even less likely to join the government than a soft Eurosceptic party.

11 Translation is 'incapable to govern'.

12 Formation of this government led to 'sanctions' against Austria freezing bilateral political ties between the other fourteen member states and the Austrian government, but not affecting the participation of Austria or Austrians in EU organs. These sanctions provide a notable subject in themselves but lie outside the focus here (see Fleischhacker 2001; Manoschek 2002; Winkler 2001).

13 Much of this information comes from interviews in Bratislava in June 2001 and June 2002. See Henderson (2001, 2002) and Meseznikov (2002) for an overview of Slovak political parties, Gyárfášová and Velšic (2002) for an overview of public opinion, Bil ík (2001) for Slovakia's negotiations with the EU, and www.sme.sk/volby for 2002 electoral data.

14 The array of governing parties is bewildering. In 1998–2002, the largest party, SDK, was in fact a coalition of four parties (the KDH, DS, LDÚ, and SZS) that gradually left the party coalition (but not the government), leaving a rump SDKÚ in the place of the former SDK. It was joined in government by the SDL, SOP, and the SMK (itself a coalition of Hungarian-speaking parties across the political spectrum).

15 This elite would include cabinet and sub-cabinet level people as well as anyone who benefits from their patronage at lower levels of government (or business). Obviously, patronage systems such as the Austrian *Proporz* give the party rank-and-file some personal benefits from government membership.

16 The Netherlands saw some tactical Eurosceptic positioning of traditionally pro-EU parties in response to the rise of Pim Fortuyn before the elections of 2002, but these positions seem not to have persisted.

17 France also seems to be moving toward a majoritarian system of Socialists and the Union for a Presidential/Popular Majority/Movement. If this occurs, divisions over the EU may come to follow the more haphazard British pattern.

18 However, many professionals and middle-class SPÖ loyalists have moved to the Greens, in part out of frustration with the SPÖ's moves toward Haider's anti-immigration position. In 1999, 58 per cent of Green voters said that they had chosen this party 'because it is engaged against hostility to immigrants and against right radicalism' [weil sie engagiert gegen Ausländerfeindlichkeit und gegen Rechtsradikalismus eintrete] (Pelinka 2000: 64). Green leader Alexander van der Bellen is also highly regarded by many Austrians across the political spectrum, and is often identified as the most respected politician in Austria. As a professor of economics, he also appeals to highly educated professionals, who often find the left-libertarianism of Green parties attractive in any case (see Kitschelt 1995: ch. 1).

19 The party had trouble finding someone willing to lead the party in the campaign, for it had expelled four of its promising cabinet members and many other leading candidates hesitated to lead the party into an electoral debacle. The first peak candidate, Mathias Reichhold, had a nervous breakdown during the campaign and had to withdraw in favour of Herbert Haupt, an unimpressive functionary and Haider loyalist who has since been replaced.

Bibliography

Abbott, K.W. and Snidal, D. (2000) 'Hard and Soft Law in International Governance', *International Organization* 54(4): 421–56.

Abbott, K.W. and Snidal, D. (2001) 'International Standards and International Governance', *Journal of European Public Policy* 9(3): 345–70.

Ahmad, Z.H. and Ghoshal, B. (1999) 'The Political Future of ASEAN after the Asian Crisis', *International Affairs* 75(4): 759–78.

Albonetti, A. (1963) *Préhistoire des Etats-Unis de l'Europe*, Paris: Editions Sirey.

Altvater, E. and Mahnkopf, B. (1993) *Gewerkschaften vor der europäischen Herausforderung*, Münster: Westfälisches Dampfboot.

Anderson, P. (1980) *Arguments within English Marxism*, London: New Left Books.

Anderson, S. and Eliasson, K. (1993) *Making Policy in Europe*, London: Sage.

Armstrong, K. and Bulmer, S.J. (1998) *The Governance of the Single European Market*, Manchester: Manchester University Press.

Arts, B., Noortmann, M. and Reinalda, B. (eds) (2001) *Non-State Actors in International Relations*, Aldershot: Ashgate.

Aspinwall, M. (2002) 'Preferring Europe: Ideology and National Preferences on European Integration', *European Union Politics* 3(1): 81–111.

Aspinwall, M.D. and Schneider, G. (2000) 'Same Menu, Separate Tables: The Institutionalist Turn in Political Science and the Study of European Integration', *European Journal of Political Research* 38(1): 1–36.

Atkinson, T. (2002) 'Social Inclusion and the European Union', *Journal of Common Market Studies* 40(4): 625–43.

Austen-Smith, D. (1992) 'Strategic Models of Talk in Political Decision Making', *International Political Science Review* 13(1): 45–58.

Axelrod, R. (1984) *The Evolution of Cooperation*, New York: Basic Books.

Bailer, B., Neugebaur, W. and Schiedel, H. (2000) 'Die FPÖ auf dem Weg zur Regierungspartei. Zur Erfolgsgeschichte einer rechtsextremen Partei', in H.-H. Scharsach (ed.), *Haider: Österreich und die rechte Versuchung*, Reinbek bei Hamburg: Rowolt Taschenbuch Verlag.

Baldwin, D. (1971) 'Money and Power', *Journal of Politics* 33: 578–614.

Beck, U. (2001) *What is Globalization?* Cambridge: Polity.

Berger, P.L. and Luckmann, T. (1966) *The Social Constructivism of Reality: A Treatise in the Sociology of Knowledge*, London: Penguin Books.

Berger, S. and Dore, R. (eds) (1996) *National Diversity and Global Capitalism*, Ithaca: Cornell University Press.

Bergman, T., Müller, W.C. and Strøm, K. (2000) 'Parliamentary Democracy and the Chain of Delegation', *European Journal of Political Research* 37(3): special issue.

Bertola, G., Boeri, T. and Nicoletti, G. (eds) (2001) *Welfare and Employment in a United Europe: A Study for the Fondazione Rodolfo Debenedetti*, Cambridge, MA and London: MIT Press.

Bieler, A. and Morton, A.D. (eds) (2001) *Social Forces in the Making of the New Europe: The Restructuring of European Social Relations in the Global Political Economy*, Houndsmill: Palgrave.

Bieling, H.-J. and Deppe, F. (1996) 'Internationalisierung, Integration und politische Regulierung', in M. Jachtenfuchs and B. Kohler-Koch (eds), *Europäische Integration*, Opladen: Leske & Budrich.

Bieling, H.-J. and Steinhilber, J. (2000a) 'Einleitung', in Bieling and Steinhilber (eds), *Die Konfiguration Europas: Dimensionen einer kritischen Integrationstheorie*, Münster: Westfälisches Dampfboot.

Bieling, H.-J. and Steinhilber, J. (2000b) 'Hegemoniale Projekte im Prozess der europäischen Integration', in Bieling and Steinhilber (eds), *Die Konfiguration Europas: Dimensionen einer kritischen Integrationstheorie*, Münster: Westfälisches Dampfboot.

Bil ík, V. (2001) 'Slovenská cesta do Európskej únie – vývin po vo bach 1998', *Integrace*, http://integrace.cz/integrace.

Bleich, E. (2003) *Race Politics in Britain and France: Ideas and Policy-Making since the 1960s*, Cambridge: Cambridge University Press.

Boeri, T. (2001) 'Introduction: Putting the Debate on a New Footing', in Bertola, Boeri and Nicoletti (eds), pp. 1–20.

Börzel, T.A. (1998) 'Organizing Babylon: On the Different Conceptions of Policy Networks', *Public Administration* 76: 253–73.

Börzel, T.A. (2002) 'Non-State Actors and the Provision of Common Goods: Compliance with International Institutions', in A. Héritier (ed.), *Common Goods: Reinventing European and International Governance*, Lanham, MD: Rowman & Littlefield, pp. 155–78.

Börzel, T. and Risse, T. (2002) 'Die Wirkung internationaler Institutionen: Von der Normanerkennung zur Normeinhaltung', in M. Jachtenfuchs and M. Knodt (eds), *Regieren in internationalen Institutionen*, Opladen: Leske & Budrich, pp. 141–81.

Bowles, P. (2002) 'Asia's Post-crisis Regionalism: Bringing the State back in, keeping the (United) States out', *Review of International Political Economy* 9(2): 230–56.

Bowles, P. and MacLean, B. (1996) 'Understanding Trade Bloc Formation: The Case of the ASEAN Free Trade Area', *Review of International Political Economy* 3(2): 319–48.

Branch, A.P. and Øhrgaard, J.C. (1999) 'Trapped in the Supranational Dichotomy: A Response to Stone Sweet and Sandholtz', *Journal of European Public Policy* 6(1): 123–43.

Breuning, M. (1995) 'Words and Deeds: Foreign Assistance Rhetoric and Policy Behavior in the Netherlands, Belgium, and the United Kingdom', *International Studies Quarterly* 39: 235–54.

Bulmer, S. (1994a) 'Institutions and Policy Change in the European Communities: The Case of Merger Control', *Public Administration* 72(3): 423–44.

Bulmer, S. (1994b) 'The Governance of the European Union: A New Institutionalist Approach', *Journal of Public Policy* 13(4): 351–80.

Bulmer, S. (1997) 'New Institutionalism, the Single Market and EU Governance', Arena Working Papers 97/25, Oslo: ARENA.

Bulmer, S. and Padget, S. (2003) *Policy Transfer in the European Union: An Institutionalist Interpretation*, Paper presented at the ESRC conference 'Policy Learning and the New European Governance', London, 23 May 2003.

Burley, A.-M. and Mattli, W. (1993) 'Europe Before the Court: A Political Theory of Legal Integration', *International Organization* 47(1): 41–76.

Cafruny, A.W. and Ryner, M. (2003a) 'Preface', in Cafruny and Ryner (eds), *A Ruined Fortress? Neoliberal Hegemony and Transformation in Europe*, London: Rowman & Littlefield.

Cafruny, A.W. and Ryner, M. (2003b) 'Introduction: The Study of European Integration in the Neoliberal Era', in Cafruny and Ryner (eds), *A Ruined Fortress? Neoliberal Hegemony and Transformation in Europe*, London: Rowman & Littlefield.

Callinicos, A. (1987) *Making History: Agency, Structure, and Change in Social Theory*, Cambridge: Polity Press.

Caporaso, J.A., Marks, G., Moravcsik, A. and Pollack, M.A. (1997) 'Does the European Union Represent an *n* of 1?', *ECSA Review* 10(3): 1–5.

Carr, E.H. (1981 [1939]) *The Twenty Years' Crisis: 1919–1939*, London: Papermac (Macmillan).

Chalmers, D. and Lodge, M. (2003) *The Open Method of Co-ordination and the European Welfare State*, CARR Working Paper 11, London: Centre for Analysis of Risk and Regulation, LSE.

Checkel, J.T. (1997) 'International Norms and Domestic Politics: Bridging the Rationalist–Constructivist Divide', *European Journal of International Relations* 3(1): 473–95.

Checkel, J.T. (1998) 'The Constructivist Turn in International Relations Theory', *World Politics* 50(2): 324–48.

Checkel, J.T. (1999a) 'Social Construction and Integration', *Journal of European Public Policy* 6(4): 545–60.

Checkel, J.T. (1999b) 'Norms, Institutions, and National Identity in Contemporary Europe', *International Studies Quarterly* 43: 83–144.

Checkel, J.T. (2001a) 'The Europeanization of Citizenship?', in M.G. Cowles, J.A. Caproaso and T. Risse (eds), *Transforming Europe: Europeanization and Domestic Change*, Ithaca: Cornell University Press, pp. 180–97.

Checkel, J.T. (2001b) 'Why Comply? Social Learning and European Identity Change', *International Organization* 55(3): 553–88.

Christiansen, T., Falkner, G. and Jørgensen, K.-E. (2002) 'Social Science Theory and EU Treaty Reform: Beyond Diplomacy and Bargaining', *Journal of European Public Policy* 9(1): 12–32.

Christiansen, T., Jørgensen, K.-E. and Wiener, A. (1999) 'The Social Construction of Europe', *Journal of European Public Policy* 6(4): 528–44: special issue. Christiansen, Jørgensen and Wiener (eds).

Cini, M. (2001) 'The Soft Law Approach: Commission Rule-Making in the EU's State Aid Regime', *Journal of European Public Policy* 9(2): 192–207.

Clark, A.-M. (1995) 'Non-Governmental Organizations and their Influence on International Society', *Journal of International Affairs* 48(2): 507–25.

Clark, A.-M., Friedman, E.J. and Hochstetler, K. (1998) 'The Sovereign Limits of Global Civil Society', *World Politics* 52(1): 1–35.

Clement, W. and Myles, J. (1994) *Relations of Ruling: Class and Gender in Postindustrial Societies*, Montreal–Kingston: McGill–Queen's University Press.

Clement, W. and Williams, G. (1989) 'Introduction', in Clement and Williams (eds), *The New Canadian Political Economy*, Kingston, Ont.: McGill–Queen's University Press.

Cocks, P. (1980) 'Towards a Marxist Theory of European Integration', *International Organization* 34(1): 1–40.

Coen, D. (1997) 'The Evolution of the Large Firm as a Political Actor in the European Union', *Journal of European Public Policy* 4(1): 91–108.

Cohen, B.J. (1998) *The Geography of Money*, Ithaca: Cornell University Press.

Colas, A. (2002), 'The Class Politics of Globalisation', in M. Rupert and H. Smith (eds), *Historical Materialism and Globalisation: Essays on Continuity and Change*, London: Routledge.

Coleman, J.S. (1990) *Foundations of Social Theory*, Cambridge, MA: Harvard University Press.

Collester, J.B. (2001) 'How Defence "Spilled Over" into the CFSP', in M.G. Cowles and M. Smith (eds), *The State of the European Union*, vol. 5, Oxford: Oxford University Press, pp. 369–89.

Commission of the European Communities (2000) *The European Community's Development Policy*, COM (2000) 212.

Commisssion of the European Communities (2001a) *Draft Joint Report on Social Inclusion. Communication from the Commission to the Council, the European Parliament, the Economic and Social Committee and the Committee of the Regions*, COM(2001) 565 final, Brussels, 10 October 2001.

Commission of the European Communities (2001b) *EU and Asia: A Strategic Framework for Enhanced Partnership*, Communication from the Commission, COM(2001) 469 final.

Commission of the European Communities (2002) *Towards the Enlarged Union*, Strategy paper and report of the European Commission on the progress towards accession by each of the candidate countries, COM(2002) 700 final.

Commission of the European Communities (2003) *Wider Europe – Neighbourhood: A New Framework for Relations with our Eastern and Southern Neighbours*, Communication from the Commission to the Council and the European Parliament, Brussels, COM(2003) 104 final.

Conant, L. (2001) 'Europeanization and the Courts: Variable Patterns of Adaptation among National Judiciaries', in M.G. Cowles, J.A. Caporaso and T. Risse (eds), *Transforming Europe: Europeanization and Domestic Change*, Ithaca: Cornell University Press, pp. 97–115.

Cooper, R.N. (1968) *The Economics of Interdependence*, New York: Columbia University Press (reprinted 1980).

Council (2000) Lisbon European Council: Presidency Conclusions, 24/3/2000 Nr: 100/1/00 (http://www.europa.eu.int/council/off/conclu/index.htm).

Council (2003) Brussels European Council: Presidency Conclusions, 5/5/2003 Nr: 8410/03 (http://www.europa.eu.int/council/off/conclu/index.htm).

Cowles, M.G. (1994) 'The Politics of Big Business in the European Community', PhD dissertation, American University.

Cowles, M.G. (1995) 'Setting the Agenda for a New Europe: The ERT and EC 1992', *Journal of Common Market Studies* 33(4): 501–26.

Cowles, M.G. (1996) 'The EU Committee of AmCham: The Powerful Voice of American Firms in Brussels', *Journal of European Public Policy* 3(3): 339–58.

Cowles, M.G. (2001a) 'The Transatlantic Business Dialogue: Transforming the New Transatlantic Dialogue', in M. Pollack and G. Schaffer (eds), *Transatlantic Governance in a Global Economy*, Lanham, MD: Rowman & Littlefield, pp. 159–79.

Cowles, M.G. (2001b) 'Who Writes the Rules of E-Commerce? A Case Study of the Global Business Dialogue on E-Commerce (GBDe)', Policy Paper 14, Washington, DC: American Institute for Contemporary German Studies. Downloadable from http://www.aicgs.org/publications/pubonline.shtml#policypapers.

Cowles, M.G., Caporaso, J.A. and Risse, T. (eds) (2001) *Transforming Europe: Europeanization and Domestic Change*, Ithaca: Cornell University Press.

Cox, M. (2001) 'Whatever Happened to American Decline? International Relations and the New United States Hegemony', *New Political Economy* 6(3): 311–40.

Cox, R. (1981) 'Social Forces, States and World Orders', *Millennium* 10(2): 126–55, reprinted in R.O. Keohane (ed.), *Neorealism and its Critics*, New York: Columbia University Press, 1986.

Cox, R. (1983) 'Gramsci, Hegemony and International Relations: an Essay in Method', *Millennium* 12(2): 162–75, reprinted in R. Cox and T. Sinclair, *Approaches to World Order*, New York: Cambridge University Press, 1996.

Cox, R. (1987) *Production, Power and World Order: Social Forces in the Making of History*, New York: Columbia University Press.

Cox, R. (1995) 'Critical Political Economy', in B. Hettne, *International Political Economy: Understanding Global Disorder*, Halifax: Fernwood Books, pp. 31–45.

Cram, L. (1993) 'Calling the Tune without Paying the Piper? Social Policy Regulation', *Policy and Politics* 21(2): 135.

Cram, L. (2001) 'Governance "to Go": Domestic Actors, Institutions and the Boundaries of the Possible', *Journal of Common Market Studies* 39(4): 595–618.

Crombez, C. (1996) 'Legislative Procedures in the European Community', *British Journal of Political Science* 26(2): 199–228.

Crombez, C. (1997) 'The Co-Decision Procedure in the European Union', *Legislative Studies Quarterly* 22(1): 97–119.

Crombez, C. (2002) 'Information, Lobbying and the Legislative Process in the European Union', *European Union Politics* 3(1): 7–32.

Cutler, A.C., Haufler, V. and Porter, T. (1999) *Private Authority and International Affairs*, Albany, NY: Suny University Press.

Dalton, G. (ed.) (1968) *Primitive, Archaic, and Modern Economies: Essays of Karl Polanyi*, Boston: Beacon Press.

de Búrca, G. (1999) 'Reappraising Subsidiarity's Significance after Amsterdam', Harvard Jean Monnet Working Paper 7/99, http://www.jeanmonnetprogram.org/papers/99/990701.rtf

de la Porte, C. (2002) 'Is the Open Method of Co-ordination Appropriate for Organising Activities at European Level in Sensitive Policy Areas?', *European Law Journal* 8(1): 38–58.

de la Porte, C., Pochet, P. and Room, G. (2001) 'Social Benchmarking, Policy-Making and New Governance in the EU', *Journal of European Social Policy* 11: 291–307.

Derrida, J. (1981) *Positions*, Chicago: University of Chicago Press.

De Sola Pool, Ithiel (1959) 'Trends in Content Analysis Today', in Ithiel de Sola Pool, (ed.), *Trends in Content Analysis*, Urbana: University of Illinois Press, pp. 189–233.

Deutsch, K.W., Burrell, S.A., Kann, R.A., Lee, M. Jr, Lichterman, M., Lindgren, L.E., Loewenheim, F.L. and Van Wagenen, R.W. (1957) *Political Community and the North Atlantic Area: International Organization in the Light of Historical Experience*, Princeton: Princeton University Press.

Deutsch, K.W., Edinger, L.J. and Macridis, R.C. (1967) *Study of Elite Attitudes on European Integration and World Politics*, New York: Charles Scribner and Sons.

Dewatripont, M., Giavazzi, F., Hardin, I., Persson, T., Roland, G., Sapir, A., Tabellini, G. and von Hagen, J. (1995) *Flexible Integration: Toward a More Effective and Democratic Europe*, Monitoring European Integration Series No. 6, London: CEPR.

Dieter, H. and Higgott, R. (2003) 'Exploring Alternative Theories of Economic Regionalism: From Trade to Finance in Asian Co-operation', *Review of International Political Economy* 10(3): 430–54.

Diez, T. (1997) 'International Ethics and European Integration: Federal State or Network Horizon?', *Alternatives* 22: 287–312.

Diez, T. (2001) 'Europe as a Discursive Battleground: Discourse Analysis and European Integration Studies', *Cooperation and Conflict* 36(1): 5–38.

Directorate-General for Economic and Financial Affairs (2002) *Co-ordination of Economic Policies in the EU: A Presentation of Key Features of the Main Procedures*, Euro Papers 45, European Commission: Brussels (URL: http://europa.eu.int/comm/ economy_finance).

Ditch, J. and Oldfield, N. (1999) 'Social Assistance: Recent Trends and Themes', *Journal of European Social Policy* 9: 65–76.

Dogan, M. and Pahre, R. (1989) 'The Fragmentation and Recombination of the Social Sciences', *Studies in International Comparative Development* 24(2): 1–18.

Dogan, M. and Pahre, R. (1990) *Creative Marginality: Innovation at the Intersections of Social Sciences*, Boulder, Colorado: Westview Press.

Dogan, R. (1997) 'Comitology: Little Procedures with Big Implications', *West European Politics* 20(3): 31–60.

Doleys, T.J. (2000) 'Member States and the European Commission: Theoretical Insights from the New Economics of Organization', *Journal of European Public Policy* 7(4): 532–53.

Drazen, A. (2000) *Political Economy in Macroeconomics*, Princeton: Princeton University Press.

Dunning, J.H. (1958) *American Investment in British Manufacturing Industry*, London: George Allen Unwin, revised edition, London: Routledge (1998).

'Dzurinda vyhlásil, e predreferendovú kampa vyhodnotí chladnokrvne', *Sme online*, 18 May 2003, http://www.sme.sk/clanok.asp?cl=982481

Eden, L. (ed.) (1991), 'Special Section. Sovereignty at Bay: An Agenda for the 1990s', *Millennium* 20(2): 187–8.

Egan, M. (1998) 'Regulatory Strategies, Delegation and European Market Integration', *Journal of European Public Policy* 5(3): 485–506.

Egan, M. (2001) *Constructing a European Market: Standards, Regulation, and Governance*, Oxford: Oxford University Press.

Eichener, V. (1993) 'Social Dumping or Innovative Regulation?', EUI Working Paper 92/28, Florence: European University Institute.

Elster, J. (ed.) (1998) *Deliberative Democracy*, Cambridge: Cambridge University Press.

Epstein, D. and O'Halloran, S. (1999) *Delegating Powers*, Cambridge: Cambridge University Press.

Escobar, A. (1995) *Encountering Development: The Making and Unmaking of the Third World*, Princeton: Princeton University Press.

Esping-Andersen, G. (1990) *The Three Worlds of Welfare Capitalism*, Princeton: Princeton University Press.

Esping-Andersen, G. (1999) *Social Foundations of Postindustrial Economies*, Oxford: Oxford University Press.

Falkner, G. (1998) *EU Social Policy in the 1990s: Towards a Corporatist Policy Community*, London and New York: Routledge.

Falkner, G. (2000) 'EG-Sozialpolitik nach Verflechtungsfalle und Entscheidungslücke: Bewertungsmastäbe und Entwicklungstrends', *Politische Vierteljahresschrift* 41: 279–301.

Felder, M., Tidow, S. and Wolfwinkler, G. (1999) 'Jenseits von Eurooptimismus und -pessimismus. Integrationstheorie und europäische Politik vor neuen Herausforderungen',

EU-Krit Discussion Paper 4, Forschungsgruppe Europäische Gemeinschaften, Philipps-Universität, Marburg.

Ferrera, M. (1998) 'The Four "Social Europes": Between Univeralism and Selectivity', in M. Rhodes and Y. Mény (eds), *The Future of European Welfare: A New Social Model?*, Houndmills: Macmillan, pp. 81–96.

Ferrera, M. and Rhodes, M. (eds) (2000) *Recasting European Welfare States*, London: Frank Cass.

Finnemore, M. (1996a) *National Interests in International Society*, Ithaca: Cornell University Press.

Finnemore, M. (1996b) 'Norms, Culture, and World Politics: Insights from Sociology's Institutionalism', *International Organization* 50(2): 325–47.

Finnemore, M. and Sikkink, K. (1998) 'International Norm Dynamics and Political Change', *International Organization* 52(4): 887–917.

Fiorina, M.P. (1977) *Congress: Keystone of the Washington Establishment*, New Haven: Yale University Press.

Fleischhacker, M. (2001) *Wien, 4 Februar 2000, oder Die Wende zur Hysterie*, Wien: Czernin Verlag.

Florini, A. (ed.) (2000) *The Third Force: The Rise of Transnational Civil Society*, Washington, DC: Carnegie Endowment for International Peace: Brookings Institution Press.

Forster, A. (1999) 'The European Union in South East Asia: Continuity and Change in Turbulent Times', *International Affairs* 75(4): 743–58.

Foucault, Michel (1980) *Power/Knowledge* (ed. by Colin Gordon), New York: Pantheon Books.

Franchino, F. (2001) 'Delegation and Constraints in the National Execution of the EC Policies', *West European Politics* 24(4): 169–92.

Franzese, R.J., Jr (2002) *Macroeconomic Policies of Developed Countries*, Cambridge: Cambridge University Press.

Frieden, J.A. and Lake, D. (eds) (1995) *International Political Economy: Perspectives on Global Power and Wealth*, London: Routledge.

Garrett, G. (1992) 'International Cooperation and Institutional Choice: The European Community's Internal Market', *International Organization* 46(2): 533–58.

Garrett, G. (1993) 'The Politics of Maastricht', *Economics and Politics* 5(2): 105–25.

Garrett, G. (1995a) 'From the Luxembourg Compromise to Codecision: Decision Making in the European Union', *Electoral Studies* 14(3): 289–308.

Garrett, G. (1995b) 'The Politics of Legal Integration in the European Union', *International Organization* 49(1): 171–81.

Garrett, G. (1995c) 'Capital Mobility, Trade, and the Domestic Politics of Economic Policy', *International Organization* 49(4): 657–87.

Garrett, G. (1998) *Partisan Politics in the Global Economy*, Cambridge: Cambridge University Press.

Garrett, G. (2000) 'Capital Mobility, Exchange Rates and Fiscal Policy in the Global Economy', *Review of International Political Economy* 7(1): 153–70.

Garrett, G. and Tsebelis, G. (1996a) 'Agenda Setting Power, Power Indices, and Decision Making in the European Union', *International Review of Law and Economics* 16: 345–61.

Garrett, G. and Tsebelis, G. (1996b) 'An Institutional Critique of Intergovernmentalism', *International Organization* 50(2): 269–299.

Garrett, G. and Weingast, B. (1993) 'Ideas, Interests, and Institutions: Constructing the European Community's Internal Market', in J. Goldstein and R.O. Keohane (eds), *Ideas and Foreign Policy: Beliefs, Institutions, and Political Change*, Ithaca: Cornell University Press, pp. 173–206.

George, J. (1994) *Discourses of Global Politics: A Critical (Re)Introduction to International Relations*, Boulder, CO: Lynne Rienner.

Germain, R.D. and Kenny, M. (1998) 'International Relations Theory and the New Gramscians', *Review of International Studies* 24(1): 3–21.

Geyer, R. (2003) 'European Integration, the Problem of Complexity and the Revision of Theory', *Journal of Common Market Studies* 41(1): 15–35.

Giavazzi, G. and Pagano, M. (1988) 'The Advantage of Tying One's Hands: EMS Discipline and Central Bank Credibility', *European Economic Review* 32: 1055–82.

Giddens, A. (1979) *Central Problems in Social Theory: Action, Structure and Contradiction in Social Analysis*, Berkeley: University of California Press.

Gill, S. (1992) 'The Emerging World Order and European Change: The Political Economy of European Union', in R. Miliband and L. Panitch (eds), *The Socialist Register 1992*, New York: Monthly Review Press, pp. 157–96.

Gill, S. (1993a) 'Gramsci and Global Politics: Towards a Post-hegemonic Research Agenda', in S. Gill (ed.), *Gramsci, Historical Materialism and International Relations*, Cambridge: Cambridge University Press, pp. 1–20.

Gill, S. (1993b) 'Epistemology, Ontology, and the "Italian School"', in S. Gill (ed.), *Gramsci, Historical Materialism and International Relations*, Cambridge: Cambridge University Press, pp. 21–48.

Gill, S. (ed.) (1993c) *Gramsci, Historical Materialism, and International Relations*, Cambridge: Cambridge University Press.

Gill, S. (1995) 'Globalisation, Market Civilization and Disciplinary Neoliberalism', *Millennium* 24(3): 399–423.

Gill, S. (1997) 'An EMU or an Ostrich? EMU and Neo Liberal Economic Integration, Limits and Alternatives', in P. Minkkinen and H. Patomäki (eds), *The Politics of Economic and Monetary Union*, Helsinki: Finnish Institute of International Affairs, pp. 207–31.

Gill, S. (1998) 'European Governance and New Constitutionalism: Economic and Monetary Union and Alternatives', *New Political Economy* 3(1): 5–26.

Gilpin, R. (1987) *The Political Economy of International Relations*, Princeton: Princeton University Press.

Ginsberg, R.H. (1999) 'Conceptualizing the European Union as an International Actor: Narrowing the Theoretical Capability – Expectations Gap', *Journal of Common Market Studies* 37(3): 429–54.

Ginsberg, R.H. (2001) *The European Union in International Politics*, Oxford: Rowman & Littlefield.

Goffman, E. (1974) *Frame Analysis: An Essay on the Organization of Experience*, Cambridge: Harvard University Press.

Goodin, R.E. (1996) *The Theory of Institutional Design*, Cambridge: Cambridge University Press.

Gramsci, A. (1971) *Selections from the Prison Notebooks of Antonio Gramsci*, Q. Hoare and G. Nowell-Smith (eds), New York: International Publishers.

Greenwood, J. (1997) *Representing Interests in the European Union*, Houndmills: Macmillan.

Greenwood, J., Grote, J. and Ronit, K. (1992) *Organised Interests and the European Community*, London: Sage.

Grieco, J.M. (1995) 'The Maastricht Treaty Economic and Monetary Union and Neo-Realist Research Programme', *Review of International Studies* 21(1): 21–40.

Gurowitz, A. (1999) 'Mobilizing International Norms: Domestic Actors, Immigrants, and the Japanese State', *World Politics* 51: 413–45.

Gyárfášová, O. and Velšic, M. (2002) 'Public Opinion', in G.M. Nikov, M. Kollár and T. Nicolson (eds), *Slovakia 2001: A Global Report on the State of Society*, Bratislava: Institute for Public Affairs.

Haas, E.B. (1958) *The Uniting of Europe* (1st edition), London: Stevens.

Haas, E.B. (1964) *Beyond the Nation State: Political, Social, and Economic Forces 1950–1957*, Stanford: Stanford University Press.

Haas, E.B. (1968) *The Uniting of Europe* (2nd edition), Stanford: Stanford University Press.

Haas, E.B. (1971) 'The Study of Regional Integration: Reflections on the Joy and Anguish of Prethorizing', *Regional Integration*: 3–44.

Haas, E.B. (1975) *The Obsolescence of Regional Integration Theory*, Research Studies, 25, Institute of International Studies, Berkeley, California.

Haas, E.B. (1976) 'Turbulent Fields and the Theory of Regional Integration', *International Organization* 30(2): 173–212.

Haas, P. (ed.) (1992) 'Knowledge, Power, and International Policy Coordination', *International Organization* 46: special issue.

Habermas, J. (1989) *The Structural Transformation of the Public Sphere*, Cambridge, MA: MIT Press.

Hall, P.A. (1989) 'Conclusion', in Peter Hall (ed.), *The Political Power of Economic Ideas: Keynesianism across Nations*, Princeton: Princeton University Press, pp. 361–91.

Hall, P.A. (1993) 'Policy Paradigms, Social Learning and the State: The Case of Economic Policy-Making in Britain', *Comparative Politics* 25(3): 275–96.

Hall, P.A. (1994) 'Central Bank Independence and Coordinated Wage Bargaining: Their Interaction in Germany and Europe', *German Politics and Society* 31: 1–23.

Hall, P.A. and Franzese, R.J., Jr (1998) 'Mixed Signals: Central Bank Independence, Coordinated Wage Bargaining, and European Monetary Union', *International Organization* 52(3): 505–35.

Hall, P.A. and Soskice, D. (eds) (2001) *Varieties of Capitalism: The Institutional Foundations of Comparative Advantage*, Oxford: Oxford University Press.

Hall, P.A. and Taylor, R.C.R. (1996) 'Political Science and the Three New Institutionalisms', *Political Studies* 44(5): 936–57.

Hall, S. (1996) 'The Problem of Ideology: Marxism without Guarantees', in D. Morley and K.H. Chen (eds), *Stuart Hall: Critical Dialogues*, London: Routledge.

Hamilton-Hart, N. (2003) 'Asia's New Regionalism: Government Capacity and Cooperation in the Western Pacific', *Review of International Political Economy* 10(2): 222–45.

Hansen, Jørgen Drud and Finn, Olesen (2001) 'From European Economies towards a European Economy?', in Jørgen Drud Hansen (ed.), *European Integration: An Economic Perspective*, Oxford: Oxford University Press, pp. 227–45.

Haufler, V. (2000) 'Private Sector International Regimes: An Assessment', in R.A. Higgott, G.R.D. Underhill and A. Bieler (eds), *Non-State Actors and Authority in the Global System,* London, New York: Routledge, pp. 121–37.

Haufler, V. (2001) *A Public Role for the Private Sector: Industry Self-Regulation in a Global Economy*, Washington, DC: Carnegie Endowment for International Peace Press.

Haughton, T. (2002) 'Slovakia's Robert Fico: A Man to be Trusted or Feared?', *RFE/RL East European Perspectives* 4(1) 29 May 2002, http://wwww.rfel.org

Hawes, M.K. (1996) 'APEC and the New Regionalism in Asia: Problems and Prospects', *Dokkyo International Review* 9: 239–59.

Hemerijck, A.C. and Schludi, M. (2000) 'Sequences of Policy Failures and Effective Policy Responses', in F.W. Scharpf and V.A. Schmidt (eds), *Welfare and Work in the Open Economy*, Oxford: Oxford University Press, pp. 125–228.

Henderson, K. (2001) 'Euroscepticism or Europhobia: Opposition Attitudes to the EU in the Slovak Republic', Sussex European Institute Working Paper No. 50, Opposing Europe Research Network Paper No. 5.

Henderson, K. (2002) 'Europe and the Slovak Parliamentary Election of September 2002', RIIA/OERN Election Briefing No. 7.

Hennis, M. (2001) 'Europeanization and Globalization: the Missing Link', *Journal of Common Market Studies* 39(5): 829–50.

Héritier, A. (1999) *Policy-making and Diversity in Europe: Escaping Deadlock*, Cambridge: Cambridge University Press.

Héritier, A. (2001) 'New Modes of Multiarena Governance in Europe: Policy-making without Legislation', Paper presented at the conference 'Linking Law and Politics', 1–2 February, Bonn.

Héritier, A. (ed.) (2002) *Common Goods: Reinventing European and International Governance*, Lanham, MD: Rowman & Littlefield.

Héritier, A., Knill, C. and Mingers, S. (1996) *Ringing the Changes in Europe*, London: Walter de Gruyter.

Hettne, B. (1995) 'Introduction: The International Political Economy in Transformation', in B. Hettne (ed.), *International Political Economy: Understanding Global Disorder*, London: Zed Books, pp. 1–30.

Higgott, R. and Stubbs, R. (1995) 'Competing Conceptions of Economic Regionalism: APEC versus EAEC in the Asia Pacific', *Review of International Political Economy*, 2(3): 516–35.

Higgott, R.A., Underhill, G.R.D. and Bieler, A. (2000) *Non-State Actors and Authority in the Global System*, London: Routledge.

Hindley, B. (1999) 'New Institutions for Transatlantic Trade?', *International Affairs* 75(1): 45–60.

Hinich, M.J. and Munger, M.C. (1994) *Ideology and the Theory of Political Choice*, Ann Arbor: University of Michigan Press.

Hirsch, J. (1992) 'Regulation, Staat und Hegemonie', in A. Demirovic *et al.* (eds), *Hegemonie und Staat. Kapitalistische Regulation als Projekt und Prozess*, Münster.

Hirsch, J. (1995) *Der nationale Wettbewerbsstaat. Staat, Demokratie und Politik im globalen Kapitalismus*, Berlin: Edition ID-Archiv.

Hirschman, A.O. (1970) *Exit, Voice and Loyalty: Responses to Decline in Firms*, Cambridge: Cambridge University Press.

Hirschman, A.O. (1981) 'Exit, Voice and Loyalty: Further Reflections and a Survey of Recent Contributions', in Albert O. Hirschman's *Essays in Trespassing. Economics to Politics and Beyond*, Cambridge: Cambridge University Press, pp. 213–35.

Hirschman, A.O. (1989) 'How the Keynesian Revolution was Exported from the United States, and other Comments', in P. Hall (ed.), *The Political Power of Economic Ideas: Keynesianism across Nations*, Princeton: Princeton University Press, pp. 347–59.

Hirschman, A.O. (1992) 'Exit and Voice: An Expanding Sphere of Influence', in his *Rival Views of Market Society*, Cambridge, MA: Harvard University Press, pp. 77–101.

Hirschman, A.O. (1993) 'Exit, Voice, and the Fate of the German Democratic Republic. An Essay in Conceptual History', *World Politics* 45 (2): 173–202.

Hix, S. (1994) 'The Study of the European Community: The Challenge to Comparative Politics', *West European Politics* 17(4): 1–30.

Hix, S. (1999) *The Political System of the European Union*, Houndsmill and New York: Palgrave.

Hix, S. (2002) 'Parliamentary Behavior with Two Principals: Preferences, Parties, and Voting in the European Parliament', *American Journal of Political Science* 46(3): 688–98.

Hobsbawm, E.J. (1982) 'Gramsci and Marxist Political Theory', in A. Showstack Sassoon (ed.), *Approaches to Gramsci*, London: Writers and Readers.

Hodson, D. and Maher, I. (2001) 'The Open Method as a New Mode of Governance: The Case of Soft Economic Policy Co-ordination', *Journal of Common Market Studies* 39(4): 719–46.

Hoffmann, S. (1966) 'Obstinate or Obsolete? The Fate of the Nation-state and the Case of Western Europe', *Daedalus* 95(3): 862–916.

Hoffmann, S. (1978) *Primacy or World Order? American Foreign Policy since the Cold War*, New York: McGraw-Hill.

Holland, M. (2002) *The European Union and the Third World*, London: Palgrave.

Hollingsworth, J.R. and Boyer, R. (eds) (1997) *Contemporary Capitalism: The Embeddedness of Institutions*, Cambridge: Cambridge University Press.

Holman, O. (1992) 'Transnational Class Strategy and the New Europe', *International Journal of Political Economy* 22(1): 3–22.

Holman, O. and Van der Pijl, K. (1996) 'The Capitalist Class in the European Union', in G.A. Kourvetaris and A. Moschonas (eds), *The Impact of European Integration: Political, Sociological and Economic Changes*, Westport: Praeger, pp. 55–74.

Holman, O. and Van der Pijl, K. (2003) 'Structure and Process in Transnational European Business', in A.W. Cafruny and M. Ryner (eds) *A Ruined Fortress? Neoliberal Hegemony and Transformation in Europe*, London: Rowman & Littlefield, pp. 71–93.

Holmstrom, B. (1979) 'Moral Hazard and Observability', *Bell Journal of Economics* 10: 74–91.

Holsti, K.J. (1970) 'National Role Conceptions in the Study of Foreign Policy', *International Studies Quarterly* 14: 233–309.

Hooghe, L. (2002) *The European Commission and the Integration of Europe*, Cambridge: Cambridge University Press.

Horn, M.J. and Shepsle, K.A. (1989) 'Administrative Process and Organizational Form as Legislative Responses to Agency Costs', *Virginia Law Review* 75: 499–509.

Hosli, M.O. (1993) 'Admission of European Free Trade Association States to the European Community: Effects on Voting Power in the European Community Council of Ministers', *International Organization* 47(4): 629–643.

Hosli, M.O. (1995) 'The Balance Between Small and Large: Effects of a Double-Majority System on Voting Power in the European Union', *International Studies Quarterly* 39(3): 351–70.

Hosli, M.O. (1996) 'Coalitions and Power: Effects of Qualified Majority Voting in the Council of the European Union', *Journal of Common Market Studies* 34(2): 255–73.

Hug, S. and König, T. (1999) 'Ratifying Amsterdam', Paper prepared for presentation at the Annual Meeting of the American Political Science Association, Atlanta, September 2–5, 1999.

Hurd, I. (1999) 'Legitimacy and Authority in International Politics', *International Organization* 53(2): 379–408.

Hurrell, A. (1995) 'Regionalism in Theoretical Perspective', in L. Fawcett and A. Hurrell (eds), *Regionalism and World Politics*, Oxford: Oxford University Press, pp. 39–40.

Hurrell, A. (1998) 'Security in Latin America', *International Affairs*, 14(3): 529–46.

Ikenberry, J.G. (2002) *America Unrivaled: The Future of the Balance of Power*, London: Cornell University Press.

Imig, D. and Tarrow, S. (eds) (2001) *Contentious Europeans: Protest and Politics in an Emerging Polity*, Lanham, MD: Rowman & Littlefield.

Ingebritsen, C. (1998) *Nordic States and European Unity*, Ithaca: Cornell University Press.

Iversen, T. (1998) 'Wage Bargaining, Central Bank Independence, and the Real Effects of Money', *International Organization* 52(3): 469–504.

Iversen, T. (1999) *Contested Economic Institutions: The Politics of Macroeconomics and Wage Bargaining in Advanced Democracies*, Cambridge: Cambridge University Press.

Iversen, T. (2001) 'The Dynamics of Welfare State Expansion: Trade Openness, De-industrialization and Partisan Politics', in P. Pierson (ed.), *The New Politics of Welfare States*, Oxford: Oxford University Press, pp. 45–79.

Iversen T. and Cusack, T.R. (2000) 'The Causes of Welfare State Expansion: Deindustrialization or Globalization?', *World Politics* 52(3): 313–49.

Jachtenfuchs, M. (2001) 'The Governance Approach to European Integration', *Journal of Common Market Studies* 39(2): 245–64.

Jackson, R. and Sørensen, G. (2003) *Introduction to International Relations* (2nd edition), Oxford: Oxford University Press.

Jenson, J. and Mahon, R. (1993) 'Representing Solidarity: Class, Gender and the Crisis of Social Democratic Sweden', *New Left Review* 201: 76–100.

Jessop, B. (1988) *Conservative Regimes and the Transition to Post-Fordism: The Cases of Britain and West Germany*, Essex: Dept. of Government, University of Essex.

Jessop, B. (1990a) *State Theory: Putting the Capitalist State in its Place*, Cambridge, UK: Polity Press.

Jessop, B. (1990b) 'Regulation Theory in Retrospect and Prospect', *Economy and Society* 19(2): 153–216.

Jobert, B. (1992) 'Représentations sociales, controverses et débats dans la conduite des politiques publiques', *Revue Française de Science Politique* 42(2): 219–34.

Jobert, B. (2001) 'Europe and the Reshaping of National Forums: The French Case', paper presented at a conference on 'Ideas, Discourse, and European Integration', European Union Center, Harvard University.

Johnson, J. (1993) 'Is Talk Really Cheap? Prompting Conversation between Critical Theory and Rational Choice', *American Political Science Review* 87: 74–86.

Johnson, R. (2000) 'Toward Democratic Governance for Sustainable Development: Transnational Civil Society Organizing around Big Dams', in A. Florini (ed.), *The Third Force: The Rise of Transnational Civil Society*, Washington, DC: Carnegie Endowment for International Peace: Brookings Institution Press.

Jones, E. (2001) 'The Politics of Europe 2000: Unity *through* Diversity', *Industrial Relations Journal* 32(5): 362–79.

Jones, E. (2002) *The Politics of Economic and Monetary Union: Integration and Idiosyncrasy*, Lanham, MD: Rowman & Littlefield.

Jones, E. (2003) 'Liberalized Capital Markets, State Autonomy, and European Monetary Union', *European Journal of Political Research* 42(2): 111–36.

Jordan, G. and Schubert, K. (eds) (1992) *European Journal of Political Research,* special issue: *Policy Networks* 21(1/2): 7–27.

Jørgensen, K.-E. (ed.) (1997) *Reflectivist Approaches to European Governance*, London: Macmillan.

Jupille, J. and Caporaso, J.A. (1999) 'Institutionalism and the European Union: Beyond International Relations and Comparative Politics', *Annual Review of Political Science* 2: 429–44.

Kahler, M. and Lake, David A. (eds) (2003) *Governance in a Global Economy: Political Authority in Transition*, Princeton: Princeton University Press.

Kanner, A. (2002) 'European Union – Mercosur Relations: The Institutionalisation of Cooperation', Robert Schuman Papers, Jean Monnet European Union Centre, Miami: University of Miami.

Kassim, H. (1994) 'Policy Networks, Networks and EU Policy Making: A Sceptical View', *West European Politics* 17(4): 15–27.

Kassim, H. (2000) 'Conclusion', in H. Kassim, B.G. Peters and V. Wright (eds), *The National Co-ordination of EU Policy: The Domestic Level*, Oxford: Oxford University Press, pp. 235–64.

Kassim, H. (2003) 'The European Administration: Between Europeanization and Domestication', in J. Hayward and A. Menon (eds), *Governing Europe*, Oxford: Oxford University Press.

Kassim, H. and Menon, A. (2003) 'The Principal–Agent Approach and the Study of the European Union: A Provisional Assessment', European Research Institute Working Paper.

Kassim, H. and Menon, A. (2004) 'Europe in the 1990s: The Re-assertion of Member State Control', in Dionyssis Dimitrakopoulos (ed.), *The Prodi Commission*, Manchester: Manchester University Press.

Kassim, H. and Wright, V. (1991) 'The Role of National Administrations in the Decision-making Processes of the European Community', *Rivista Trimestrale di Diritto Pubblico* 3: 832–50.

Kassim, H., Menon, A., Peters, B.G. and Wright, V. (2001) *The National Co-ordination of EU Policy: The European Level*, Oxford: Oxford University Press.

Katzenstein, P.J. (1996a) *Cultural Norms and National Security: Police and Military in Postwar Japan*, Ithaca: Cornell University Press.

Katzenstein, P.J. (ed.) (1996b) *The Culture of National Security. Norms and Identity in World Politics*, New York: Columbia University Press.

Katzenstein, P.J., Keohane, R.O. and Krasner, S.D. (1998) '*International Organization* and the Study of World Politics', *International Organization* 52(4): 645–85.

Keck, M.E. and Sikkink, K. (1998) *Activists beyond Borders: Advocacy Networks in International Politics*, Ithaca: Cornell University Press.

Kennedy, P. (1988) *The Rise and Fall of the Great Powers*, London: Unwin Hyman.

Keohane, R.O. (1984) *After Hegemony*, Princeton: Princeton University Press.

Keohane, R.O. (ed.) (1986) *Neorealism and its Critics*, New York: Columbia University Press.

Keohane, R.O. (1989) *International Institutions and State Power*, Essays in International Relations Theory, Boulder, CO: Westview Press.

Keohane, R.O. (2002) 'Ironies of Sovereignty: The European Union and the United States', *Journal of Common Market Studies* 40(4): 743–65.

Keohane, R.O. and Hoffmann, S. (1991) 'Institutional Change in Europe in the 1980s', in R.O. Keohane and S. Hoffmann (eds), *The New European Community: Decisionmaking and Institutional Change*, Boulder, CO: Westview Press, pp. 1–39.

Keohane, R.O. and Nye, J. (eds) (1972) *Transnational Relations and World Politics*, Cambridge, MA: Harvard University Press.

Kerremans, B. (1996) 'Do Institutions Make a Difference? Non-Institutionalism, Neo-Institutionalism and the Logic of Common Decision-Making in the European Union', *Governance* 9(2): 217–40.

Khong, Y.F. (1992) *Analogies at War: Korea, Munich, Dien Bien Phu, and the Vietnam Decisions of 1965*, Princeton: Princeton University Press.

Kiewiet, D.R. and McCubbins, M.D. (1991) *The Logic of Delegation: Congressional Parties and the Appropriations Process*, Chicago: University of Chicago Press.

Kindleberger, C. (1970) *Power and Money: The Economics of International Politics and the Politics of International Economics*, New York: Basic Books.

Kingdon, J. (1995) *Agendas, Alternatives and Public Policies* (2nd edition), New York: HarperCollins.

Kirshner, J. (2000) 'The Study of Money', *World Politics* 52: 407–36.

Kitschelt, H., Lange, P., Marks, G. and Stephens, J.D. (eds) (1999) *Continuity and Change in Contemporary Capitalism*, Cambridge: Cambridge University Press.

Klom, A (2003) 'Mercosur and Brazil: A European Perspective', *International Affairs*, 79(2): 351–68.

Klotz, A. (1995) *Norms in International Relations: The Struggle against Apartheid*, Ithaca: Cornell University Press.

Knight, J. (1992) *Institutions and Social Conflict*, Cambridge: Cambridge University Press.

Knill, C. (2001) 'Private Governance across Multiple Arenas: European Interest Associations as Interface Actors', *Journal of European Public Policy* 8(2): 227–46.

Knill, C. and Lehmkuhl, D. (2002) 'Private Actors and the State: Internationalization and Changing Patterns of Governance', *Governance* 15(1): 41–63.

Knill, C. and Lenschow, A. (2001) ' "Seek and Ye Shall Find!" Linking Perspectives on Institutional Change', *Comparative Political Studies* 34(2): 187–215.

Kohler-Koch, B. (1996) 'Catching up with change: the transformation of governance in the European Union', *Journal of European Public Policy* 3(3): 359–80.

Kohler-Koch, B. (1997) 'The European Union Facing Enlargement: Still a System sui generis?', Working Paper 20, Mannheimer Zentrum für Europäische Sozialforschung, Arbeitsbereich III, ISSN 0948-0099.

Kohler-Koch, B. and Eising, R. (eds) (1999) *The Transformation of Governance in the European Union*, London: Routledge.

König, T. and Hug, S. (2000) 'Ratifying Maastricht: Parliamentary Votes on International Treaties and Theoretical Solution Concepts', *European Union Politics* 1(1): 93–124.

König, T. and Mirja, P. (2001) 'Examining the EU Legislative Process: The Relative Importance of Agenda and Veto Power', Universität Konstanz: Manuscript.

Kooiman, J. (1993) 'Social-Political Governance: Introduction', in J. Kooiman (ed.), *Modern Governance: New Government-Society Interactions*, London: Sage, pp. 1–9.

Kopecký, P. and Cas, M. (2002) 'The Two Sides of Euroscepticism: Party Positions on European Integration in East Central Europe', *European Union Politics* 3(3): 297–326.

Krasner, S. (1976) 'State Power and the Structure of International Trade', *World Politics* 28(3): 317–47.

Kratochwil, F.V. (1989) *Rules, Norms and Decisions: On the Conditions of Practical and Legal Reasoning in International Relations and Domestic Affairs*, New York: Cambridge University Press.

Kreppel, A. (2002) 'Moving Beyond Procedure: An Empirical Analysis of European Parliament Legislative Influence', *Comparative Political Studies* 35(7): 784–813.

Kuhn, T.S. (1996 [1962]) *The Structure of Scientific Revolutions* (3rd edition), Chicago: University of Chicago Press.

Kühnhardt, L. (2002) 'Implications of Globalization on the Raison d'Être of European Integration', ARENA Working Paper 02, Oslo: ARENA.

Kupchan, C.A. (2002) 'Hollow Hegemony or Stable Multipolarity', in G.J. Ikenberry, *America Unrivaled: The Future of the Balance of Power*, Ithaca: Cornell University Press, pp. 68–97.

Lakatos, I. (1970) 'Falsification and the Methodology of Scientific Research Programmes', in I. Lakatos and A. Musgrave (eds), *Criticism and the Growth of Knowledge*, Cambridge: Cambridge University Press, pp. 91–195.

Lake, D.A. (2001) 'Beyond Anarchy: The Importance of Security Institutions', *International Security* 26 (1): 129–60.

Larson, D.W. (1988) 'Problems of Content Analysis in Foreign-Policy Research: Notes from the Study of the Origins of Cold War Belief Systems', *International Studies Quarterly* 32: 241–55.

Laver, M. and Shepsle, K. (1990) 'Coalitions and Cabinet Government', *American Political Science Review* 84(3): 873–90.

Lawton, T.C., Rosenau, J.N. and Verdun, A.C. (2000) 'Introduction: Looking Beyond the Confines', in T.C. Lawton, J.N. Rosenau and A.C. Verdun (eds), *Strange Power: Shaping the Parameters of International Relations and International Political Economy*, Aldershot: Ashgate, pp. 3–18.

Legro, J.W. (1997) 'Which Norms Matter? Revisiting the "Failure" of Internationalism', *International Organization* 51(1): 31–63.

Lehmbruch, G. and Schmitter, P.C. (1982) *Patterns of Corporatist Policy-making*, London: Sage.

Lehmkuhl, D. (2000) 'Commercial Arbitration – A Case of Private Transnational Self-Governance?', Working Paper, Max-Planck Group on 'Common Goods: Law, Politics and Economics', Bonn.

Lewis, J. (1998) 'Is the "Hard Bargaining" Image of the Council Misleading?', *Journal of Common Market Studies* 36(4): 457–77.

Lewis, J. (1999) 'Administrative Rivalry in the Council's Infrastructure: Diagnosing the Methods of Community in EU Decision-Making', paper delivered at the Sixth Biennial ECSA International Conference, 2–5 June 1999.

Leys, C. (1985) 'Thatcherism and British Manufacture: A Question of Hegemony', *New Left Review* 181: 5–25

Lijphart, A. (1968) *The Politics of Accommodation: Pluralism and Democracy in the Netherlands*, Berkeley: University of California Press.

Lipietz, A. (1987) *Mirages and Miracles: The Crises of Global Fordism*, London: Verso.

Lipietz, A. (1991) 'Regulation', in T. Bottomore (ed.), *A Dictionary of Marxist Thought*, Oxford: Basi Blackwell, pp. 461–3.

Lohmann, S. (2000) 'Sollbruchstelle: Deep Uncertainty and the Design of Monetary Institutions', *International Finance* 3(3): 391–411.

Lowi, T.J. (1969) *The End of Liberalism*, New York: Norton.

McAdam, D., McCarthy, J.D. and Zald, M.N. (eds) (1996) *Comparative Perspectives on Social Movements: Political Opportunities, Mobilizing Structures, and Cultural Framings*, New York: Cambridge University Press.

McCarthy, J.D. (1997) 'The Globalization of Social Movement Theory', in J. Smith, C. Chatfield and R. Pagnucco (eds), *Transnational Social Movements and Global Politics: Solidarity beyond the State,* Syracuse: Syracuse University Press, pp. 243–59.

McCubbins, M.D. and Page, T. (1987) 'A Theory of Congressional Delegation', in M.D. McCubbins and T. Sullivan (eds), *Congress: Structure and Policy*, Cambridge: Cambridge University Press, pp. 409–25.

McCubbins, M.D. and Schwartz, T. (1984) 'Congressional Oversight Overlooked: Police Patrols versus Fire Alarms', *American Journal of Political Science* 28: 165–79.

McCubbins, M.D., Noll, R. and Weingast, B. (1987) 'Administrative Procedures as Instruments of Political Control', *Journal of Law, Economics and Organization* 3: 242–79.

McCubbins, M.D., Noll, R. and Weingast, B. (1989) 'Structure and Process, Politics and Policy: Administrative Arrangements and the Political Control of Agencies', *Virginia Law Review* 75: 431–83.

McKelvey, R.D. (1976) 'Intransitivities in Multidimensional Voting: Models and Some Implications for Agenda Control', *Journal of Economic Theory* 12: 472–82.

McNamara, K. (1998) *The Currency of Ideas: Monetary Politics in the European Union*, Ithaca: Cornell University Press.

McNamara, K. (1999) 'Consensus and Constraint: Ideas and Capital Mobility in European Monetary Integration', *Journal of Common Market Studies* 37(3): 455–76.

McNamara, K. and Jones, E. (1996) 'The Clash of Institutions: Germany in European Monetary Affairs', *German Politics and Society* 14(3): 5–30.

Mahon, R. (1984) *The Politics of Industrial Restructuring*, Toronto: University of Toronto Press.

Majone, G. (1993) 'The European Community: An "Independent Fourth Branch of Government?"', EUI Working Paper SPS 93/9, Florence: European University Institute.

Majone, G. (1994) 'The Rise of the Regulatory State in Europe', *West European Politics* 17(3): 77–101.

Majone, G. (1997) 'The Regulatory State and its Legitimacy Problems', *West European Politics* 22(1): 1–24.

Majone, G. (2001a) 'Nonmajoritarian Instititutions and the Limits of Democratic Governance: A Political Transaction-cost Approach', *Journal of Institutional and Theoretical Economics* 157: 57–78.

Majone, G. (2001b) 'Two Logics of Delegation: Agency and Fiduciary Relations in EU Governance', *European Union Politics* 2(1): 103–21

Manners, I. (2002) 'Normative Power Europe: A Contradiction in Terms?', *Journal of Common Market Studies* 40(2): 235–58.

Manoschek, W. (2002) 'The Freedom Party of Austria (FPÖ) – an Austrian and a European Phenomenon?', in G. Bischof, A. Pelinka, and M. Gehler (eds), *Austria in the European Union*, Contemporary Austrian Studies, Volume 10, New Brunswick (US) and London: Transaction Publishers.

Mansfield, E.D., Milner, H.V. and Rosendorff, B.P. (2000) 'Free to Trade: Democracies, Autocracies, and International Trade', *American Political Science Review* 94(2): 305–21.

March, J.G. and Olsen, J.P. (1989) *Rediscovering Institutions: The Organizational Basis of Politics*, New York: Free Press.

March, J.G. and Olsen, J.P. (1995) *Democratic Governance*, New York: Free Press.

Marcussen, M. (1998) *Central Bankers, the Ideational Life-Cycle and the Social Construction of EMU*, EUI Working Papers 98/33, Florence: European University Institute.

Marcussen, M. (2000) *Ideas and Elites: The Social Construction of Economic and Monetary Union*, Aalborg: Aalborg University Press.

Marks, G., Hooghe, L. and Blank, K. (1996) 'European Integration from the 1980s', *Journal of Common Market Studies* 34(3): 341–78.

Marks, G., Scharpf, F.W., Schmitter, P.C. and Streeck, W. (eds) (1996) *Governance in the European Union*, London: Sage.

Marks, G., Wilson, C.J. and Ray, L. (2002) 'National Political Parties and European Integration', *American Journal of Political Science* 46(3): 585–94.

Martin, L.L. (2000) *Democratic Commitments: Legislatures and International Cooperation*, Princeton: Princeton University Press.

Martin, L.W. and Stevenson, R.T. (2001) 'Government Formation in Parliamentary Democracies', *American Journal of Political Science* 45(1): 33–50.

Marx, K. (1978) 'The Eighteenth Brumaire of Louis Bonaparte', in R.C. Tucker (ed.), *The Marx–Engels Reader* (2nd edition), New York: Norton.

Marx, K. (1987) *Der achtzehnte Brumaire des Louis Bonaparte*, reprinted in K. Marx and W Mattli, *The Logic of Regional Integration*, Cambridge: Cambridge University Press, 1999.

Mattli, W. (1999) *The Logic of Regional Integration: Europe and Beyond*, Cambridge: Cambridge University Press.

Mattli, W. (2001) 'Private Justice in a Global Economy: From Litigation to Arbitration', *International Organization* 55(4): 919–47.

Mattli, W. (2003) 'Public and Private Governance in Setting International Standards', in M. Kahler and D. Lake (eds), *Governance in a Global Economy: Political Authority in Transition*, Princeton: Princeton University Press, pp. 199–226.

Mayhew, A. (1998) *Recreating Europe: The European Union's Policy towards Central and Eastern Europe*, Cambridge: Cambridge University Press.

Mazey, S. (1998) 'The European Union and Women's Rights: From the Europeanization of National Agendas to the Nationalization of the European Agenda?', *Journal of European Public Policy* 5(1): 131–52.

Mazey, S. and Richardson, J. (eds) (1993) *Lobbying in the European Community*, Oxford: Oxford University Press.

Mazey, S. and Richardson, J. (1995) 'Promiscuous Policy-making: the European Policy Style?', in C. Rhodes and S. Mazey (eds), *The State of the European Union*, vol. 3, London: Longman, pp. 337–59.

Mecham, M. (2003) 'Mercosur: A Failing Development Project?', *International Affairs* 79(2): 369–87.

Menon, A. (2003) 'Member States and International Institutions: Institutionalising Intergovernmentalism in the European Union', *Comparative European Politics* 1(2): 171–202.

Menon, A. and Weatherill, S. (2002) 'Legitimacy, Accountability and Delegation in the European Union', in A. Arnull and D. Wincott (eds), *Accountability and Legitimacy in the EU after Nice*, Oxford: Oxford University Press, pp. 113–32.

Meseznikov, G. (2002) 'Domestic Politics', in G.M. Nikov, M. Kollár and T. Nicolson (eds), *Slovakia 2001: A Global Report on the State of Society*, Bratislava: Institute for Public Affairs.

Meunier, S. (2003) 'Trade Policy and Political Legitimacy in the European Union', *Comparative European Politics* 1(1): 67–90.

Michelmann, H.J. and Soldatos, P. (eds) (1994) *European Integration: Theories and Approaches*, Lanham, MD: University Press of America.

Milgrom, P. and Roberts, J. (1992) *Economics, Organization and Management*, New York: Prentice-Hall.

Milliken, J. (1999) 'The Study of Discourse in International Relations: A Critique of Research and Methods', *European Journal of International Relations* 5(2): 225–54.

Milner, H.V. (1997) *Interests, Institutions, and Information: Domestic Politics and International Relations*, Princeton: Princeton University Press.

Milner, H.V. and Rosendorff, B.P. (1997) 'Democratic Politics and International Trade Negotiations: Elections and Divided Government as Constraints on Trade Liberalization', *Journal of Conflict Resolution* 41(1): 117–46.

Milward, A.R. (2000) *The European Rescue of the Nation-State* (2nd edition), London and New York: Routledge.

Milward, A.S. (1992) *The European Rescue of the Nation-State*, London: Routledge.

Moe, T.M. (1984) 'The New Economics of Organization', *American Journal of Political Science* 28: 739–77.

Moe, T.M. (1987) 'An Assessment of the Positive Theory of Congressional Dominance', *Legislative Studies Quarterly* 12: 475–520.

Moe, T.M. (1989) 'The Politics of Bureaucratic Structure', in J.E. Chubb and P.E. Peterson (eds), *Can the Government Govern?*, Washington, DC: Brookings Institution, pp. 267–329.

Moe, T.M. (1990) 'The Politics of Structural Choice: Toward a Theory of Public Bureaucracy', in O.E. Williamson (ed.), *Organization Theory: From Chester Barnard to the Present and Beyond*, Oxford: Oxford University Press, pp. 116–53.

Mohanty, C.T. (1991) 'Under Western Eyes: Feminist Scholarship and Colonial Discourses', in C.T. Mohanty, A. Russo and L. Torres (eds), *Third World Women and the Politics of Feminism*, Bloomington: Indiana University Press.

Moravcsik, A. (1991) 'Negotiating the Single European Act. National Interests and Conventional Statecraft in the European Community', *International Organization* 45(1): 651–88.

Moravcsik, A. (1993a) 'Introduction: Integrating International and Domestic Theories of International Bargaining', in P.B. Evans, H.K. Jacobson and R.D. Putnam (eds), *Double-Edged Diplomacy*, Berkeley: University of California Press, pp. 3–42

Moravcsik, A. (1993b) 'Preferences and Power in the European Community: A Liberal Intergovernmentalist Approach', *Journal of Common Market Studies* 31(4): 473–524.

Moravcsik, A. (1998) *The Choice for Europe*, Ithaca: Cornell University Press.

Moravcsik, A. (1999a) 'A New Statecraft? Supranational Entrepreneurs and International Cooperation', *International Organization* 53(2): 267–306.

Moravcsik, A. (1999b) 'Is Something Rotten in the State of Denmark? Constructivism and European Integration,' *Journal of European Public Policy* 6(5): 669–81.

Moravcsik, A. (2000) 'De Gaulle between Grain and *Grandeur*: The Political Economy of French EC Policy, 1958–1970', *Journal of Cold War Studies* 2(1) and 2(2).

Moravcsik, A. (2002) 'In Defence of the "Democratic Deficit": Reassessing Legitimacy in the European Union', *Journal of Common Market Studies* 40(4): 603–24.

Moser, P. (1996a) 'The European Parliament as a Conditional Agenda Setter: What Are the Conditions? A Critique of Tsebelis (1994)', *American Political Science Review* 90(4): 834–838.

Moser, P. (1996b) 'A Theory of the Conditional Influence of the European Parliament in the Cooperation Procedure', Twente, Netherlands: Network on Enlargement and New Membership of the European Union Working Paper No. 96–1.

Moses, J.W. (2004) 'Exit Voice and Sovereignty: Migration, States and Globlization', *Review of International Political Economy* (forthcoming).

Mosher, J.S. and Trubek, D.M. (2003) 'Alternative Approaches to Governance in the EU: EU Social Policy and the European Employment Strategy', *Journal of Common Market Studies* 41(1): 63–88.

Moyer, H.W. (1993) 'The European Community and the GATT Uruguay Round: A Two-Level Game Approach', in W.P. Avery (ed.), *World Agriculture and the GATT*, Boulder: Lynne Rienner Publishers.

Muller, P. (1995) 'Les politiques publiques comme construction d'un rapport au monde', in Alain Faure, Gilles Pollet and Philippe Warin (eds), *La Construction du sens dans les politiques publiques: débats autour de la notion de Référentiel*, Paris: L'Harmattan.

Murphy, C.N. (1994) 'Review of Overbeek', in H. (1993) (ed.) *Restructuring Hegemony in the Global Political Economy: The Rise of Transnational Neo-Liberalism in the 1980s*, London: Routledge, *Review of International Political Economy* 1(1): 193–7.

Murphy, C.N. (1998) 'Understanding IR: Understanding Gramsci', *Review of International Studies* 24(3): 417–25.

Myrdal, G. (1956) *An International Economy: Problems and Prospects*, New York: Harper and Brothers.

Nadelmann, E.A. (1990) 'Global Prohibition Regimes: The Evolution of Norms in International Society', *International Organization* 44(4): 479–526.

Naillant, M. and Ons, A. (2002) 'Preferential Trading Arrangements between the European Union and South America: The Political Economy of Free Trade Zones in Practice', *World Economy* 25(1): 1433–68.

Nelson, D. (1988) 'Endogenous Tariff Theory: A Critical Survey', *American Journal of Political Science* 32(3): 796–837.

Newman, A. and Bach, D. (2002a) 'The Transnationalization of Regulation', paper presented at the 13th International Conference of Europeanists, Chicago, 14–16 March 2002.

Newman, A. and Bach, D. (2002b) 'Self-Regulatory Trajectories in the Shadow of the State: Resolving Digital Dilemmas in Europe and the United States', unpublished manuscript.

Nicolaïdis, K. and Howse, R. (2002) 'This is my Eutopia…: Narrative as Power', *Journal of Common Market Studies* 40(4): 767–92.

Nisbett, R. and Ross, L. (1980) *Human Inference: Strategies and Shortcomings of Social Judgment*, Englewood Cliffs: Prentice-Hall.

Noury, A.G. (2002) 'Ideology, Nationality and Euro-Parliamentarians', *European Union Politics* 3(1): 33–58.

Nye, J. (1990) *Bound to Lead: The Changing Nature of American Power*, New York: Basic Books.

Nye, J. (2000) 'The US and Europe: Continental Drift?', *International Affairs* 76(1): 51–9.

Oatley, T. (1999) 'How Constraining is Capital Mobility? The Partisan Hypothesis in an Open Economy', *American Journal of Political Science* 43(4): 1003–27.

Ötsch, W. (2000) *Haider Light: Handbuch für Demagogie*, Wien: Czernin Verlag.

Oye, K.A. (1986) (ed.) *Cooperation under Anarchy*, Princeton: Princeton University Press.

Pahre, R. (1996) 'Mathematical Discourse and Crossdisciplinary Communities: The Case of Political Economy', *Social Epistemology* 10(1): 55–73.

Pahre, R. (1997) 'Endogenous Domestic Institutions in Two-Level Games: Parliamentary Oversight in Denmark and Elsewhere', *Journal of Conflict Resolution* 41(1):147–74.

Pahre, R. (1998) 'Reactions and Reciprocity: Tariffs and Trade Liberalization in 1815–1914', *Journal of Conflict Resolution* 42(4): 467–92.

Pahre, R. (2001) 'Divided Government and International Cooperation in Austria-Hungary, Sweden-Norway, and the European Union', *European Union Politics* 2(2): 131–62.

Palan, R. (1992) 'The Second Structuralist Theories of International Relations: A Research Note', *International Studies Notes* 17(3): 22–9.

Palan, R., Abbott, J. and Deans, P. (1996) *State Strategies in the Global Political Economy*, London: Pinter.

Panagariya, A. (2002) 'EU Preferential Trade Arrangements and Developing Countries', *World Economy* 25(1): 1415–32.

Parsons, C. (2003) *A Certain Idea of Europe*, Ithaca: Cornell University Press.

210   *Bibliography*

Patomäki, H. and Teivainen, T. (2002) 'Critical Responses to Neoliberal Globalization in the Mercosur Region: Roads towards Cosmopolitan Democracy', *Review of International Political Economy* 9(1): 37–71.

Payne, A. and Gamble, A. (1996) 'Introduction: The Political Economy of Regionalism and World Order', in A. Gamble and A. Payne (eds), *Regionalism and World Order*, New York: Macmillan, pp. 1–20.

Payne, R.A. (2001) 'Persuasion, Frames and Norm Construction', *European Journal of International Relations* 7(1): 37–61.

Pedersen, T. (2002) 'Cooperative Hegemony: Power, Ideas and Institutions in Regional Integration', *Review of International Studies* 28(4): 677–96.

Pelinka, A. (2000) 'Die rechte Versuchung. SPÖ, ÖVP und die Folgen eines falschen Tabus', in H.-H. Scharsach (ed.), *Haider: Österreich und die rechte Versuchung*, Reinbek bei Hamburg: Rowolt Taschenbuch Verlag.

Peters, G.B. (1999) *Institutional Theory in Political Science: The 'New Institutionalism'*, London: Pinter.

Peterson, J. (1995) 'Decision-Making in the European Union: Towards a Framework for Analysis', *Journal of European Public Policy* 2(1): 69–93.

Peterson, J. (2001) 'The Choice for EU Theorists: Establishing a Common Framework for Analysis', *European Journal of Political Research* 39: 289–318.

Peterson, M.J. (1992) 'Whalers, Cetologists, Environmentalists, and the International Management of Whaling', *International Organization* 46(1): 147–86.

Phillips, N. (2003) 'Hemispheric Integration and Sub-regional in the Americas', *International Affairs* 79(2): 327–49.

Pierson, P. (1994) *Dismantling the Welfare State? Reagan, Thatcher, and the Politics of Retrenchment*, Cambridge, MA: Cambridge University Press.

Pierson, P. (1996) 'The Path to European Integration: A Historical Institutionalist Analysis', *Comparative Political Studies* 29(2): 123–63.

Pierson, P. (2000) 'Increasing Returns, Path Dependence, and the Study of Politics', *American Political Science Review* 94(2): 251–67.

Pierson, P. (ed.) (2001) *The New Politics of the Welfare State*, Oxford: Oxford University Press.

Pistor, M. (2002) 'European Integration as Accumulation Strategy: The European Integration Policy of the Federation of German Industries (BDI) from Eurosclerosis to Economic and Monetary Union', Ph.D. dissertation, Queen's University, Kingston, Ontario.

Plasser, F. and Ulam, P.A. (2000) 'Protest ohne Parteibindung. Die Wählerschaft der FPÖ', in H.-H. Scharsach (ed.), *Haider: Österreich und die rechte Versuchung*, Reinbek bei Hamburg: Rowolt Taschenbuch Verlag.

Plummer, M.G. (2002) 'The EU and ASEAN: Real Integration and Lessons in Financial Cooperation', *World Economy* 25(1): 1469–500.

Pochet, P. (2003) 'OMC: A Way to Democratise Europe or/and Europeanise Social Rights?', paper presented at the 'Workshop on the Open Method of Coordination and Economic Governance in the European Union', Minda de Ginzburg Center, Harvard University, 28 April 2003 (http://www.ces.fas.harvard.edu/conferences/omc.html).

Polanyi, K. (1957 [1944]) *The Great Transformation: The Political and Economic Origins of our Times*, Boston: Beacon Press.

Pollack, M. (1996) 'The New Institutionalism and EU Governance: The Promise and Limits of Institutionalist Analysis', *Governance* 9(4): 429–58.

Pollack, M. (1997) 'Delegation, Agency and Agenda Setting in the European Community', *International Organization* 51(1): 99–135.

Pollack, M. (2001) 'International Relations Theory and European Integration', *Journal of Common Market Studies* 39(2): 221–44.

Pollack, M. and Shaffer, G. (eds) (2001) *Transatlantic Governance in a Global Economy*, Lanham, MD: Rowman & Littlefield.

Pollack, M.A. (1999) 'Delegation, Agency and Agenda Setting in the Treaty of Amsterdam', *European Integration Online Papers* 3(6) April 1999, http://eiop.or.at/eiop/texte/1999-006a.htm

Pollack, M.A. (2000) 'The End of Creeping Competence? EU Policy-making since Maastricht', *Journal of Common Market Studies* 38(3): 519–38.

Poole, K.T. and Rosenthal, H. (1985) 'A Spatial Model for Legislative Roll Call Analysis', *American Journal of Political Science* 29(2): 357–84.

Prakash, A. (2000) *The Greening of the Firm*, Cambridge: Cambridge University Press.

Price, R. (1998) 'Reversing the Gun Sights: Transnational Civil Society Targets Land Mines', *International Organization* 53(3): 613–44.

Price, R. and Reus-Smit, C. (1998) 'Dangerous Liaisons? Critical International Relations Theory and Constructivism', *European Journal of International Relations* 4(3): 259–94.

Pridham, G. (1999) 'Complying with the European Union's Democratic Conditionality: Transnational Party Linkages and Regime Changes in Slovakia, 1993–1998', *Europe-Asia Studies* 51(7): 1221–244.

Pridham, G. (2002) 'EU Enlargement and Consolidating Democracy in Post-Communist States: Formality and Reality', *Journal of Common Market Studies* 40(3): 953–73.

Puchala, D.J. (1975) 'Domestic Politics and Regional Harmonization in the European Communities', *World Politics* 27(4): 496–520.

Putnam, R.D. (1988) 'Diplomacy and Domestic Politics: The Logic of Two-Level Games', *International Organization* 42(3): 427–60.

Radaelli, C.M. (2003) 'Policy Learning and the Open Method of Coordination', paper presented at the ESRC conference 'Policy Learning and the New European Governance', London, 23 May 2003.

Radtke, K.W. and Wiesebron, M. (2002) *Competing for Integration: Japan, Europe, Latin America and their Strategic Partners*, New York: M.E. Sharpe.

Ramirez, F.O., Soysal, Y. and Shanahan, S. (1997) 'The Changing Logic of Political Citizenship: Crossnational Acquisition of Women's Suffrage Rights, 1890–1990', *American Sociological Review* 62: 735–45.

Rauscher, H. (2000) 'Ein geschlossene Verdrängungskette. Warum Österreichs Konservative der Haider-Partei zur Regierungsmacht verhalfen', in H.-H. Scharsach (ed.), *Haider: Österreich und die rechte Versuchung*, Reinbek bei Hamburg: Rowolt Taschenbuch Verlag.

Rein, M. and Schön, D. (1993) 'Reframing Policy Discourse', in F. Fischer and J. Forester (eds), *The Argumentative Turn in Policy Analysis and Planning*, Durham: Duke University Press, pp. 145–66.

Reinicke, W. (1998) *Global Public Policy: Governing without Government?*, Washington, DC: Brookings Institution Press.

Rhodes, M. (2000) 'Lisbon: Europe's "Maastricht for Welfare" ?', *ECSA Review* 13(3): 2–4.

Rhodes, M. and Mény, Y. (eds) (1998) *The Future of European Welfare: A New Social Contract?*, Houndsmill, and New York: Palgrave.

Rhodes, R.A.W. (1996) 'The New Governance: Governing without Government', *Political Studies* 44: 652–67.

Richards, G.A. and Kirkpatrick, C. (1999) 'Reorienting Interregional Cooperation in the Global Political Economy: Europe's East Asian Policy', *Journal of Common Market Studies* 37(4): 683–710.

Rieger, E. (2001) 'Eine Regierung für Regierungen. Territoriale Organisation und Sozialpolitik in der Europäischen Union und in den Vereinigten Staaten', in W. Müller, O. Fromm, and B. Hansjürgens (eds), *Regeln für den europäischen Systemwettbewerb*, Marburg: Metropolis, pp. 307–35.

Riker, W. (1980) 'Implications from the Dis-equilibrium of Majority Rule for the Study of Institutions', *American Political Science Review* 74: 432–47.

Risse, T. (2000) 'Let's Argue: Communicative Action in World Politics', *International Organization* 54(1): 1–40.

Risse, T. (2002) 'Transnational Actors and World Politics', in W. Carlsnaes, T. Risse and B. Simmons (eds), *Handbook of International Relations*, London: Sage, pp. 255–74.

Risse, T., Engelmann-Martin, D., Knopf, H.J. and Roscher, K. (1999) 'To Euro or not to Euro: The EMU and Identity Politics in the European Union', *European Journal of International Relations* 5(2): 147–87.

Risse-Kappen, T. (1994) 'Ideas Do Not Float Freely: Transnational Coalitions, Domestic Structures, and the End of the Cold War', *International Organization* 48(2): 185–214.

Risse-Kappen, T. (ed.) (1995) *Bringing Transnational Relations Back in: Non-State Actors, Domestic Structures and International Institutions*, Cambridge: Cambridge University Press.

Rodrik, D. (1996) 'Understanding Economic Policy Reform', *Journal of Economic Literature* 34(1): 9–41.

Rodrik, D. (1997) *Has Globalization Gone Too Far?*, Washington: Institute for International Economics.

Rogowski, Ronald (1987) 'Political Cleavages and Changing Exposure to Trade', *American Political Science Review* 81(4): 1121–37.

Rogowski, Ronald (1989) *Commerce and Coalitions*, Princeton: Princeton University Press.

Rokkan, Stein (1966) 'Norway: Numerical Democracy and Corporate Pluralism', in R.A. Dahl (ed.), *Political Oppositions in Western Democracies*, New Haven: Yale University Press, pp. 70–115.

Roland, G. (2000) *Transition and Economics: Politics, Markets and Firms*, Cambridge, MA, and London: The MIT Press.

Ronit, K. and Schneider, V. (1999) 'Global Governance through Private Organisations', *Governance* 12(3): 243–66.

Rosamond, B. (2000) *Theories of European Integration*, Houndsmill and New York: Palgrave.

Ross, F. (2000) 'Interests and Choice in the "Not Quite so New" Politics of Welfare', *West European* Politics 23(2): 1–34.

Ross, S.A. (1973) 'The Economic Theory of Agency: The Principal's Problem', *American Economic Review* 63(2): 134–9.

Röttger, B. (1994) 'Hegemonie und Weltmarktmacht. Kritische Theorieglobal-kapitalistischer Regulation', in H.-J. Bieling, F. Deppe and B. Röttger, *Weltmarkt, Hegemonie und europäische Integration. Kritische Beiträge zur Theorie internationaler Beziehungen*, Arbeitspapier 15, Forschungsgruppe Europäische Gemeinschaften, Philipps-Universität, Marburg, pp. 5–44.

Röttger, B. (1995) 'Über die "Krise der Politik" und die Malaisen einer Regulationstheorie des transnationalen Kapitalismus – Anmerkungen zu Bob Jessop, Josef Esser und Ingeborg Tömmel', in *Europäische Integration und politische Regulierung: Aspekte,*

Dimensionen, Perspektiven, Studien der Forschungsgruppe Europäische Gemeinschaften 5, Forschungsgruppe Europäische Gemeinschaften, Philipps-Universität, Marburg, pp. 65–79.

Röttger, B. (1997) *Neoliberale Globalisierung und Eurokapitalistische Regulation. Die Politische Konstitution des Marktes*, Münster: Westfälisches Dampfboot.

Ruggie, J.G. (1975) 'International Responses to Technology: Concepts and Trends', *International Organization* 29: 557–84.

Ruggie, J.G. (1998) *Constructing the World Polity*, London: Routledge.

Rüland, J. (2001) 'ASEAN and the European Union: A Bumpy Inter-Regional Relationship', ZEI Discussion Paper C95, Bonn: ZEI.

Rupert, M. and Smith, H. (2002) 'Editors' Introduction', in M. Rupert and H. Smith (eds), *Historical Materialism and Globalisation: Essays on Continuity and Change*, London: Routledge, pp. 1–13.

Sabel, C.F. and Zeitlin, J. (2003) 'Active Welfare, Experimental Governance, Pragmatic Constitutionalism: The New Transformation of Europe', paper presented at the Conference of the Hellenic Presidency of the European Union, 'The Modernisation of the European Social Model and EU Policies and Instruments', Ioannina, 21–22 May 2003.

Sally, R. (1995) *States and Firms: Multinational Enterprises in Institutional Competition*, London: Routledge.

Sanchez Bajo, C. (1999) 'The European Union and Mercosur: A Case of Inter-regionalism', *Third World Quarterly* 20(5): 927–41.

Sandholtz, W. (1993) 'Choosing Union: Monetary Politics and Maastricht', *International Organization* 47(1): 1–39.

Sandholtz, W. (1996) 'Membership Matters: Limits of the Functional Approach to European Institutions', *Journal of Common Market Studies* 34(3): 403–29.

Sandholtz, W. and Zysman, J. (1989) '1992: Recasting the European Bargain', *World Politics* 42(1): 95–128.

Sapir, A. (2000) 'Trade Regionalism in Europe: Towards an Integrated Approach', *Journal of Common Market Studies* 38(1): 151–62.

Saussure, Ferdinand de (1974) *Course in General Linguistics*, London: Fontana.

Sayer, D. (1987) *The Violence of Abstraction: the Analytic Foundations of Historical Materialism*, New York: Basil Blackwell.

Scharpf, F. (1997) *Games Real Actors Play*, Boulder, CO: Westview Press.

Scharpf, F. (1999) *Governing in Europe: Effective and Democratic?* Oxford: Oxford University Press.

Scharpf, F.W. (2002) 'The European Social Model: Coping with the Challenges of Diversity', *Journal of Common Market Studies* 40(4): 645–70.

Scharpf, F.W. and Schmidt, V. (eds) (2000a) *Welfare and Work in the Open Economy*, vol. 1: *From Vulnerability to Competitiveness*, Oxford: Oxford University Press.

Scharpf, F.W. and Schmidt, V. (eds) (2000b) *Welfare and Work in the Open Economy*, vol. 2: *Diverse Responses to Common Challenges*, Oxford: Oxford University Press.

Scharsach, H.-H. (ed.) (2000) *Haider: Österreich und die rechte Versuchung*, Reinbek bei Hamburg: Rowolt Taschenbuch Verlag.

Schelkle, W. (2002) 'Disciplining Device or Insurance Arrangement? Two Approaches to the Political Economy of EMU Policy Coordination', European Institute Working Papers 1/02, London School of Economics.

Schimmelfennig, F. (2001) 'The Community Trap: Liberal Norms, Rhetorical Action, and the Eastern Enlargement of the European Union', *International Organization* 55(1): 47–80.

Schmidt, S.K. (1996) 'Sterile Debates and Dubious Generalisations: European Integration Theory Tested by Telecommunications and Electricity', *Journal of Public Policy* 16(3): 233–71.

Schmidt, V. (2001) 'The Politics of Adjustment in France and Britain: When Does Discourse Matter?', *Journal of European Public Policy* 8(2): 247–64.

Schmidt, V. (2002) *The Futures of European Capitalism*, Oxford: Oxford University Press.

Schmidt, V.A. (2000a) 'Values and Discourse in the Politics of Adjustment', in Scharpf and Schmidt (eds), pp. 229–309.

Schmidt, V.A. (2000b) 'Democracy and Discourse in an Integrating Europe and a Globalising World', *European Law Journal* 6(3): 277–300.

Schmitter, P.C. (1974) 'Still the Century of Corporatism?', *Review of Politics* 36: 85–131.

Schneider, G. (2000) 'The Two-Level Dilemma of European Politics: The Empirical Relevance of Threats and Promises in Interstate Negotiations', Universität Konstanz: Manuscript, October.

Schneider, G. and Cederman, L.-E. (1993) 'The Change in Tide in Political Cooperation: A Limited Information Model of European Integration', *International Organization* 48(4): 633–62.

Schorske, C.E. (1961) *Fin-de-siècle Vienna: Politics and Culture*, New York: Vintage.

Schumpeter, J.A. (1962 [1950]) *Capitalism, Socialism, and Democracy* (3rd edition), New York: Harper Torchbooks (Harper & Row).

Sell, S. (1995) 'Intellectual Property and Antitrust in the Developing World: Crisis, Coercion, and Choice', *International Organization* 49(2): 315–49.

Shapiro, M. and Stone Sweet, A. (2002) *On Law, Politics, and Judicialization*, Oxford: Oxford University Press.

Shaw, J. (1999) 'Postnational Constitutionalism in the European Union', *Journal of European Public Policy* 6(4): 579–97.

Shepsle, K.A. (1979) 'The Institutional Foundations of Committee Power', *American Economic Review* 81: 85–104.

Shepsle, K.A. (1985) 'Comment', in R. Noll (ed.), *Regulatory Policy and the Social Sciences*, Berkeley: University of California Press, pp. 231–7.

Shepsle, K.A. (1992) 'Bureaucratic Drift, Coalitional Drift and Time Consistency', *Journal of Law, Economics and Organization* 8: 111–18.

Shepsle, K.A. and Bonchek, M.S. (1997) *Analyzing Politics: Rationality, Behavior, and Institutions*, New York: Norton.

Simon, H.A. (1957) *Models of Man: Social and Rational: Mathematical Essays on Rational Human Behavior in a Social Setting*, New York: Wiley.

Simon, H.A. (1982) *Models of Bounded Rationality: Behavioral Economics and Business Organization*, vol. 2. Cambridge MA: MIT Press.

Simon, R. (1982) *Gramsci's Political Thought: An Introduction*, London: Lawrence & Wishart.

Sinclair, T. (1996) 'Beyond International Relations Theory: Robert W. Cox and Approaches to World Order', in R. Cox and T. Sinclair (eds), *Approaches to World Order*, New York: Cambridge University Press, 85–123.

Sinn, S. (1992) 'The Taming of Leviathan: Competition among Governments', *Constitutional Political Economy* 3: pp.177–95.

Sisson, K. and Marginson, P. (2001) 'Benchmarking and the "Europeanisation" of Social Policy', in *One Europe or Several?* ESRC Programme Briefing Note, 3/01.

Sitter, N. (2001) 'The Politics of Opposition and European Integration in Scandinavia: Is Euro-Scepticism a Government-Opposition Dynamic?', *West European Politics* 24(4): 22–39.

Sjursen, H. (2002) 'Why Expand? The Question of Legitimacy and Justification in the EU's Enlargement Policy', *Journal of Common Market Studies* 40(3): 491–513.

Smith, H. (2002) 'The Politics of "regulated liberalism": A Historical Materialist Approach to European Integration', in M. Rupert and H. Smith (eds), *Historical Materialism and Globalisation: Essays on Continuity and Change*, London: Routledge, pp. 257–83.

Smith, J., Pagnuco, R. and Chatfield, C. (1997) *Transnational Social Movements and World Politics: Solidarity beyond the State*, Syracuse, NY: Syracuse University Press.

Smith, S. (2001) 'Reflectivist and Constructivist Approaches to International Theory', in J. Baylis and S. Smith (eds), *The Globalization of World Politics: An Introduction to International Relations*, Oxford: Oxford University Press, pp. 224–49.

Snyder, F. (1993) 'Soft Law and Institutional Practice in the European Community', European University Institute working paper, LAW 93/5, Florence: European University Institute.

Snyder, J. (1991) *Myths of Empire: Domestic Politics and International Ambition*, Ithaca: Cornell University Press.

Sokolowski, A. (2001) 'Bankrupt Government: Intra-Executive Relations and the Politics of Budgetary Irresponsibility in Yeltsin's Russia', *Europe–Asia Studies* 53(4): 541–72.

Solingen, E. (1998) *Regional Orders at Century's Dawn: Global and Domestic Influences on Grand Strategy*, Princeton: Princeton University Press.

Solomon, M.S. and Rupert, M. (2002) 'Historical Materialism, Ideology, and the Politics of Globalizing Capitalism', in M. Rupert and H. Smith (eds), *Historical Materialism and Globalisation: Essays on Continuity and Change*, London: Routledge, pp. 284–300.

Soskice, D. and Iversen, T. (1998) 'Multiple Wage-Bargaining Systems in the Single European Currency Area', *Oxford Review of Economic Policy* 14(3): 110–24.

Spar, D.L. (1999) 'Lost in (Cyber)space', in A. Claire Cutler, V. Haufler and T. Porter (eds), *Private Authority and International Affairs*, Albany, NY: Suny University Press, pp. 31–52.

Staniland, M. (1985) *What is Political Economy?* New Haven: Yale University Press.

Steinmo, S., Thelen, K. and Longstreth, F. (eds) (1992) *Structuring Politics: Historical Institutionalism in Comparative Analysis*, Cambridge: Cambridge University Press.

Stetter, S. (2000) 'Regulating Migration: Authority and Delegation in Justice and Home Affairs', *Journal of European Public Policy* 7(1): 80–103.

Stone Sweet, A. (2002) *On Law, Politics, and Judicialization*, Oxford: Oxford University Press.

Stone Sweet, A. and, Sandholtz, W. (1997) 'European Integration and Supranational Governance', *Journal of European Public Policy* 4(3): 297–317.

Stone Sweet, A. and, Sandholtz, W. (eds) (1998a) *European Integration and Supranational Governance*, Oxford: Oxford University Press.

Stone Sweet, A. and Sandholtz, W. (1998b) 'Integration, Supranational Governance, and the Institutionalization of the European Polity', in W. Sandholtz and A. Stone Sweet (eds), *European Integration and Supranational Governance*, Oxford: Oxford University Press, pp. 1–26.

Strange, S. (1970) 'International Economics and International Relations: A Case of Mutual Neglect', *International Affairs* 46(2): 304–15.

Strange, S. (1971) *Sterling and British Policy: A Political Study of An International Currency in Decline*, Oxford: Oxford University Press.

Strange, S. (1972) 'International Economic Relations I: The Need for an Interdisciplinary Approach', in R. Morgan (ed.), *The Study of International Affairs: Essays in Honour of Kenneth Younger*, London: RIIA/Oxford University Press, pp. 63–84.

Strange, S. (1988a) *States and Markets*, New York: Basil Blackwell.

Strange, S. (1988b) *States and Markets: An Introduction to International Political Economy*, London: Pinter.

Strange, S. (1996) *The Retreat of the State: The Diffusion of Power in the World Economy*, New York: Cambridge University Press.

Streeck, W. and Schmitter, P.C. (1985) *Private Interest Government: Beyond Market and State*, London: Sage.

Strom, K. (1990) *Minority Government and Majority Rule*, Cambridge: Cambridge University Press.

Surel, Y. (2000) 'The Role of Cognitive and Normative Frames in Policy-Making', *Journal of European Public Policy* 7(4): 495–512.

Szczerbiak, A. (2001) 'Polish Public Opinion: Explaining Declining Support for EU Membership', *Journal of Common Market Studies* 39(1): 105–22.

Sztompka, P. (1994) 'Evolving Focus on Human Agency in Contemporary Social Theory', in P. Sztompka (ed.), *Agency and Structure: Reorienting Social Theory*, Langhorne, PA: Gordon & Breach, pp. 25–60.

Taggart, P. (1998) 'A Touchstone of Dissent: Euroscepticism in Contemporary Western European Party Systems', *European Journal of Political Research* 33(3): 363–388.

Taggart, P. and Szczerbiak, A. (2002) 'The Party Politics of Euroscepticism in EU Member and Candidate States', paper presented at the European Consortium for Political Research Joint Workshops, Turin, March.

Tancsits, W. (2001) 'Die Entstehung des Koalitionsabkommens zwischen ÖVP und FPÖ', in C.P. Wieland (ed.), *Österreich in Europa*, Wien: Amalthea.

Tarrow, S. (1994) *Power in Movement: Social Movements, Collective Action and Politics*, New York: Cambridge University Press.

Tharakan, P.K.M. (2002) 'European Union and Preferential Arrangements', *World Economy* 25(1): 1387–97.

Thatcher, M. and Stone Sweet, A. (eds) (2002) 'Delegation to Non-Majoritarian Institutions', *West European Politics* 25(1): special issue.

'The same peculiar team?', *The Economist*, 1 March 2003, p. 48.

Thomas, G.M., Meyer, J.W., Ramirez, F.O. and Boli, J. (eds) (1987) *Institutional Structure: Constituting State, Society and the Individual*, Newbury Park, CA: Sage.

Thomsen, N. (1993) 'EF som stridpunkt i dansk politik 1972–1979', in B.N. Thomsen (ed.), *The odd man out? Danmark og den europæiske integration*, Odense: Odense Universitetsforlag.

Tolstoy, L. (2000) *Anna Karenina*, C. Garnett, trans., New York: The Modern Library.

Tömmel, I. (1995) 'Die Europäische Integration: ökonomische Regulierung und Politikgestaltung zwischen Staat und Markt', in *Europäische Integration und politische Regulierung: Aspekte, Dimensionen, Perspektiven*, Studien der Forschungsgruppe Europäische Gemeinschaften 5, Philipps-Universität, Marburg, pp. 49–64.

Trachtenberg, Marc (2000) 'De Gaulle, Moravcsik, and Europe', *Journal of Cold War Studies* 2(3): 101–16.

Tranholm-Mikkelsen, J. (1991) 'Neofunctionalism: Obstinate or Obsolete? A Reappraisal in the Light of the New Dynamism of the European Community', *Millennium* 20: 1–22.

Tsebelis, G. (1994) 'The Power of the European Parliament as a Conditional Agenda Setter', *American Political Science Review* 88(1): 128–42.

Tsebelis, G. and Garrett, G. (2000) 'Legislative Politics in the European Union', *European Union Politics* 1(1): 9–36.

Tsebelis, G. and Garrett, G. (2001) 'The Institutional Foundation of Intergovernmentalism and Supranationalism in the European Union', *International Organization* 55(2): 357–90.

Tucker, R.C. (ed.) (1978) *The Marx–Engels Reader* (2nd edition), New York: Norton.

Tung, R. Ko–Chi (1981) *Exit-Voice Catastrophes: Dilemma between Migration and Participation*, Stockholm: University of Stockholm.

Van Apeldoorn, B. (2000) 'Transnationale Klassen und europäisches Regieren: Der European Round Table of Industrialists', in H.-J. Bieling and J. Steinhilber (eds), *Die Konfiguration Europas: Dimensionen einer kritischen Integrationstheorie*, Münster: Westfälisches Dampfboot; originally published as 'Transnational Class Agency and European Governance: The Case of the European Round Table of Industrialists', *New Political Economy* 5(2): 157–81.

Van Apeldoorn, B. (2002) *Transnational Capital and the Struggle over European Integration*, London: Routledge.

Van Apeldoorn, B., Overbeek, H. and Ryner, M. (2003), 'Theories of European Integration: A Critique', in A.W. Cafruny and M. Ryner (eds), *A Ruined Fortress? Neoliberal Hegemony and Transformation in Europe*, London: Rowman & Littlefield, pp. 17–45.

Van der Pijl, K. (1998) *Transnational Classes and International Relations*, London: Routledge.

Van der Wurff, R. (1992) 'Neo-Liberalism in Germany? The "Wende" in Perspective', in H. Overbeek (ed.), *Restructuring Hegemony in the Global Political Economy: The Rise of Transnational Neo-Liberalism in the 1980s*, London: Routledge.

Van Tulder, R. and Junne, G. (1998) *European Multinationals in Core Technologies*, New York: Wiley.

Väyrynen, R. (2003) 'Regionalism: Old and New', *International Studies Review* 5(1): 25–51.

Verdun, A. (1996) 'An "Asymmetrical" Economic and Monetary Union in the EU: Perceptions of Monetary Authorities and Social Partners', *Journal of European Integration/Revue d'intégration européenne* 20(1): 59–81.

Verdun, A. (1999) 'Book review of Andrew Moravcsik, *The Choice for Europe*, Ithaca, NY: Cornell University Press, 1998', *ECSA Review* 12(1): 14–15.

Verdun, A. (2000) *European Responses to Globalization and Financial Market Integration: Perceptions of Economic and Monetary Union in Britain, France and Germany*, Houndmills: Palgrave-Macmillan.

Verdun, A. (2002) 'Merging Neofunctionalism and Intergovernmentalism: Lessons from EMU', in A. Verdun (ed.), *The Euro: European Integration Theory and Economic and Monetary Union*, Lanham, MD: Rowman & Littlefield, pp. 9–28.

Walker, R.B.J. (1989) 'History and Structure in the Theory of I.R.', *Millennium* 18(2): 163–83.

Wallace, H. (2001) 'The Changing Politics of the European Union: An Overview', *Journal of Common Market Studies* 39(4): 481–49.

Wallace, W. (1983) 'Less than a Federation, More than a Regime: The Community as a Political System', in H. Wallace, W. Wallace and C. Webb (eds), *Policy-Making in the European Community* (2nd edition), Chichester: Wiley, pp. 403–36.

Wallace, W. (1990) 'Introduction: The Dynamics of European Integration', in W. Wallace (ed.), *The Dynamics of European Integration*, London: Pinter/RIIA, pp. 1–24.

Waltz, K. (1979) *Theory of International Politics*, New York: Random House.

Waltz, K.N. (1986) 'Reflections on *Theory of International Politics*: A Response to my Critics', in Robert O. Keohane (ed.), *Neorealism and its Critics*, New York: Columbia University Press, pp. 322–46.

Weaver, R.K. and Rockman, B.A. (eds) (1993) *Do Institutions Matter? Government Capabilities in the United States and Abroad*, Washington, DC: Brookings Institution.

Webb, C. (1983) 'Theoretical Perspectives and Problems', in H. Wallace, W. Wallace and C. Webb (eds), *Policy-Making in the European Community* (2nd edition), Chichester: Wiley, pp. 1–41.

Weber, S. (ed.) (2001) *Globalization and the European Political Economy*, New York: Columbia University Press.

Weingast, B.R. and Marshall, W.J. (1988) 'The Industrial Organization of Congress; or, Why Legislatures, Like Firms, Are Not Organized as Markets', *Journal of Political Economy* 96(1): 132–63.

Weingast, B.R. and Moran, M.J. (1983) 'Bureaucratic Discretion or Congressional Control?', *Journal of Political Economy* 91: 765–800.

Weldes, J. (1999) *Constructing National Interests: The U.S. and the Cuban Missile Crisis*, Minneapolis: University of Minnesota Press.

Wendt, A. (1987) 'The Agent–Structure Problem in International Relations Theory', *International Organization* 41(3): 335–70.

Wessels, W. (1997) 'An Ever Closer Fusion? A Dynamic Macropolitical View on Integration Processes', *Journal of Common Market Studies* 35(2): 267–99.

White, S., McAllister, I. and Light, M. (2002) 'Enlargement and the New Outsiders', *Journal of Common Market Studies* 40(1): 135–53.

Wiener, A. and Diez, T. (eds) (2004) *Theories of European Integration: Past, Present and Future*, Oxford: Oxford University Press.

Williamson, J. (ed.) (1994) *The Political Economy of Policy Reform*, Washington, DC: Institute for International Economics.

Williamson, J. and Haggard, S. (1994) 'The Political Conditions for Economic Reform', in J. Williamson (ed.), *The Political Economy of Policy Reform*, Washington, DC: Institute for International Economics, pp. 525–96.

Williamson, O.E. (1985) *Economic Institutions of Capitalism*, New York: Free Press.

Willis, F.R. (1968) *France, Germany, and the New Europe: 1945–1967*, revised and expanded edition, London: Oxford University Press.

Wincott, D. (1995) 'The Role of the Law or the Rule of the Court of Justice? An "institutional" Account of Judicial Politics in the European Community', *Journal of European Public Policy* 2(4): 583–602.

Winkler, G. (2001) 'Eine staatsrechtliche und europarechtliche Analyse der Sanktionen der 14 EU-Mitgliedern', in C.P. Wieland (ed.), *Österreich in Europa*, Wien: Amalthea.

Wodak, R. (2000) ' "Echt, anständig und ordentlich." Wie Jörg Haider und die FPÖ Österreichs Vergangenheit, Gegenwart und Zukunft beurteilen', in H.-H. Scharsach (ed.), *Haider: Österreich und die rechte Versuchung*, Reinbek bei Hamburg: Rowolt Taschenbuch Verlag.

Woods, N. (2001) 'International Political Economy in an Age of Globalisation', in J. Baylis and S. Smith (eds), *The Globalization of World Politics: An Introduction to International Relations*, Oxford: Oxford University Press, pp. 277–98.

Wrobel, P.S. (1998) 'A Free Trade Area of the Americas in 2005?', *International Affairs* 74(3): 547–61.

Zaller, J.R. (1992) *The Nature and Origins of Mass Opinion*, Cambridge: Cambridge University Press.

Zöchling, C. (1999) *Haider: Eine Karriere*, Munich: Econ Taschenbuch Verlag.

Index